AUTHENTIC

VOICES

Women of Insight Talk about Real-Life Challenges

AUTHENTIC VOICES:

Women of Insight Talk about Real-Life Challenges

EDITED BY

Jewell Reinhart Coburn, Ph.D.   Joyce Smith Helyer

Taylor University Press

Authentic Voices: Women of Insight Talk About Real-Life Challenges.

We gratefully acknowledge permission to reprint excerpts from previously published material:

God's Ordinary People: No Ordinary Heritage, Jessica Rousselow and Alan Winquist, Taylor University Press, 1996, by permission of the authors who hold all rights.

Excerpts from *Parnassus* by Esther Lewis, 1943, Kristen Prillwitz, 2000, Jessica St.Clair, 2004, by permission of Professor Thom Satterlee, *Parnassus* Advisor.

Excerpts from *Survival of the Unfit,* Mary Ellen Gudeman, Xlibris Corporation, 2001, by permission of the author who holds all rights.

Excerpts from *To Bend Without Breaking: Addendum 1994,* Mary Ella Rose Stuart by permission of the Stuart family to whom Abingdon Press has returned all rights.

Excerpts from *Underground Manual for Ministers Wives,*1974, and *Spaghetti from the Chandelier*, 1984, Ruth Dixon Truman, by permission of the author to whom Abingdon Press has returned all rights.

Excerpts from personal letters of Susan Davis Marsters Smith, Fort Wayne Female College student, 1848, by permission of Dr. Robert Lay and the Lilly Library, Indiana University.

Scripture quotations marked (NIV) taken from the *Holy Bible, New International Version.* Copyright @1973, 1978, 1984 by International Bible Society. Used by permission of Zondervan Publishing House. All rights reserved. The "NIV" and "New International Version ®" trademarks are registered in the United States Patent and Trademark Office by International Bible Society. Use of either trademark requires the permission of International Bible Society.

Excerpts from *A Lone Woman in Africa,* Agnes McAllister, copyright by Hunt and Eaton, 1896, currently in the public domain.

ATTENTION: Women's Study Groups, Churches, Colleges and Schools – *Authentic Voices* is available at quantity discounts with bulk purchase for educational and group study use. For information, please write to the Editors, Taylor University Press, 236 West Reade Avenue, Upland, Indiana 46989-1001.

Editor/Publisher Note: Each author whose words appear herein assumes full responsibility for the information and views expressed by her. Neither the content nor the views expressed are those of the editors or the publisher.

Cover Art by Katharina Jeong-Hwa Kang

Library of Congress Control Number: 2004113704

ISBN 0-9740758-3-3

TABLE OF CONTENTS

Authentic Voices: Women of Insight Talk about Real-Life Challenges

IN PURSUIT OF MEANING: Life's Significant Firsts and
Highly Charged Life Events, Incidents that Serve to Influence,
Challenge, Define, and Advance Life Attitudes, Inclinations,
Compulsions, Inhibitions, Callings, or Sense of Mission
Questions to Ponder: My Companion Journal

THE POWER OF RELATIONSHIP
Family, Friendships, Mentors, Caregivers, Love Relationships,
Marriage, Parenting, Separation, Divorce
Questions to Ponder: My Companion Journal

MY BODY / MY MIND / MY SPIRIT / MYSELF:
Transitioning, Transforming, Transcending, Honoring One's
Body, Attitudes Toward Reproduction, Physical, Psychologi-
cal and Emotional Illness, Depression, Perfectionism, Negative
Thinking, Panic Syndrome, Self Destruction, Death, Grief
Questions to Ponder: My Companion Journal

THROUGH A GLASS DARKLY: Dusk and Dawning
The Perplexing, Unexpected, Confusing, Lonely, Dark Night of
the Soul / Singing a New Song, The Power of Humor, of
Affirmation, of Forgiveness, of Praising God in All Things
Questions to Ponder: My Companion Journal

BROAD HORIZONS / OPEN OPTIONS:

Historical Shifts in Views of the Roles of Women: National,
International, the Worlds of Business, Science, Politics,
The Professions
Questions to Ponder: *My Companion Journal*

VENERABLE VOICES / MODERN MESSAGES:

From the founding of Fort Wayne Female College (1848)
forward, voices of women past speak to the universality of
shared life concerns across time and circumstance. Messages
from the heart both penetrate and persist throughout historical
and cultural shifts.

Women's voices, with their clear potential to contribute to the essential composition and continuance of many of the most revered and longed for values in human life, have not always been easy to hear.

But, no more – not as we journey into the new millennium. *Authentic Voices: Women of Insight Talk About Real-Life Challenges* places women's considerable capability fully within the massive paradigm shift predicted following World War II, launched with zest in the '60s and '70s, and becoming ever more normative now in the 21st century.

Perhaps both in spite of, as well as because of, events that have transpired historically, religiously, and culturally, women's voices can be more readily heard and their messages of peace, civility, stability, and compassion – vital complements to existing forces – can now be acknowledged.

FOREWORD

The voices contained within this book bring to mind a symphony, lush and varied. There is the captivating theme of rich, life experience that runs throughout. It is a theme that touches the mind and heart as well as the spirit and does so in universal ways, for who of us has not known the restlessness of loneliness, the exuberance of love, the hollowness of grief, or any of the array of feelings and passions common to us all? Within this theme are variations, such as staccato (brief flashes of insight), adagio (the ponderings of a sensitive heart), amoroso (the stuff of love and tenderness), appassionatamente (the stirrings of the soul) and, of course, crescendo (the powerful understandings that can come through powerful life experience).

Each contributor to this book brings her authentic self, expressed through her authentic life experience. Each life represented is unique yet, in some ways, similar. Each response to life is particularized by the specific characteristics of the life challenges within which the writer has found herself.

Surely *Authentic Voices* is a testament to the truism that the heart is a many splendored thing, and that the writers' willingness to share their lives within these pages is to be honored.

Much about the way life tends to work is contained within these pages. There may be found life's paradoxes (the contrapuntal), as well as the sense of entropy (fugues of formlessness, chaos and confusion). There are the disillusionments (the requiems to lost dreams, to cherished notions set aside), just as there are the illuminati (those melodies that elevate and illuminate). When blessed with the gift of honest and forthright accounts of life as lived by the many writers within this book, no one needs to feel alone in times of trial. With pretenses set aside, with openness available to us, each of us is the beneficiary of the encouragement and healing that can be ours through the sharing of these writers' real-life stories.

Dr. Hazel Butz Carruth Anderson (1938)
Chair Emeritus, Department of English and
Division of Language Arts
Taylor University

PREFACE

The founding of Taylor University as Fort Wayne Female College in 1846 is an event largely ignored and unknown in the milieu of modern culture. In context, the fact that women were provided fine opportunities for higher education constitutes a defining era in American history. The emergence of the other fifty percent of the world's population into political, economic, literary, scientific and indeed all areas of human endeavor is a well established reality in the 21st century. This did not happen without insight, intent, and perseverance. The thoughts, aspirations, insights, anguish, resignation, humor, anger and restraint to name only a few of the facets of the female heart tell a story beyond and deeper than the mere documentation of the struggle of "women's rights."

It is for me a revealing, but almost totally overlooked detail that it was in the church related colleges that this "right" of women was first acknowledged and in conjunction with the "frontier revival" at that. Interestingly, it is Charles G. Finney and Oberlin College that first opened the door and Taylor was soon to follow. These frontier evangelicals read their Bibles, believed them to be true and found in Jesus and Paul not a restriction upon woman but the liberating reality always known by believers. They read in the book of Genesis God's declaration that all of humankind was created in the "image of God – male and female." This book is about the interior reflections and experiences of women energized by the knowledge that the image of God was theirs, who without abandoning the Christian graces, rejected venom and hatred, persevered in their own ways and added to the weight of the reality that in Christ there is "neither male nor female" but one complementary human race. These representative Taylor women, past and present, document the hand of God in their lives with compelling power.

Women will enjoy this book but so will men who, like me, have been immeasurably enriched by their relationships with women. Mothers, sisters, wives, classmates, colleagues and stimulating rivals in the classroom have taught us that man cannot prosper alone.

This glimpse into the souls of Taylor women is an enriching journey into the deeper part of the story of redemption. "God was in Christ reconciling the world unto Himself" and a major part of that healing is the understanding of the complementary relationship of woman and man.

Dr. Jay Kesler
President Emeritus
Taylor University

ACKNOWLEDGMENTS

Assembling, editing, and arranging writing of nearly 80 different women has been a challenge and a privilege. Dr. Julie (Jewell Reinhart Coburn '55) provided the seed idea leading to this anthology of women's voices, and her research has taken her to many valuable resources for past material, as well as into countless rich encounters with contemporary contributors. Dr. Julie found her relationship with writers to reveal women of great heart and compelling vision.

Joyce Smith Helyer is deeply appreciated for her reservoir of talent, her organizational and editing skills, and her warm interface with all who contributed to this publication. Joyce is to be thanked for her commitment and perseverance that challenged her to work many hours beyond the requirements of her daily professional demands.

Our unending appreciation is most sincerely expressed to the many women who opened their hearts and lives, committed themselves to the rigors of written expression, and generously gifted the reader with their valuable life-insights.

Heather Myers Kittleman from Taylor University archives provided valuable hours of research assistance and editorial expertise. For their enthusiasm in tracking sometimes illusive historical leads, many thanks are expressed to Roselyn Baugh Kerlin, Rebecca Ringenberg, and Dr. Mildred Chapman. The editorial assistance of Dr. Hazel Butz Carruth Anderson, Dr. D. G. Newton, Elizabeth Freese and Arna Smith was exhaustive and invaluable. For clerical assistance, appreciation is expressed to Amanda Schaffer, Sheila Moorman and Serena Thrush Duke. Deeply appreciated are the permissions granted by the following persons: Dr. Robert Lay for his generous offer to make available the personal letters of Fort Wayne Female College student, Susan Davis Marsters Smith, 1848, found in the Lilly Library, archives of Indiana University, and for the Lilly Library's permission to reprint not only excerpts from the letters but also to make use of their staff transcriptions for better reader comprehension of the handwritten letters. Thank you to Professor Thom Satterlee, *Parnassus* Advisor, who granted permission to reprint selected

Parnassus entries. Appreciation is expressed to the family of Mary Ella Rose Stuart, '30, who generously granted permission to reprint an excerpt from her 1994 *Addendum* to her previously published book, *To Bend Without Breaking*. All permissions to reprint are also listed on the copyright page.

INTRODUCTION

Authentic Voices grew out of the observation and acknowledgement that real-life experiences are valuable resources for learning, testing, and communicating important wisdoms for living. This book constitutes a forum for women to express themselves and to reveal the rich lessons they derived from the events that have made up their lives. This book represents a "first" in the 159-year history of Taylor University, and, to that end, voices from the institution's past are also included in the special chapter devoted exclusively to historically posthumous voices: *Venerable Voices/Modern Messages,* an unabridged version of which is housed in the University archives for additional study or research.

Names of persons other than the writer have been omitted or changed in the contemporary entries, as have many specific location names. We honor each writer's openness and willingness to communicate with courage the often deep inner conflicts, sufferings, and victories they have experienced along life's road. Each author whose words appear herein assumes full responsibility for the information and views expressed by her. Neither the content nor the views expressed are those of the editors or the publisher.

IN PURSUIT OF MEANING
Life's Significant Firsts and Highly Charged Life Events

*I keep asking that the God of our Lord Jesus Christ, the
glorious Father, may give you the Spirit of wisdom and
revelation, so that you may know him better. I pray also
that the eyes of your heart may be enlightened in order
that you may know the hope to which he has called you,
the riches of his glorious inheritance in the saints.*
Ephesians 1:17-18 NIV

If we choose to live out our lives in a somewhat moment-to-moment manner, hemmed in
and pressured by the demands of day-to-day life,
we may fail to be consciously aware of the layers of significance hidden within our existence. This
book of personal accounts records the life events of
its writers and is meant for readers who wish to push the pause
button on what may have become a merry-go-round life. Herein
is the invitation to look at the ups and downs, the ins and outs, of
our lives to see what lies beneath and within.

When one chaotic event seems to overlay another and they
appear to have little relationship to one another, we can all too
easily assume a fatalistic view that, for us, things seem to be
leading no place in particular. The car must be taken to the repair
shop. Our daughter's dress for graduation must be picked up
from the cleaners. Our son already told us his soccer team faces
its season's final game. Our neighbor insists that not another
night pass before we do something about our barking dog. Then,
the minister's wife is ill again and it's my turn to take the expected casserole to her.

Or, take a CNN's eye view of things. Our nation's major political parties are attempting to undermine each other while the nation is in prolonged recession. We take pride in our national security while crime rages in our cities and burgs. The polar ice cap is melting and the ozone layer is thinning. We're admonished to slather ourselves with lotions to block the sun's rays while our cars and factories spew pollutants. Fifty-two of the some 193 countries of the world are engaged in either civil war or conflict with international implications. The 1997 international treaty for the banning of landmines has still not been accepted by China or the United States. Regardless of the Code of Universal Human Rights drawn up and adopted in 1948, many nations continue to practice slavery, subjugation of women, denial of self-determination, and in many cases foster only the barest level of human subsistence. To top it all, the three greatest religions of the world, all claiming descent from Abraham, are at each other's necks.

If we hope to live a life of meaningfulness then our greatest need and most significant achievement is to be mindful of what makes up our lives.

Closing down our awareness and our sensitivities to what makes up our personal and larger life is tantamount to renunciation of such human attributes as the ability to learn, the power of imagination, positive thought and action, and certainly access to divine wisdom.

If we hope to live a life of meaningfulness, then our greatest need and most significant achievement is to be mindful of what makes up our lives. With minimum reflection, we can each cite numerous acquaintances who have gone to their graves never having resolved, attempted, or attended to the gaping holes either within their own lives or within the significant relationships that have made up their lives.

An understanding of the meanings behind the events in our lives is not necessarily acquired at any particular age, not even when we have reached chronological maturity. Pausing, taking stock, looking across the larger scenery of our lives, asking ourselves what it has all meant – these are exercises valuable to the pursuit of psychological, emotional, and spiritual maturity. Take, for example, our very first remembered experiences with life, be they positive or negative, those events that speak to us, that show us their colors, that grab our attention. These incidents, together with our response to them, may have an intrinsic power to influence us both immediately and throughout our lives.

Consider our very first sense of secure, nurturing environment or, conversely, our first encounter with feelings of loneliness, even abandonment; our first sense of love or our meeting with rejection; our initial sensation of great goodness, or our sense of foreboding, even evil. Reflect on the first time we came face to face with the incomprehensible, the impossible. For some of us, there may have been an inclination to turn away. For others, there may have arisen an inner urgency to make attainable what appeared unachievable. Consider the first time we felt a power beyond ourselves, a power we came to identify as God. Regardless of race, education, or social status, we all share in the essential human condition. We all know joy and sorrow, abundance and want, dreams and disappointments, security and fear. Human existence, no matter how we may attempt to protect ourselves and our loved ones, will contain the unexpected, the unjust, the tragic, the evil, and also the unexplainable.

The manner in which we observed ourselves responding or reacting to these signal "firsts" or highly charged events in our life has an ability to aid or hinder the ultimate revealing of our authentic selves. We are by no means robots, responding robotically to a predetermined, mechanistic game plan of life. Instead, we are complex, unique, glorious persons, each on our own pilgrimage in the direction we sense will offer our soul its highest fulfillment.

Life events, reviewed thoughtfully, serve to assist us to master the psychological and emotional problems of growing up – overcoming narcissistic disappointments, sibling rivalry, oedi-

pal dilemmas, the relinquishing of childhood dependencies, growing into a sense of selfhood, of healthy self-worth, and developing a sense of moral clarity and responsibility.

Our positive feelings give us the strength to develop our rationality, and our developed hope for the future can sustain us through the adversities we unavoidably encounter. Our negative sensations can function helpfully as deterrents, setting up an inner sense of caution.

Adversity, while viewed with fear and revulsion, can function in our lives in many positive ways. Facing and grappling with the negative forces in life can stimulate the development of a range of valuable coping skills. Learning to face the hard stuff of life with courage, resourcefulness and level-headedness equips us to be more understanding of catastrophe and random misfortune and how to deal better with the great tragedies that can befall any one of us. Consider first our basic survival needs of food, shelter, clothing; then move on to the next level of needs, our health and education in order to function within whatever social system we find ourselves; then move on to the social needs of fundamental rights to information and skills to work out our lives within community. Just as the reviewed life has the potential to deepen our understandings, yet greater understanding develops as we become familiar with those dynamics that lie beneath.

When bothersome feelings are repressed and therefore denied entry into our awareness, it is only a matter of time before a person's thinking will become influenced by the remnants of these unaddressed problem areas. But when we give ourselves permission to invite all that is within us to present itself to our conscious thinking, and we encourage ourselves to work it through, the potential for causing distress to ourselves or others is much reduced.

Today's era of highly developed and generally available therapeutic tools, that include helpful medications, frees us to be about the heady adventure of exploring and reviewing our lives for the rich meanings that lie within.

These occurrences need not be major events. They can, but need not be. For many, a profoundly meaningful occurrence may be no more than a look, a gesture, a tone of voice, the dip of a wing, or drop of a petal. Taking note of such an occurrence – as do a number of our writers – and reflecting upon it, and the meaning it may have for our lives, can provide us with greater self-knowledge as well as empathy for others.

Take courage and comfort from the defining events expressed by women throughout this book. Shared experiences can offer direction, a sense of companionship, and make our own path easier and richer in meaning.

As an example of just such an event, the following was inspired by a phone conversation I had with **Mrs. Jean Frances Bergwall, whose husband was the president of Taylor University from 1951 to 1959.** During the course of our friendly conversation, she spoke warmly of numerous reminiscences when the following presented itself without either drama or fanfare. With her permission to use this incident, Jean related to me an occurrence likely common to most of us. A treasured gift, broken by an unintentional gesture, triggered the emergence of an insight. What came to her was both poignant and profound, and with such potential power as to influence her personally, as well as many who might come within the circle of her expanded perception.

I was tying up some newspapers and, close by, there was a little shelf on which stood a precious vase. My husband had brought that vase to me from one of his travels to Athens, Greece, back in the 1950s. You guessed it – I bumped it and off it fell! I looked at the shattered vase and I was heartbroken.

I'll try to mend it, I thought to myself, *but, surely, glued back together, it will never be the same.* I worked hard on that vase. I tried a shard here and another there. For a time I was disheartened, but I persevered and finally, to my delight, the pieces came together. I marveled at the beauty of that mended vase and couldn't help thinking how its restoration gave it added character. Then I thought about life and the way it can get all broken and twisted. I thought about its mending process. It came to me that beauty can reside within brokenness. I learned that day that perfection can easily be rivaled by the potentials within imperfection.

It held me in awe, that simple revelation.

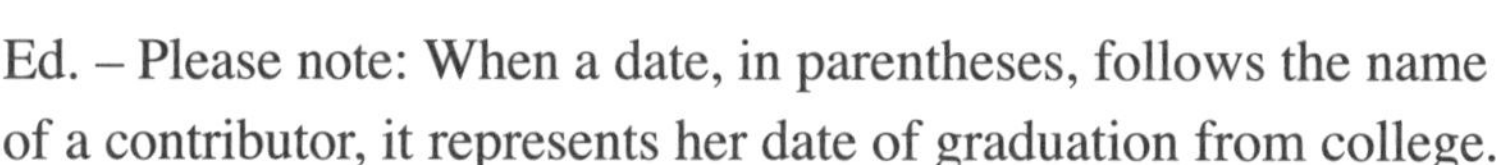

Ed. – Please note: When a date, in parentheses, follows the name of a contributor, it represents her date of graduation from college. For all other names, see *Writers' Index*.

Back when she was a teenager, **Wendy Loney Dechert (1996)** wanted only to have a little carefree fun in the snow with her friends. Who could have known the terrible turn of events she was about to encounter. Full of energy and playfulness, Wendy, a bright, accomplished young girl thought no further ahead than the fresh, cold air on her cheeks, camaraderie with her friends, the *joie de vivre* of the moment. None of us can know what awaits us around the corners of life, and yet we aren't meant to cower in fear of the unknown, nor are we, as Wendy tells us, left without resources despite the limitations life can impose on us.

All I wanted to do was go on a youth retreat that winter. I was 15 back then in the late '80s and, admittedly, a stir-crazy teenager. I had not been outside much during that Ohio winter, and on this particular day the fresh, new snow was especially inviting.

Four of us jumped onto a huge inner tube. We all pushed hard; then down the hill we tore, gaining momentum as we went. The faster we went the less control we had. The two guys rolled off. I was left only with the other girl, and the lighter load caused us to travel even faster. Then we started to spin. We were careening backwards at an unstoppable speed.

I don't remember what happened next, only what I was told much later.

They said blood spattered everywhere; red stains were all over the new snow. I had hit a boulder, they told me, opening a gash the width of my head. Then they described how the spinning of the tube caused me to hit again – this time face first.

What I do remember was waking up groggy, with my parents and the doctor at my side. A large tube, going straight down my throat, was gagging me. I panicked and tried to pull it out. As a result, I was tied down and left to drift in and out of consciousness. I learned later that the hospital Chaplain had been asked to speak with my parents. He was sent to prepare them to make the decision to keep me on or take me off life support.

The doctor warned my parents that my brain was swelling. If it ruptured, the condition would likely cause considerable brain damage.

As it turned out, I survived, but not without some memory impairment. Even now, 15 years later, I'm very thankful that I'm able to reflect somewhat. I admit my memory is far from perfect; still, I can think back and capture flashes of that life-changing incident. When I was 15 years of age, I did not realize that life is precious. In fact, I felt I was almost invincible.

The disorientation of this experience confused me at first and I found myself crying out, "Why me?" But as time passed, I grew to cherish these pieces of memories because what they offer to my life is a deep appreciation for each breath I take. I realize now that I am not indestructible; however, how can I *not* believe I was destined to have more time on this earth? To me, this is a powerful gift. The trauma I experienced has affected so many parts of my life that I have come to relish every moment of every day.

What intrigues me is that I wasn't left feeling fearful, nor am I inclined to try to make my life smaller with the hope that somehow it will be safer for me. Instead, my desire is to experience more of life. I have a great thirst for knowledge and a huge longing for meaningful relationships. I am deeply thankful for my time on earth, and I do not want to miss out on a single day's experiences.

Mary Ellen Gudeman (1964) arrived in Japan as a missionary soon after her college graduation. Faced with considerable culture shock together with a compelling urge to be about the business for which she had committed so much of her life and personal resources, Mary Ellen takes us with her as she jostles her way through the pressing Tokyo crowds in her attempt to keep her schedule and catch the right train. But what Mary Ellen also succeeds in doing is bringing us into a moment of horror – an incident resulting from the intersecting of time and event and fraught with a juxtaposition of overlaying intentions and of mixed assumptions; all of which led to a burst of insight – Mary Ellen's perception of an opportunity lost.

If I had spoken to her, I would have missed my train.

I was waiting at Shukugawa, one of Japan's Hankyu train stations. People were lined up around me at the four automatic ticket dispensers. Two 70-yen lights – the cost for one stop and the cost for a platform ticket – flashed on. But she just stared at the dispenser.

She's not getting on the train, I thought. *Maybe she's meeting someone on the platform.*

She hesitated. I was going to miss my train if she didn't

hurry.

Finally, she reached out and pushed the platform ticket button. The ticket dropped into the tray below, but she only stared at it.

Exasperated at having to wait, I reached over her shoulder, brushing it, to insert money for my train fare.

Momentarily, I forgot her. Then, out of the corner of my eye, I saw her go through the gate on my left. Pausing, she looked at the timetable overhead.

What a thin coat to wear on this chilly March day, I thought. *She must not have much of this world's goods. And 70 yen is a lot to pay just to get on a platform.*

As I went down the steps and crossed over to the Osaka side, the young woman hurried up the steps to the platform for passengers going to Kobe. I forgot the incident as I waited for my train. The 1:29 Super-Express bound for Kobe would need to pass through first. My ears, grown accustomed to the roar, almost tuned out the thundering sound of its fast approach.

Suddenly, an eerie thud, screeching brakes, then flying fragments and train's bed-rocks flew around me.

Oh, no, the train had left the tracks! I grabbed my coat to shield my face.

Then, just as suddenly as the horrifying experience had begun, it ended. Out of the deafening silence someone across the platform from me shrieked, "Niku Niku" (Flesh! Flesh!). A couple of hundred yards down the tracks was the motionless Super-Express. From everywhere, people hurried down the platform.

Scattered bits of a mutilated body confirmed the tragedy. Below, in front of me, lying inside the train tracks, there was the gray coat, grease-and-blood-stained.

I had touched that gray coat moments before, without understanding and without caring.

She paid 70 yen for her leap into eternity; I had paid thousands of dollars to come to Japan to reach her before she leaped.

If I had spoken to her, I would have missed my train.

And so would she.*

*Ed. – The above firsthand experience is reprinted by permission of Mary Ellen Gudeman and appears in her book of personal life experiences, *Survival of the Unfit* (Xlibris Corporation, U.S., 2001, p.9).

Severe difficulties that life places before us cannot always be traced to a specific cause. Although studied predictability is the subject of sophisticated mathematical inquiry, life events can elude our heart's desires, and certainly our firmest attempts at control. **Valerie Wilson Boado (1987)** brings us into just such a personal dilemma when she finds herself alone and bereft on a hospital operating room table in a foreign country. She tells us her experience of thinking that surely little more could go wrong than already has, but it does. What she encounters offers richness to her life and could indeed speak to ours as well.

I had been left there, alone on the operating room table. The air conditioner blew cold air across me, and I shivered under the thin hospital sheet. I was grateful to be at the best place at that

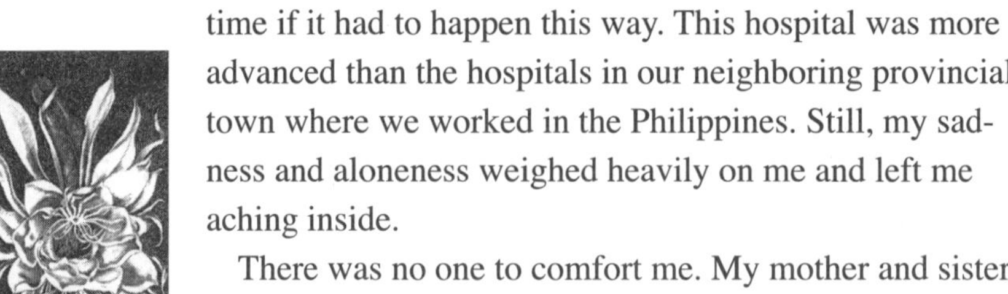

time if it had to happen this way. This hospital was more advanced than the hospitals in our neighboring provincial town where we worked in the Philippines. Still, my sadness and aloneness weighed heavily on me and left me aching inside.

There was no one to comfort me. My mother and sisters were thousands of miles from me, and my husband left our other two children with friends so he could be with me at the hospital. I was overwhelmed with sadness and grief.

No one had prayed with me before I entered the operating room. There were no friends in the waiting room praying for me. There was just my Father God and me. As the tears fell, I prayed silently for comfort and strength. I was weak, alone and scared as I waited for the D & C procedure to begin.

Through my tears, I suddenly became aware that I was not alone. How long had he been sitting there, I wondered? A young male nurse, dressed in hospital scrubs, complete with mask, looked over at me, paused, and then spoke to me in faltering English. When I responded in his national Tagalog dialect, he switched easily into his own language.

The young nurse then began to ask me questions – questions about where I was from, my reason for being in the Philippines, how many children I had, and much more. All the while, he worked swiftly and expertly attaching me to the myriad of machines. And at the same time, I felt a sense of calm come over me. By the time the doctor arrived I was no longer crying. God had answered my prayer for comfort and strength.

We spent a few more days in the city relaxing and resting before returning to our provincial home. Though my body regained strength, my heart felt open and bare. For a month I grieved about the loss of my unborn child. Then, one day, God's small voice spoke to me from within. It acknowledged my need to express my sorrow, it honored my loss, then it nudged me ever so gently to move on.

As hard as it was to move on, I knew my family members were alive and needed me. I had to be there for them. I gathered myself together and, in time, pushed forward and through my pain. God had not left me alone in my sadness. He had been with me, carried me through, and I had grown closer to Him in the process.

As I reflect on that experience, I cannot help being moved by the ways that God worked. How did it happen that when I miscarried, we just happened to be in the city, which provided us with immediate access to quality health care? Or how was it that special friends were able to care for our children so that my husband could be with me in the hospital? And then there was the 'angel' in the operating room. I didn't know him. I couldn't see his face, and yet with his gentle ways he calmed my fears and caused me to relax while I was waiting for the procedure to begin. The timing was such that we were granted the added benefit of staying in the city a few more days to rest after the procedure. Perhaps the best gift of all was the birth of our daughter less than one year later. She is a joy to our lives.

No matter how difficult or painful the situation, I have learned that God is with me. Even though emotionally I feel alone, intellectually I know that I am not alone. God uses these difficult times as opportunities for me to grow closer to Him. As I grow closer to God, He gently reminds me of His great love for me.

I never knew the name of my 'angel' in the operating room and I will never be able to identify his face. Yet, he was with me when I so desperately needed comfort. He diverted my attention when I was nearly consumed by my pain and loss. Am I surprised at that? Not at all; God is like that. He knows just what I need and He never fails to meet that need. God works that way, I've found.

The visual, as well as the auditory quality of a scene before us, can have great potential to impress our thinking and influence our emotions. What we bring to our encounters offers color, texture, and ultimately meaning. To the fatalist, events can unfold before her, and little if anything positive is taken from them. For one of a compassionate heart, she may be touched in a manner that stirs her in ways so profound that she opens herself to fresh ways of viewing life events.

Communicating her impressions by stream-of-consciousness, **Frances Valberg Ringenberg (1978)** welcomes us to join a festivity that she finds at once lighthearted and comedic, yet profoundly moving.

❦   ❦   ❦

It was an ice cream sundae event of sorts ... held in the playroom in honor of Superbowl Sunday… any cause for celebration… anything for a little lightness… a moment of diversion. My son, then 17, was in the pediatric department that covers ages up to 21. The whole hospital floor, in fact, is given to pediatric neurological cases of one sort or another.

The event had the air of the Mad Hatter's party in *Alice in Wonderland*. We ran out of spoons, then came the search for whipped cream. After looking everywhere, even among the watercolors, somebody found it… where else, but in the refrigerator.

The staff person made a fine Mad Hatter, pattering about and muttering that this was his first ice cream party. Chocolate syrup made a late arrival, too,… then cherries.. and chips… and sprinkles… and even bananas appeared.

A small, leathery volunteer… ah, the March Hare?… whispered to me in conspiratorial tones, "I feel so bad for him…" I had no idea who she meant… per-

The event had the air of the Mad Hatter's party in Alice in Wonderland.

haps the child out in the hall who couldn't eat ice cream? I didn't know, but I nodded sympathetically.

The kids gathered around the table with all the aplomb of Carroll's characters. Among them, a friendly teenage boy with a body bent at a seemingly impossible angle… a girl radiating various sized braids and wearing a Pooh Bear robe… and a little guy with a wild configuration of hair… poking out through head bandages… and very thick glasses and a squeaky, weepy voice. *Ah yes, the Mouse,* I thought.

And there, around the edges of the gaiety hovered the parents, the ones I couldn't fit into Wonderland. Their party spirits were far too carefully contrived, their pain too cautiously controlled....

Do I look like that? I wondered.

And taking in the scene, I couldn't help thinking, *it's often the parents who make me cry.* Then I thought of that verse, about many coming to recline at the table with Abraham, Isaac, and Jacob in the Kingdom of Heaven... and I was left to ponder.

For middle class, white Americans, the 1950s were undeniably characterized by a certain decorum of restraint. Following World War II, America was invested in bringing itself back together – men returning from military service and women reentering a domestic role, the departure from which was, in many sectors, a matter of national need for additional aid with the war effort. The 1960s saw a social revolution that spilled into the 1970s and on into the '80s, but for many there remained a carry-over, if not overtly then certainly as an undercurrent, of restraints practiced in those years leading up to the cultural explosion of the '60s.

The social prohibition against offering affirmation to each other was one of these deeply ingrained attitudes. "A compliment will give her the big head," was all too often the rationale for withholding verbalized support among family members and to those in the wider community as well.

To avoid being labeled a "show off," or appearing to be "too full of one's self," or being "stuck up," or having "airs," or being found guilty of, or victimized by, insincere flattery – many tended to submit to the psychology of limitation. Viewing one's self as humble and thus of unassailable character served as a form of personal protection and tended to guarantee a secure place of acceptance within one's immediate and powerful peer group. What was found later upon the softening of these social constraints was an underbelly of potentially crippling suppression of one's viable attributes that, otherwise, could make a

positive contribution to many areas of life. What was accepted as
a behavioral norm was a compressed, if not almost extinguished,
authenticity.

**Joyce Smith Helyer (affiliated with Taylor University
since 1985; presently Associate Vice President for University
Advancement)** takes us with her into a zone characterized by
overriding attitudes that rendered her unaware of her unusual
talents. It took but a single, simple inquiry by a respected educa-
tor to penetrate the culturally constructed boundaries of Joyce's
world. Her response to this occurrence rises above the expected
and exposes valuable insight.

It was following one of my summer school classes back in
1996: Critical Issues in Higher Education. As for completing
the requirements for my master's degree program, I was on the
home stretch. Our kids had long since been on their own, and
my husband was involved in his academic pursuits. My gruel-
ing schedule of juggling full-time university development work
at Taylor University, together with taking graduate courses, was
nearly behind me.

I had never worked so hard. Preparation for my final class
presentation had tied me tightly to my "to do" lists and my
demanding time schedule. My *Day Timer* had long since become
an essential part of me, like an arm or a leg. When I reviewed the
requirements for the class, I wondered how all of this could be
accomplished in a five-week course. I remembered that previous courses and life experiences had taught me to work my way
through step by step, take each project separately and realize there would be very few "free" moments during those five
weeks. My self-talk included thoughts such as, *You can do this.
Don't struggle. Accept the challenge and move forward.*

The class drew to a close. My presentation was over. I gathered my books and started for the door when my professor spoke
to me. Matter-of-factly, and without emotion, she asked, "Joyce,

are you considering a doctoral program? We need women like you in academia."

If I thought my sense of elation at completing my final course project had been excessive, it was nothing to the way I felt upon hearing those words from a person of undisputed reputation and for whom I had developed great respect.

A sense of pleasure washed over me at this affirmation of my abilities. I thanked her for her inspiration and left the classroom. It wasn't until later, when I piled my books into my car and slipped the key into the ignition, that my feelings crystallized. Suddenly, tears came to my eyes. What surprised me the most was that my tears were not tears of gratitude and pleasure. Rather, they were tears of grief and anger: grief for wasted years of self-doubt and lack of confidence, anger for not believing in myself and my God-given abilities and gifts.

I felt myself weeping for the losses: loss of time, loss of opportunities, loss of knowing who I had most surely always been. Somehow, I had invited or allowed self-doubt to delay my pursuit of graduate studies. Somehow, I had allowed myself, with all the very best of intentions, to become blinded.

Through the weeks and months that followed this moment of self-revelation, set in motion by that simple, straightforward question by a professor to a student, there began to open in me something illuminating and joyous. I found myself responding confidently to new opportunities, new life challenges. I was able to dismiss, more easily, feelings of self-doubt and petty fears. What has perhaps spoken most clearly to me is the realization that I was being introduced to whom I most surely had always been; I was awakening to my authentic self.

So deeply embedded within me is this experience that whenever I have opportunity to interact with others, and in particular with women whose need for affirmation I sense, I am compelled to offer them the gift of confidence and affirmation so freely given to me. I doubt that I will ever cease to be amazed at the power of affirmation.

━━━━━━━━━━━━━━━ ❧ ❧ ❧ ━━━━━━━━━━━━━━━

Janice Spaulding Miller (1972) describes circumstances in which she finds herself that are so different from what she expected from life that she is challenged in ways she could not have foreseen. And yet, there are themes that run throughout Janice's account: themes of hope, encouragement, endurance, and high creativity. What Janice learns from this experience, she may not have been able to learn so effectively or personally had this particular set of forces not converged in her life.

❧ ❧ ❧

"What are we going to do, Lord?" I asked silently one January morning. "Here I am, four months pregnant with our second child, and my husband has just received a call announcing that his job is eliminated." I was in shock.

There had been no inkling, no clue that this would happen. How could a hard-working, loyal employee be terminated? It wasn't fair. Besides, why would God let this happen to His children who were trying to live for Him? This wasn't starting off as a good year at all.

It was the early 1980s. The country was in the midst of a mini-recession. The job market, especially in rural Indiana, was difficult. What were we to do? With a three-year-old to care for and a baby on the way, I was not in a position to look for employment had there been a job available.

After the initial shock, our questions intensified. Had we done something wrong? What could we do now? Where could my husband find employment? How could we pay our bills? How would we pay upcoming medical expenses?

This was not the first time we had been unemployed, but this time it was far different. Without responsibilities, we could look on previous hard times as adventures. This time we had little ones depending on us. During the course of the next several very scary months, I had the opportunity to think back to other times when things looked bleak. I reflected on how things seemed to work out back then: jobs coming along just before we got married, finding housing when we needed it, finding jobs after we were laid off. I even thought about the way our income seemed to stretch when I quit work to care for our first child. These memories about how things eventually worked out in the past helped me face this uncertain future.

I found that during those jobless months, I had to be strong physically for the baby I was carrying as well as in caring for our preschooler. I took note of how she thrived from more play time with dad, since he was now at home and unemployed.

But still, the responsibilities wouldn't end. Tensions mounted. It felt as if a part of our lives had come to an end. There were times when I felt the only energy I had was for crying.

I knew I had to be strong mentally to figure out how to pay bills and provide food. I had to cut corners, to spend wisely, and to discern needs from wants. It helped that I had grown up in a family that "made do" with what was available. Fortunately, this

practice was not new to me. It proved helpful that I had always been conservative in my spending; now I had to be not only conservative but also creative. Think, for example: garage sales, growing our own food, and 101 ways with ground beef.

I also knew I had to be strong emotionally, to be *up* when my husband was *down*. This was a very depressing time for him. He needed to hear how important he was to us and that we loved him. We would not be better off without him. He needed my strength and my encouragement. He needed to be reassured, just as I had reaffirmed within my own thinking, that the right job would appear at the right time.

Throughout this difficult time, I was thankful that in the face of my husband's pessimism I could maintain optimism, even though, at times, I tired of being the strong one. I was tempted to say, "Snap out of it and let's get on with life." I am confident that because of God's grace I was able, however, to be the encourager and cheerleader that my husband and family needed at that time.

I knew, too, that I had to be strong spiritually. Our obstacles soon became bigger than we were. How could we face them alone? Once again, I thought of the many times my own family had come through difficulties when I was young. I thought again about the problems that we had to face before we started our own family, and the ways we had come through them. I thought of the larger picture, that God was at work for our good in all things.

During those months, I learned to be the gracious recipient of others' giving. There were a restaurant's leftover chicken and noodles, and our neighbor's extra strawberries. I learned there is no shame in asking for help, whether from church or government, though it is, admittedly, humbling.

Above all, I sensed all over again that God does indeed keep His promises. During those months we did have food to eat and our bills were paid. As it so happened, just before our son was born, my husband found another job, and the company even paid the medical bills connected with our son's birth. Through the whole experience, I learned far more about what it is to face adversity, to be creative and to work hard within times of need, to humble myself before what appears to be forces much larger than I, yet to hold my head erect in the confidence that things do indeed have a way of working out. That our faith can be rewarded and our sense of being protected and provided for are, indeed, real.

Family, to many of us, is merely a fact of life – a given. We are brought up within our own unique family structure and our usual response to it is an unquestioned acceptance. Our family is our immediate and most important social environment and, as such, many of us interact with it on a kind of auto-pilot. We tend to act and react, adapt, and assimilate – usually with limited questioning.

It is not until we emerge from the family unit and begin to observe other ways of life beyond our own private world, that comparisons and contrasts begin to show themselves and we begin to ask questions about what we have previously accepted without challenge.

Many of us carry along through life portions of the family philosophy and practice. If we were the fortunate recipients of an essentially healthy upbringing, we will find ourselves forming judgments about others' ways as opposed to what we have known – using our experience as the norm against which we measure the quality of others. If we are the product of a dysfunctional family unit, what we take from those interactions may be varied and reactionary.

Sometimes considerable amounts of time can pass before some unexamined family tradition, implemented repeatedly and comfortably by us over the years, either suddenly or gradually begins to show itself ready to be re-evaluated within a broader context.

Hazel Butz Carruth Anderson (1938) explores what seemed in her youth to be an exemplary family philosophy. Easily, she assimilated the concept and was conscientious about fulfilling its import, only to find later in life that its broad and unquestioned applicability may be appropriate only in carefully selected circumstances.

While I was growing up as the eldest child on my family's South Dakota farm during the 1920s, I adopted with ease and without question the attitude of my parents that *anything worth doing is worth doing well*. Without giving this inclination a name, in time I became, quite simply, a perfectionist. Failure upset me. I became devoted to doing all things well, and for me that meant doing them right.

I recall crying in utter frustration over a high school assignment in history. My teacher assigned some pages in the textbook to outline. The problem was that no one had ever taught me *how* to outline.

As I reflect on that highly distressing moment, it would have been impossible then to have imagined that later on in my life, once I learned the method, I would outline many of my own assignments; that I would, with no difficulty, outline numerous speeches and sermons given by others; and that I would choose this highly effective organizational method for my own teaching materials used in the classroom.

What I came to understand with time and circumstance, however, was that the effort expended in trying to be perfectly prepared and perfectly organized resulted too often in a sense of impatience both with myself and with others. I think I must have prayed for patience more than for any other Christian virtue.

I think I must have prayed for patience more than for any other Christian virtue.

Having made it a priority to organize the day's materials as well as the day's schedule, I found myself sometimes nearly defeated because of disruptions to my carefully laid plans.

Time passed… as did events that challenged my earnest inclination to have my life arranged according to my concepts of orderliness. I began to wonder eventually if the thinking I had cultivated was, in reality, its own private interpretation of those words from my past: *anything worth doing is worth doing well.* Emerging from my misgivings was another option, and that different rendering brought into play what was to become a vital shift in my thinking. What finally became clear to me, in life's larger picture, was that the needs of others have greater significance for me than my resolute adherence to my own painstakingly constructed time lines and systems. As much as I respected the well-organized life, I learned that people and their needs are most important by far.

Humor, good-natured banter, exaggeration, laying hold of the incongruous – all can lighten circumstances grown heavy, tedious, and lifeless. *Joie de vivre* – the french expression for "joy of living" – erupts with a flash of recognition when perceived seriousness is juxtaposed against enlightened irrelevance. **Kayleen Brewer Reusser (1982)** shares just this cleverness that triggers a comic and healing response.

My two daughters turned up their cards: "M" and "Cereal," respectively. The eldest yelled "Mueseli" and won the point.

We were at a local coffee house playing "ASAP," a game in which two groups of cards, one alphabetical and the other subject-oriented, are turned up by the players simultaneously. Players have to think of a common denominator between the two cards and call out a legitimate answer. Whoever does so first, wins the point.

My teenager was ahead of her younger sister by six points. I had no points at all and was silently hoping at least to get on the scoreboard. After several more rounds, I was feeling embarrassed by my lack of brainpower. But, I hung in.

Then came the next move. Up came the card printed with the letter "T" and the subject card, "TV Show."

With no hesitation, I shouted out, "Tell It to Your Mom!" and felt wonderfully smug inside.

"Tell It to Your Mom?" my eldest looked at me quizzically. What in the world is, 'Tell It to Your Mom?'"

"What do you mean, 'What in the world is that'?" I questioned her right back, knowing all the while that she couldn't possibly know about a show that I had watched as a youngster. So, I explained how it was that this particular TV show, back when I was a kid, had a youngster sit behind a screen. He was to ask three different moms questions about growing up. The mom who was judged to come up with the best answers would be the winner.

At this explanation, my girls first looked at me, then at each other, rolled their eyes, and burst into laughter. In no time, I was right there with them – laughing uproariously. Each of us, coming from our own vantage point, was united in rollicking good humor – laughing at, laughing with, laughing because. Whatever its origins, that moment of lightheartedness was beautiful to me.

Besides being mighty glad the coffeehouse was empty at just that time, my respect for the value of humor in my family was reaffirmed.

I have often read the position of mental health professionals on the significance of laughter in life. I have read that people who laugh at their mistakes recover faster from illness than do perfectionists. And from Proverbs 17, I was reminded that *a merry heart doeth good like medicine.*

More than merely making a moment of good pleasure, I have found that humor can be a great bonding agent among my family members. Take, for example, an incident that remains a source of good humor to this very day.

My then 16-year-old son had pushed my final button that particular day. I wanted to scream at him and launch into a serious lecture about the dangerous consequences of the behavior he was exhibiting, and to punch something, maybe even him. But I was hesitant to give full expression to what I was really feeling. Finally, I stood up straight, shook my finger at him and said sternly, "If you don't behave, I'll… I'll… " and I have no idea where it came from but I blurted out – "I'll tickle your toes!"

With that, my two daughters, sitting nearby and silently taking in my frustration, nearly fell off their chairs in hysterical laughter. No longer able to hold a straight face, I joined in, and then my son, too.

Even now, long after this incident, and quoted around our house at frequent intervals, "Be careful or Mom'll tickle your toes!" never fails to bring chuckles and laughter. What is for sure is that I feel far better than had I given in to my initial impulse.

To my way of seeing life, family laughter is truly a gift. To be able to ease tensions, to lift spirits, and make my own kids laugh – well, to me, that's almost sacred. *Laugh, for Family's Sake!* That's my motto.

Acknowledging our fears, and working through them, is one of the greatest gifts we can give to ourselves. **Serena Thrush Duke (2004)** takes us into an early-life experience that imprinted itself on her in such a profound and negative manner that, with time, it became, as she describes it, a phobia. A compelling convergence of circumstances forces Serena to review and deal with the phobic effect of this memory.

It wasn't death itself that I feared so much. More precisely, my fear was of everything associated with the dead, like caskets, funeral homes, and cemeteries. I know exactly where this fear came from. And I knew I should come to terms with it, but right then, in the crush of it all, there was no way I could give myself to such an undertaking. My pastor had called me – the very night before the funeral – and told me the family was requesting that I give the eulogy for a woman whose friendship had become so very important in my life, and whose death now plunged me into shock and grief.

I had come to know this wonderful lady as the result of a desire to become involved in an outreach ministry. What resulted from our ensuing visits was a powerful and highly rewarding mutual friendship. When the phone call came informing me that she had died suddenly of a heart attack, not only was I thrown into mourning, I soon learned I was about to face some of life's demands that I feared the most.

My initial response to the pastor's request was to decline.

There came immediately to my mind visions of my re-occurring nightmares: rooms full of caskets, bodies moving, corpses trying to get my attention, and being lost in a morgue. Imagining myself in a funeral home one more time, even if only for a moment, shot panic and fear through my body.

I was torn. I wanted to give my dear friend the loving tribute she deserved and also to exercise my love for public speaking and share with others how much my friend meant to me. I was afraid my paralyzing fear of death would make that impossible. Still, with the encouragement of my pastor and family, reluctantly, I agreed.

That night I cried out to the Lord for strength knowing full well that I could not accomplish this feat on my own. I hardly slept. I tossed and turned. *What am I going to do, Lord?* I asked over and over; and my restless mind suddenly tricked me back into being that six-year-old child, standing there – so small and vulnerable – with my parents at my great grandmother's casket. Everything was subdued and orderly. There was soft music. People were lingering around the casket, speaking in low tones. Then, without warning, a thunderstorm ripped through town causing a massive power outage. Suddenly, everything went black. I remember the confusion; I was stunned and terrified, and I didn't know what to do. So, perhaps it stands to reason that every time I entered a funeral home after that those same feelings of panic – the not knowing what might happen – would well up in me just as they did so many years ago.

The night was long and the next morning, waiting to leave for the funeral, seemed even longer. I was nearly consumed with anxiety. Later, when I entered the funeral home, my eyes went directly to the casket. There lay the body of my dear friend.

I sat down, and that's when I felt it – the hot sensation of panic crawling its way up inside my chest and lodging in my throat. It felt as if I could hardly breathe. More than anything I wanted to run. I wanted to leave that room. I wanted to be so far away that even the memory of it would vanish in the distance between me and that scene before me. But, I dared not move. Through that awful torment, I knew what I had to do. I had to face up to my fears.

I hardly heard the pastor as he read my friend's favorite scripture. Then it was time. The pastor nodded to me and I knew I must make my way to the podium, only a few feet from the casket. I placed my notes before me, and I looked down at my hands, quivering as though they belonged to someone else. With sheer will power, I lifted my eyes and made myself look out over the people gathered there. I drew a deep breath.

Just as I began to speak, a curious thing happened. A feeling of peace seemed to settle around me. I found I could do what I had thought, only moments before, would be impossible. Almost easily now, I began to speak about our special friendship, and the more I spoke, pleasant memories would flood my mind. I turned my head, and found I could look at the body of my dear friend lying in the casket.

That hot summer day in the funeral home was perhaps one of the most challenging moments I have ever faced. And yet, I felt assured that I touched the hearts of the people present because of the expression on their faces, and their kind remarks later. Most importantly, I feel I learned to trust God in new ways. Through this experience, I have come to understand more of what it is to face fears and push through them.

Since that time, I have also spoken at my own grandmother's funeral. To this day, I do not feel comfortable in funeral homes and I am still plagued with nightmares about them, but I draw a whole new level of confidence from Philippians 4:13 when I remind myself, *I can do all things through Christ who strengthens me.*

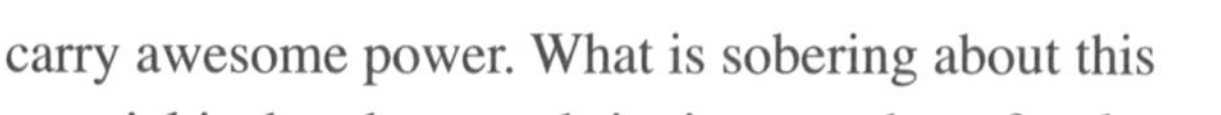

Words carry awesome power. What is sobering about this explosive potential is that the mere bringing together of a cluster of syllables to form a word or a sentence that comes from the mouth can be used as a force to create or destroy, to heal or harm, to unleash the positive or throw open the floodgates of the negative. We are reminded that out of the abundance of the heart the mouth speaks and that a soft answer has the capability of defusing the negative and, additionally, of infusing positive, up-building potential. **Nancy E. Dusckas (1975)** takes us back to her youth, back to an incident so private and so secret that, to this day, she says she has not mentioned it to any of her friends who were also present at that time. Nor has she forgotten the import of those few words said to her decades ago. Through a real-life incident, so brief it could easily have been overlooked or pushed to the back of the mind, we are challenged to be mindful of the power of the spoken word.

I am amazed that even today, as a busy professional, I can readily bring to mind and ponder words that were said to me when I was very young, words that still affect me as I make decisions in my work.

I had begun participating in a Girl Scout program at the youngest age allowed at that time. I was in the second grade and remained with the program to the very senior level, the Patrol System.

I remember clearly when it was time to elect new Patrol Leaders and I recall the high energy of the event. It wasn't my turn to hold that particular office at that time, but I always had a lot of responsibilities in the troop and I knew my opinions carried a lot of merit. When the results of the election came in, I was pleased to be elected. I paid little attention to much else that was going on.

Shortly after the election, my troop leader approached me and whispered something in my ear. Her words proved to be a defining moment, one that I have remembered to this day.

There was a girl in the troop who was a little shy and seemed to be without many strong leadership skills. Regardless of this, she had been one of the girls who was running for a Patrol Leadership position. It had to have been a brave step for her to allow herself to be considered. I had gone ahead, however, and was pleased that my name was put forward. While I knew the other girl and liked her, I never gave much thought to supporting her. Well after the election was over, my troop leader leaned toward me and whispered, "Do you know that if this girl had been elected, it might have been the only leadership position she would have held in her whole life? It wouldn't have hurt anything."

Suddenly my heart seemed to drop. How could I have been so consumed with the excitement of the moment that I overlooked a wonderful opportunity for a quiet girl who had just taken the biggest risk of her life? Did I have any way of knowing the girl could have done a good job if she had been elected? Of course not, but what I do know is that the opportunity would have given her experience that was available only in our troop at that time. The troop leader was right to say what she did.

To this day, I don't think back on the troop leader's words as scolding, just thought provoking. It doesn't take much to prompt  me to reflect on that experience. The memory of those words, said in a gentle whisper, still reminds me that I need to look beyond the boundaries of what I think is important to me. I need to pay attention to what I can do to help others grow. That brief moment served as a great lesson to me about mentoring others.

I don't know if I was the only person to whom the troop leader whispered those words after the election. Someday, I may ask some of my old Girl Scout friends if the leader had whispered the same to them. Perhaps, however, there is no need to.

From early childhood, we can be so deeply influenced by persons or events that life may assume a shape that can take to itself compensative mechanisms of a cumulative and self-perpetuating nature. These characteristics may have positive or negative attributes, or even be a mix. If we avoid opportunities to pause during our lives and in the quiet of our hearts call forth these early initial impressions, we may, as the expression goes, be doomed to perpetuate these attitudes that have, over time, grown stale and inappropriate once faced with the light of balanced maturity.

The following vignette tells of just such a dynamic. This is a vividly remembered personal experience by **Jewell Reinhart Coburn (1955)**. This incident is related as an example of the power of an early childhood sensation and how, later in life, it became important to revisit the memory with less the impressionable and reactive eyes of a child and with the more discerning mind of the adult. By so doing, did the review process minimize the positive, character-forming quality of the initial impact? Not necessarily. What a more educated, informed perspective can bring to an experience is merely refinement, not loss of its essence.

It was sometime during the early 1940s. I was six, maybe seven – old enough to lend a hand to a harried mother in a hot kitchen, but still too young to be trusted with the best family china.

It was a Sunday. The church service was behind us. Uplifted and reassured by the notion that God was indeed on duty 24 hours, seven days of every week, folks just had to feel good. Hats and gloves lay on smooth bedspreads. Suit jackets, unbuttoned. Ties loosened, slightly. This was obviously a "beyond-the-ordinary" event. I was confident of this because my mother summoned me to carry the salads to the dining room table on the very dishware I had been denied to touch many times before.

I stood fascinated while mother created on each salad plate a work of art. First, the carefully arranged iceberg lettuce leaves.

Then came the spears of delicately cooked asparagus directly from our garden. Over that, a sprinkling of egg yolk, boiled hard, then gentled through the tiny holes of the kitchen sieve. The final touches were thin, red pimento slices laid gracefully across the top for zest and color.

Swelled with excitement, sobered by nervousness, yet determined to prove myself, I placed each salad precisely to the left tip of the salad fork at each of the six place settings. I remember thinking how beautiful the table looked and how pleased Grandfather and Grandmother would be with so perfect a meal prepared by mother in their honor.

I was aware, too, that mother had cooked two meals, not one. Grandfather, she was informed, was on a rigid, salt-free diet. Just then, mother motioned from the kitchen for my father to bring everyone to the table. I recall how right it felt for my father to take his place at the head of the table. While he gestured to his parents to sit at his right, my brother and I took our seats to his left.

Things were, in that moment, silent like a church midweek. That's when it happened.

Mother appeared in the doorway, her face flushed. Hurriedly she untied her apron and tucked it behind her as she sat down. I looked on admiringly, but then, from the corner of my eye, I observed my Grandfather shift noticeably in his chair. I watched as he extended his arm forward, the palm of his hand facing outward in front of him. He took a deep breath. Then with his outstretched hand, he pushed the salad plate away from him, stating emphatically that surely his daughter-in-law could remember that this combination of vegetables he routinely avoided.

For a moment, it was as though I were seeing a double exposure. One image super-imposed upon another, each image sharp and distinct, yet together, blurred, and confused. There was Grandfather – a demeanor of unequaled imperiousness, smudging my mother – diminished and humiliated.

The stunned silence seemed crammed with feelings for which I had no words. Only later did I come to understand the language for those sensations. Injustice was one. And intolerance. Disrespect. Ruthlessness. Condescension. Abuse – words that cut like serrated knives and left deep, ragged wounds.

What I observed at that dining room table was a murder of sorts, a mini-assassination. A simple gesture packed dense with violence and cruelty. Simultaneously, something within me took form. Something palpable. Not a mere passing feeling. Rather, something that felt solid and sharp-edged, that made its own deep cut. Something I came to understand would endure.

"Never," I thought from deep within me, "never will I stand by while my mother is humiliated in this manner." To my innocent mind, this attack made no sense. What could possibly justify this act? I lacked the tools for rational, linear thought. Had one thing led to another, which finally resulted in so unfeeling a gesture? This, I had no way of knowing. But what I did know was that there was need for intervention and protection.

Psychology labels this inclination the "Protector Syndrome," one of the numerous Jungian universal archetypes. Not at all inaccurate, I'd have to agree. And certainly, not at all incorrect for what I have tended to find myself subsequently acting out.

Life lessons learned by direct observation and participation, I've experienced, can sear themselves into the neurons, slashing pathways in the brain that from then on color responses to life events. And so it has been that the rejected, the disenfranchised, the abused – they may count on attention and potential comfort where I am concerned.

Who would have known the power with which the Spirit of Compassion could speak through a plate of rejected salad topped with slices of shiny red pimento? And who could have known that in that moment, like gleaming new steel etched by acid, it would be my own innocence that would be, from that time forward, branded with deep markings of compassion that would move me to travel the world, develop educational programs, publish a collection of books – all to advance the message of Love and Understanding toward those different from us, toward those perceived to be less fortunate than we.

But, lest too grand a picture appear to be painted from the dusty pigments of a long ago memory, I hasten to add that there can be downsides to what might be, at first glance, the unfolding of noble traits. With a gift such as this, I've learned, come weighty responsibilities. Over the years and throughout events, countless of which would push my lever to unleash floods of compassion, there have emerged conditions that call for my differentiation, analysis, scrutiny, discernment, and balance. There are, I came to understand, circumstances in which "to save" can be "to enslave." And herein lies the challenge: not the generating of care and concern in my case, but rather the insight that the *greater good* may be better served by having the wisdom to know when to act and when to step aside.

**Angie Lyons Knight (1994)** tells of an incident that not only became highly meaningful to her in a personal way, but also to those who watched while it took place. She writes that she always wanted her unfortunate condition to be used to make a difference in people's lives. An unfortunate accident brings that desire into reality. From the incident, together with the skills honed during her years of training as early as a young girl, Angie shows how gracefulness, good humor, and a poignant message can emerge from adversity.

The date was August 17, 2003. It wasn't really a significant date in a large, broad sense, but it will remain emblazoned on my memory – just like June 3, 1997, the date I received my diagnosis of Multiple Sclerosis – and a happy June 8, 1999, the date of my twin daughters' birth.

On August 17, I sang two musical presentations as "special music" for our Sunday worship service. Usually, I played the piano and accompanied my own solos – many of them my own compositions. I have played the piano nearly 25 years; however, M.S. has seen fit within the last two years to limit the dexterity of my left hand.

For this reason, when my mother heard a particular musical piece, "If You Want Me To," and she thought its message about rising above life's struggles so appropriate to my own story, I was pleased when I found suitable background accompaniment on a CD. The recording would serve in place of my own piano accompaniment.

I have felt from the start of this journey, now more than six years ago, that my life would somehow be used to impart understanding through my struggle. I planned to speak briefly before I sang because I really wanted to share the song's personal meaning – how I leaned on the scripture that, *His strength can be made perfect in my weakness*. I also wanted the opportunity to share about the significance of my favorite hymn, the second musical selection I was to offer, but which I was to play on my flute for the offertory. "It is Well" has the beautiful message about those times when life is peaceful and flowing like a river, and when the waves crash in on the shores of life, God enables me to continue to have the peace of Christ in my soul. This is what I had hoped to say.

When I was in high school, I was not very athletic, but I did love to speak and perform. As president of the Drama Club and captain of the Speech Team, I was accustomed to being in front of people. In fact, I won the state championship in "impromptu speaking," an event in which the student received a topic, and then was given only 30 seconds to prepare a three to five minute presentation on the subject.

When I became a middle-school teacher, I realized immediately how impromptu speaking was the perfect preparation for my career in the classroom. What I didn't know was that it would also prepare me for a certain day in church when things didn't go as planned.

This year for our annual small town Labor Day Festival, our

church would be distributing cups of cold water to passers-by. The plastic cups were prepared and stacked in readiness in two pyramids on a narrow folding table near the steps leading to the stage in the church sanctuary. This arrangement replaced the sturdy, wooden table that usually stood there.

Everything went well as the Sunday program began to unfold. I played my flute for the offertory and was pleased because it is not my entire hand but only my fingers that are called upon to move when I play the instrument.

The vocal presentation of "If You Want Me To" was to follow. I set down my flute and prepared to step up to the stage. My first step, using my right foot, went well. But then, I felt shaky. What I have learned to do at times like this is to reach out to the right to steady myself.

Suddenly, I noticed the pulpit was too far away for support, and the slender, folding table supporting the plastic cups was all that was available to me. Instinctively, I reached for the table. I should have seen it coming. That slight jostling of the table sent the carefully constructed pyramid of cups careening to the floor and clattering down the steps.

I have never been extremely well-coordinated, and M.S. has greatly exacerbated the problem, especially with my left leg and hand; so along with the crash of cups I, too, tripped and fell.

Recently, tripping had become a more common occurrence for me. Shakily, I went on, as I had learned to do from my past, not noticing that somebody had rushed forward to help. Although I may have appeared stubbornly independent, the truth was that I was in a bit of shock as I took the microphone to follow through with my vocal presentation.

Dramatic entrances and creative introductions are one thing. But during this otherwise formal Sunday morning service, it was not my intention to get everyone's attention this way. I was quite concerned about the cups I had scattered; it didn't occur to me that people were concerned about my having hurt myself.

What I managed to say first was to let the audience know that, though unplanned, the entrance was actually related to what

I was about to share. I went on to tell of my M.S., and how it was
having more and more of an effect on my life since it was first
diagnosed more than six years ago. Then I spoke of how happy
I was to share the hymn, "It is Well," as the offertory, and went
on to say something about its meaning in my life. What I wanted
others to know that morning was that it truly *is* well with my
soul, although it may not be so well with my body just now.

I made it through the song without crying – although in all
honesty I came very close.

It wasn't until I was back in my seat (going down on the
farther side of the staircase, the only one with a railing) that I
realized I had completely forgotten to talk about the meaning in
my life of that wonderfully empowering scripture, *His strength is
made perfect in my weakness.*

Later, after the church service, I was approached by several church members and told, in one way or another, that my
introduction was just what they needed. Had I walked up and
performed as planned, it wouldn't have been at all as powerful or
as meaningful as what actually occurred. Of course, I didn't want
to have happen what took place that morning; but then, maybe
it was meant to be. Maybe it was important for everyone to see
firsthand… my weakness.

A mother's heart can feel as if it has a memory all of its own.
Evidence now points to our very biology as having the capacity
to carry the effects of life impressions. Regardless of the passage of time or the accumulation of events, a parent's heart is its
own crucible, storing memories that refuse to diminish or fade
with time. It follows, therefore, that there can be times when
the holder of distant memories feels deeply the sensation of
isolation, being alone in her private place of stored reveries and
without connection to those who would reinforce the warmth of
a time gone by.

Marilyn Willett Heavilin (1959) has had all of these sensa-

tions. She wondered on an especially difficult anniversary if
anyone now shared the knowledge of that painful part of her life
so long ago.

December 7, 1941 – Pearl Harbor Day. For our nation,
that was "a day that shall live in infamy," announced President
Franklin Roosevelt. For me personally, the day that will live forever in my own private infamy is February 10, 1983 – the night
our 17-year-old son went to a basketball game and never came
home.

That night, our son was killed in a car crash caused by a
drunk driver. He was our third son to die. Our first died of SIDS
in 1964. Then our next son's twin died of pneumonia in 1966
when he was only 10 days old. We raised this remaining twin,
watched him grow into a handsome, highly intelligent, multi-tal-
ented 17-year-old. Then he was gone, too.

Our house fell silent. It seemed the phone seldom rang. Ac-
tivities ground to a halt. In a split second, we faced the empty nest. Our lives were forever changed.

As we approached the 20th anniversary of his death, I dreaded the day. For one thing, it didn't seem possible he had actually been gone for that length of time. Secondly, I feared how 20 years could diminish the significance of
our loss. After all, two decades is a long time. Our society tends
to put little value on an event that happened so long ago. Surely,
I thought, others would have forgotten our son by now.

Shortly before the anniversary of his death, a close friend of
mine phoned one evening to say she had something wonderful
to tell me. She happened to have attended a college English class
earlier that night. The professor told the students they were to

As we approached the 20th anniversary
of his death, I dreaded the day.

select someone to proofread and critique their work before they handed it in. My friend explained to the professor that she was fortunate to have a good friend who was a writer and asked if it would be all right for her to proof her work. When the professor asked the name of her friend, she gave him mine.

"Why, I know who she is," responded the professor. "Her son was my paper boy, the best paper boy I ever had!"

Someone remembered our son. No anniversary gift could have been more deeply appreciated. Our son was not forgotten.

When **Mary Ellen Bidwell Rothrock** is feeling at her lowest and most vulnerable, the phone rings. Because of the message she receives, she must break through her despondency with lightning speed. Mary Ellen's touch of humor brings a lightness and "can-do" spirit to the otherwise heavy subject of an over-stressed life and an inclination to depression.

In 1994, after enduring eight years of acute "Sandwich Generationitis," I suddenly lost both sides of the "sandwich." My mother died from Alzheimer's, and our angry teenager moved to a state-funded boarding school for academically gifted juniors and seniors. Instead of feeling a sense of release, I felt a slow unraveling in the hollow of my heart, and then… depression. Days passed during which I moved as if through thick soup, accomplishing little or nothing.

One Friday morning I lay in bed overwhelmed and depressed. Our daughter was bringing a carload of teenagers home from her boarding school. By that evening I had to have cleaned not only the downstairs but also the upstairs. Kids were staying overnight and I was determined to house the males upstairs and the females downstairs.

"I have to clean the *whole* house!" I moaned deep inside,

pulling the covers over my head. Then suddenly it came to me. I remembered my three-step formula for coping with major stress.

I had discovered it during my Mom's last year. I was visiting her almost daily in the nursing wing of her retirement home. Exiting one day through the foyer, after being pummeled by staff with what seemed like their endless questions demanding my informed and immediate decisions about procedures and final arrangements in the face of my Mom's worsening condition, I spotted a devotional booklet on the coffee table nearby. It's title: *"Come Ye Apart."*

"I'm coming apart, all right," I responded. Of course, I knew what the words really meant, but what I wanted to do was scream to God, "I'm breaking down! Do something!"

Under the covers of my bed that Friday, I could almost smile at how my articulated, honest feelings had become helpful triggers to apply my three-step coping formula.

"Step One: I'm Coming Apart." What this meant to me was that I could go to God for help, not all spruced up with my best, positive attitude, but in honest desperation.

After praying about the task at hand, I reached for the notebook beside my bed to apply "Step Two: I'm Breaking Down." So what I did was literally break down the cleaning of the whole house into distinct tasks to be done.

Then I progressed to "Step Three: Do Something!" Among the countless, mostly worthless self-help books I owned was one gem: *Feeling Good* by Dr. David Burns. Motivation, Burns maintains, follows action, not the reverse. Doing something – almost anything – brightens one's mood. What I was learning firsthand was that nothing is so harmful to one's self-esteem as staying in bed.

From my bed, I spied the basket of clean laundry. I chose to see it as just a basket of socks. I dragged myself out of bed, rolled the socks into little bundles, and placed them in my husband's sock drawer.

Already I could feel my sense of self rising a notch, just as Dr. Burns had written. Next, I tackled the kitchen, and then moved on to the family room. Step by step, task by task, I followed the list I'd made. I focused tightly on each project and ignored the chaos around me. I persevered.

By evening, when the kids arrived, in soft lighting the house looked quite respectable. The beds were made up. Things were in order.

Seeing our daughter did wonders for my aching heart. But trying to keep the boys upstairs, separated from the girls, took some doing. One young man in a bedroom with aquariums kept wandering downstairs complaining, "But I'm not used to sleeping with fish."

Confidently, I sent him back upstairs. I had standards, and he would have to understand that. After all, I had a clean house to prove it!

An abrupt break in an otherwise ordered daily life can course its way through every level of our thinking and feeling. **Dorothy Hislop Miller (1942)** gives a finely honed focus on the moment, and through her ensuing journey along what she calls her "rainbow trail," she opens our hearts to fresh perspectives.

The doctor stood fingering his chart. I felt a stab of fear. When he finally spoke, his words were numbing. The test results revealed the presence of breast cancer. But this was not all. There were complications. Surgery, chemotherapy, and radiation – all were indicated. He asked if I had questions. I couldn't answer him. My mind was frozen.

This was two weeks before Christmas. Surgery was scheduled for the end of January. Encouraged by the support and love of my family and friends, I faced surgery feeling optimistic, only to have the post-surgery information send my spirits plummeting again. The cancer had spread. I felt chilling despair.

After that, it was as though I were losing my way. I felt smothered with lethargy. Night terrors awakened me – my heart pounding. Was it true? Was I really facing death?

Spring sometimes comes early to Northern California. That's the way it was one sun-drenched afternoon when my husband helped me into the car. Our purpose was to ride through the foothills. The forest greens, the wildflowers, drifts of blues and yellows were glorious. Rows of fruit trees stood haloed with blossoms: white, pink, and pale yellow. We drove through quaint little old gold-rush towns. We stopped for a delicious snack. In time, I became aware that my anxiety let go its grip. Tension faded. There was laughter, even contentment. That night, exhausted, I went to bed, my mind teeming with the images of the day. Gratitude spread through my mind and heart.

The next morning I looked for a quiet place, a place to be alone with my thoughts. Somehow, I had lost my way. I had been given loving support and care and I was grateful, but where was the inner peace, the sense of confidence? What, I wondered, really is the *Goodness of God*? Was I to accept it as a collection

of loving, happy events in my life? Or was it something beyond that?

I resolved to set out on a new path. Each night before I slept, I would review my day. I would pause and reflect on all things loving, beautiful, and funny, and for each, I would express my gratitude to God. My awareness of positive qualities and events grew daily. And then it came to me with perfect clarity – a grateful heart is a truly rapturous heart.

It has been a little over a year now that I have been on this rainbow trail. I share my happiness with others. It multiplies. It even turns into inexplicable joy.

Could it be that I am closer to understanding what the *Goodness of God* really means?

Dana Tucker Boxell (1977) describes an occurrence that logic suggests would cause her to be highly agitated. Instead, her serene, controlled demeanor prevailed as she focused her mind on the goodness of God. Dana shows how this practice had the power to elevate her spirit and render her calm and in charge of her thoughts and emotions midst chaos.

There it was again – the words of that song playing over and over again in my head and reaching way down into my heart: *I love You, Lord, and I lift my voice to worship You. Oh, my soul, rejoice.*

"Are you all right, Dear? You've been so quiet," said my mother, sitting next to me just outside the hospital emergency room.

Her voice broke through the strains of the song that had been going on repeatedly in my head for what seemed like several hours now. How could I convey to her the enveloping peace I was feeling throughout all this?

The words of this song came into my mind shortly after the call first came in. There had been an accident. My 14-year-old son had been seriously hurt while riding in a friend's four-wheeler a few miles from home.

The refrain continued through the frenzied ambulance ride to the hospital, and on through the countless tests and scans. Even then, seven hours into the ordeal, as my son lay in surgery, an unexplainable inner peace overrode my shock and quieted my anxiety.

The words persisted while the doctors came out of surgery to explain my son's grave situation: compound fracture of the femur, broken humerus and patella, lacerations to the lung, lacerations and contusions to the upper quadrant of his liver, as well as significant blood loss.

"You're right, Mom, I guess I have been quiet. I want you to know how much I appreciate your being here with me through all this. But I haven't been quiet because I'm worried or scared. It's just that my head and my heart keep singing this refrain over and over. The words lift my spirit. They bring me peace. I don't know the outcome of all this, Mom, but somehow I have a sense that whatever happens, it is securely in God's care."

Then I leaned back against the hospital waiting room chair and marveled inwardly at the power of the simple act of praising God in all things.

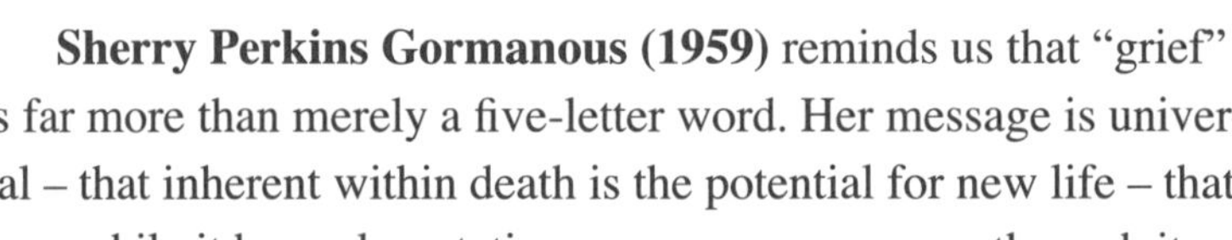

Sherry Perkins Gormanous (1959) reminds us that "grief" is far more than merely a five-letter word. Her message is universal – that inherent within death is the potential for new life – that loss, while it has a devastating power, once we pass through its down-pull and move toward acceptance, there emerges the sense of new beginnings.

This morning, quite early, I went out to inspect my garden. The drought had been severe this Spring. There were my five lilac bushes, dry and forlorn-looking. And to think that my hometown is known as The Village of Lilacs. And there in the corner of the garden, the part devoted to my husband, David, were the plants from his funeral. Even the white Rose of Sharon tree, a special birthday gift from my Dad nearly 20 years ago, like all my plants, looked fragile and lonely.

Death came into my life when I really wasn't expecting it. One day, like the Rose of Sharon tree, my loved one was healthy and robust, and the next, a dreadful disease overtook him. It was cold that February when doctors at the Mayo Clinic told me that a rare disease, Pulmonary Fibrosis, had attacked my husband's entire respiratory system. I was told that he would not live through the year.

I remember holding his kind face in my hands, looking into his eyes, and telling him how much I loved him. I promised to myself I would make each of his remaining days special. Then, only three months later, he passed away. I had wanted to do so many things for him. But now that wasn't possible. He was gone. He died in my arms and his last words were, "I love you." Even now as I write this, 11 years later, my heart and my eyes are clouded with tears. I miss him terribly. He wasn't here to see his children grow up, or to see his grandchildren born.

The word, *grief*, is only a five-letter word, but it encompasses so very much. At one point, I was so despondent I was considering my own way out. I felt I was no good to anyone the way I was. But with time, like the fragile Rose of Sharon tree in my garden, what once looked wasted and forlorn, began to show tiny signs of life. I took notice that there were others who were depending on me. Surely my departure would make life very painful for them. I tried to listen beyond my grief. I tried to open my eyes to needs around me. I struggled to hear the still, small voice deep within. The more I opened myself to God, the more my eyes dried and my heart began to mend.

I think again about that morning when I went out to survey my garden and found so many of my plants affected by the drought. But I also remember what I saw that had been almost hidden from sight then. I think about the tiny, new buds I found, so small they were barely visible at first glance. Yet, there they were, and I knew that with care they would grow larger and in time they would bloom again.

Then I think about my life and how it has taken time to heal, too. From this, I take courage.

Roselyn Baugh Kerlin (1955) brings us into a setting common to many, yet all too seldom spoken about or discussed. Inherent within the scene she describes are elements worthy of consideration.

The kaleidoscopic impact of visual images serves to trigger reminiscences that engage the senses and touch the heart. The left-overs from a lifetime of those dear to us are not unlike the findings of an archaeological dig, but at an intensely personal level. The traces-of-life stuff that survives one's existence has a language of its own. That language speaks of life goals, of life's preoccupations, of commitments. It speaks of relationships. It can offer insights into life's events. Taken together, such messages can be revelations beyond price.

❧ ❧ ❧

His mother died midsummer of 1972. We are now several years into the new millennium and her underwear is still in her underwear drawer… her clothes still hang in the closet… nothing has been touched on her desk.

His father died on New Year's Day, 1980. The same is true for him. Nothing was touched after his death… or picked up… it's all just as it had been before.

Their eldest offspring, now in his late '80s, continued to live there in the original family home. He never threw away a piece of string… a rubber band… or even the napkins from McDonalds. There was a guest room never again used after his parents passed, except for storage. Christmas and birthday presents dating more than 10 years past were piled high on the bed… 15 new shirts in various colors, never removed from their boxes. Even things like assorted teas and Harry and David goodies were still unwrapped, now years old and covered with mold.

And even the attic. Piled high, box upon box, old school supplies from his teaching job… from which he retired more than 20 years ago… and stacks of old posters…some as old as 50 years.

And the kitchen cabinets… there were Jell-O boxes… marked three for a dime… assorted napkins from an endless array of short-order food places… some used.

After a couple of very hot days sorting and trying to lay a plan for the best elder care for his aging bachelor brother, my husband sat down, surrounded by cartons… and wept.

I thought he was grieving for his parents, so I was silent and didn't say much… just got him some cool juice and sat quietly beside him. Then, in time, he began to talk… and talk… and remember. Memories and more memories tumbled out. And revelations… and insights… and finally acknowledgement of that subtle stuff, for so long a time dense and unclear, not understood … yet layered, year after year… until, like the rooms piled high and the attic packed full of things… it became its own life accumulation… not just of things, but far more importantly, of what those things spoke of… the intangibles… the unspoken dynamics… of a life.

Looking for the proverbial silver lining to life's dark clouds, the conscious choice to see life as a cup-half-full rather than a cup-half-empty – these inclinations can be subject to deliberate decision. **Jewell Reinhart Coburn (1955)** reveals this value by inviting us into an incident that served to give impetus to her conscious expression of the positive over the negative in her life.

Refusing to go with our negative feelings, and taking a stand against the urge to focus on lack and limitation is a possibility for all of us. Negativity robs us of possibility thinking. Seeing only the unpleasantness of life results in limiting our perspective and warping our imagination.

Mornings, for me as a child, were dramatic and personal. They presented themselves right in my bedroom window every day. My room faced east, and our house was at such a distance from neighbors that I never remembered Mom putting up curtains. There just wasn't any need for them.

That particular early March morning, there in the Ohio Cuyahoga River Valley, the sunlight streamed across the sky spreading a pallet of colors from north to south, so enthralling I couldn't scramble fast enough for my colors. I just had to capture that scene, I felt. But no sooner did I pull out my crayons and flip open my notebook then the colors shifted, then shifted again – all that beauty riding fast on thin, high clouds driven by early Spring winds.

How I wished I had one of those giant boxes of Crayolas, the kind with three rows of crayons with all sorts of shades in between the primary colors. How I wished I could lay down those stripes and swirls of light just the way the sky looked then.

Scrambling to translate all that glory to my note pad while it danced across the sky was difficult at best. But I wasn't ready to give up. There, beside my bed was the stub of a pencil. I grabbed it up and started to draw the scene, then write out, by name, all the colors and shades of colors I was observing in the sky. Of course, all this was completely unsatisfactory. Nature that morning was enticing, but capricious. Delightful, but disappointing.

And then, as misfortune would have it, the show was abruptly over. Gone. Like some gigantic, sullen ogre, envious of the sprightly beauty of the wood nymphs dancing across his turf, a heavy dark cloud smudged out the morning sun that I was trying to recreate on my notepaper.

I remember lying back on my bed, the comforter strewn with Crayolas. I pulled my pillow over my eyes, filled with disappointment that I couldn't work fast enough to capture the stunning, short-lived hint of Spring before it was blotted out by winter's blustery return.

I must have been about seven, maybe eight at the time. I loved that view from my first-floor, bedroom window. There was the big, old, English walnut tree to one side, and next to it the aged twin pear trees that no longer bore fruit, but spread welcome shade on a hot, sultry summer day. The lawn spread all the way to the place where the rolling fields began with their orchards and low-lying berry patches.

On Saturdays, Dad often called for a hired boy or two to give him a hand with the day's work. Sometimes we all pitched in. But this particular morning, things were off to an early start. The swift shift from the sun-streaked early morning sky all the way to dark, threatening clouds made me feel as if I'd lived through several seasons and I hadn't even eaten breakfast.

My face was turned to my pillow and, still clutching my stubby pencil, I heard voices outside. I sat up, attempting to take a closer reading of what I was hearing, when suddenly, from the heavy, purple cloud that had erased the beauty earlier, huge, heavy snowflakes began to fall. This was one of those times Mom never tired in reminding us how March came in like a lion and would likely go out like a lamb.

That's when I saw him. He was talking with someone off to the side of the house. Perhaps a hired boy had just arrived. I wasn't sure. I couldn't see beyond the corner of the house. From where I was, on my bed inside my room, I could see only one person outside. And what I saw and what I heard will remain with me all my days – no matter the season, the time, or the weather.

There was my father, greeting someone. On his face was his usual smile, along with his easy banter. But then something different, "… beautiful day," he was saying. "Isn't this something else again?" And I saw him turn, looking out over the fields now veiled in the flurry of early spring snow. "It's gotta be that God's in His heaven because all's right with the world." At that, I watched as Dad threw back his head and raised his arms high. The heavy snowflakes fell on his face and quickly covered his cap and his jacket. Then he turned to whomever he was talking and said, "Isn't it great to be alive!" With that there was laughter and sounds of enormous joy. Dad and whomever he was greeting hailed the new day, their spirits soaring. All the while a massive snow cloud had forced its way across the sky, blotting out the sun and, with it, any hint of that promising early spring day.

From my place behind my bedroom window, my heart joined

them out there. What a gift Dad gave me that day, just taking in
his exuberance. *Yes, it is great to be alive*, I thought. *Snow or
rain or sun or slush – it is great to be alive.*

From that wondrous morning, now so long ago, to this very
date, mornings are fabulous times of day to me. If they happen to
be drizzly and dull, well, were I to scramble for my crayons and
try to capture their colors, it's for sure I wouldn't go for the grays
or dark purples, and certainly not the blacks. What I'd reach for
would be the platinums and silvers – colors that, despite life's
dark, sullen days, would speak for the brilliance of life and hope.

QUESTIONS TO PONDER

The questions that follow, like those at the end of each chapter, are meant to help you take a fresh and creative look at your own life. Each of the women who have contributed to chapter one experienced an event that served as a compelling and defining moment in her life. For some, the event happened at a young, impressionable age. For others, the incident took place later in life. Some events were deeply traumatic; some small, yet highly significant. These questions are designed to help you look at your own life, and to derive both life- and spirit-enhancing meanings from it.

Alone, or in a group, here are some questions to consider:

1) What was your first, deeply-felt crisis or challenge?

2) What did you learn from the incident?

3) What qualities did it bring out in you?

4) How did it affect others around you?

5) What challenge are you facing now?

6) What opportunities does this challenge offer you?

7) Stand outside of yourself and look at the manner in which you responded to the event. Now, move away from what you actually thought or did. Consider other possible ways you might have interpreted this event. Are some reactions more constructive, or less so? With the passing of time, do you see aspects of your response that could benefit from a different, more loving, more life-enhancing approach?

MY COMPANION JOURNAL

Developing a journal is a helpful way to bring clarity and increased understanding to your life. A journal is not meant to be a diary of daily events, but a record of experiences and impressions, perhaps even questions. Writing down your thoughts and feelings helps you remember at numerous levels: where you were, what was happening around you, how you felt, what you were thinking, and how you responded. Writing can help you see the growth that is taking place in your life.

Life is a gift, and it is a journey. Your own unique journey deserves to be acknowledged. It deserves to be reflected upon and remembered. Your account will serve as a witness to the purpose and direction of your life, together with the many unique ways you lived out your life story.

1) Each of our lives contains its own stories, complete with chapters and subheadings, plots and counter-plots. Find a quiet, comfortable place and invite yourself as your own companion to review your own sacred storyline.

2) In your journal, draw a line graph in an ascending order, starting with your earliest memories. Enter on your graph those incidents that represent your personal, significant *Firsts* and *Highly Charged Life Events*. Your experiences may be positive, negative, or a mix. Affix a date and perhaps a location to each event. List, if you wish, other important players in your life at that time. Then move on. Continue your graph until you come to the present – taking as much time as you wish.

3) When completed, review your graph and take note of those incidents that may have characteristics in common. See if you can detect a theme or themes running throughout your lifeline. Are there stops, starts, repeats, dead ends, open ends?

4) The remembered incidents that cause you to pause, and that seem to call for your attention, may be signaling areas of your life in which there remains unfinished business, such as: a) negative or unproductive thinking or behaviors, or b) people or happenings yet to be forgiven and dismissed from the negative hold you sense they exert on you, or c) blessings for which you have not expressed gratitude.

5) The objective is to bring to every person, and every event, a forgiving and a grateful heart for the challenge that presented itself to you – both positive and negative, even though you may not fully understand the contributing reasons. With time, glimpses of meaning may emerge. Praying through an incident, forgiving those you felt brought you pain, allowing God to intervene, then detaching yourself from the emotional hook that held you will allow you to retrieve the part of your spirit that is important for your spiritual restoration and vigor.

If you consider some form of action, important guidelines will always include these questions: *(1) Will what I do or say bring the highest good to others, as well as to myself? (2) What will be appropriate to the situation, and be without intent to harm?*

THE POWER
OF RELATIONSHIP

Let us therefore make every effort to do what leads
to peace and to mutual edification.
Romans 14:19 NIV

veryone's life is a unique story of many components. We are who we are not only because of our genetic makeup, but because of the early and subsequent influences brought to bear on us by those closest to us interacting with our own distinctive qualities. Some of us had a rough go of it and perhaps vowed to ourselves we'd never pass on the hurts, disillusionments, and disappointments we had experienced that would negatively influence our own marriage, our own children - only to find that strongly-felt motivations may be insufficient to guarantee a desired result.

Or, perhaps we are grateful for the warm, consistent, and loving family in which we grew up and we made the subtle resolve to perpetuate those positive values, with expected or even unexpected outcomes.

Perhaps divorce made its mark. Or delinquency. Pregnancies out of wedlock. Perhaps addictions, mental or perhaps emotional or physical disorders, violence, poverty, neglect, abuse.

To become a caring, responsible adult is, of course, an admirable objective for each of us whether we look to a parent or a youngster looks to us. Some of us moved with ease into our adult roles. Others of us found we'd have to look elsewhere for positive models, or to our own resources.

Family relationships, whether we reflect on our place within our immediate family unit, or the generation past or future, or even an extra-family, caregiving relationship all have their own unique characteristics. All are in varying stages of shift and change and, as such, all become their own stories that, in turn, can become important life challenges to us.

Often it is not until we move away, replace the familiar with the unfamiliar, that we are challenged to look with different eyes at the habits, the values, the life perspectives we previously internalized.

The power of friendship, mentoring, caregiving, of being mentored, being cared for all provide potent ingredients, both positive and negative, for the shaping and directing of our lives. Group dynamics can bring unique and forceful pressures to bear upon us. Some for good; some less so. Our desire to "fit in," to feel the warm fuzzies of acceptance and affirmation, all can serve to shape us.

The first time we were picked for the team, or the times we were rejected, the experience of a teacher's encouraging remarks about our abilities, or the time an authority figure misunderstood our intent and held us up to criticism and ridicule. Church affiliations, our school environment, the communities in which we live, the era through which we lived – all constitute ongoing interactions with us on both feeling and thinking levels of our lives.

Often it is not until we move away, replace the familiar with the unfamiliar, that we are challenged to look with different eyes at the habits, the values, the life perspectives we previously internalized. Perhaps we never thought to question the wisdom of an old friend, a teacher, or others who exerted influence in our life.

A time may have come when rethinking began to lead us to redoing, when an old belief or habit simply would not work in a new setting. It can be agonizing to cut free from the old and familiar in order to release ourselves into new considerations. Change can be tough. People who touch us, whether for good or ill, introduce power for remarkable growth in our lives.

There are those who, from hearts large with respect, give voice to honoring mothers, fathers, grandparents – those they loved much and from whom they learned much. Honoring the memories of these people, influential in our lives, both validates age-old wisdoms and encourages validation of core relationships, thus serving to keep alive valued traits for future generations.

Some have struggled with basic family relationships. For some, friends and mentors have assumed places of honor and in-fluence. Also, there may be found revisions in relationship roles. Sometimes these less normative affiliations may be accepted with ease, sometimes with considerable inner, as well as outer, trauma.

And then there are those relationships that force upon us their sense of foreboding and threat. There are the severed relationships that prompt sensations of shock and disorienta-tion, with the menacing prospect of causing disruption to family harmony for years to come.

The women who speak to us through these pages generously share a variety of life experiences, all of which have, in their own right, served either to confront unquestioned assumptions or enhance life perspectives.

Regardless of the specific place on the timeline of his-tory that the writers – whose experiences appear in this chapter – made their appearance, their wisdom shows itself to have both enduring and universal qualities. The importance, for example, of honoring our parents, those who gave us life and nurture – and advocated in the Old Testament Commandment #5 – comes across as excellent advice no matter what the era.

You will find grandparent-grandchild relationships, sibling relationships, friends, and mentors. You will encounter relation-

ships altered by separation and divorce. The decision to live singly is also included. Each writer has her own life story and each offers us valuable insights.

Mother/Daughter Relationships

Mothers ... whether we look to our own mother, or our children look to us ... can provide a powerful relationship and be highly influential. A mother's words, her conduct, and demeanor – all present a comprehensive language to the young. And then, there is the power within the unspoken. **Mary Ellen Gudeman (1964)** reflects on an incident from her early life in which few words were exchanged, but from it important lessons were learned.

Some things Mama taught by example, not by word – even though Mama was indisputably good at words. But then, she was good with ideas, too.

Like shopping for a pair of new shoes. That was invariably a time of both joy and disappointment to me. Mama always insisted on buying them at least two sizes too big – "So they'll last longer," she'd tell us. That meant resoling them, but Papa was good at that. *Making do* was what we did back in the 1930s – back when we lived in the little house Papa built out there in the Indiana farm country. But when it was finally time to toss out those shoes, when they had given their very best, only then did they seem to fit just right.

Or, still another shopping trip I shall always remember. Choosing one of those less expensive dry goods stores, we headed for the counter. Mama longingly touched some thick Turkish towels. Noting the price, she laid them back and asked the clerk for some thinner ones. Although I was only 10 at the time, how my heart longed for her to have the expensive ones. After a weary day of shopping, tired feet headed for our Essex (one step from the old Model-T Ford), and back home again to unload our purchases.

"These aren't the ones I paid for!" Mama exclaimed as she opened the package with the thick Turkish towels. "The clerk must have made a mistake," she added, carefully scanning her sales receipt. "We'll have to take them back the next time we go to town."

"Mama," I protested, "they'll never know the difference if we keep them. It was the store that made the mistake, not us."

Mama made no reply.

From time to time, I went into the little closet downstairs and felt those thick, soft towels stored there on a shelf. Had she forgotten them?

The answer to that question became clear as we headed for that same dry goods store again on our next trip to town. She hadn't!

Mama probably had no idea that standing beside her, as she explained the mistake to the clerk, and handing back across the counter those thick, luxurious towels, there was a little girl learning a great lesson in honesty.

Life with Mama was like that.

The relationship between mother and daughter can be highly complex. Many helpful studies are readily available on this subject. **Pauline Getz Medhurst (1952)** is forthright in her account of a relationship with her mother that is characterized by issues not uncommon to many of us and from which we may learn.

As a child, followed by growing into a young woman, I found much of my life and many of my choices controlled by my mother's expectations. "You will pick strawberries (at two cents per quart in those days), make an extra cake for 4-H, and fold the laundry."

As I look back on those situations, they were not particularly out-of-the-ordinary requests. In fact, as I review them, it is good for every child to take on tasks that contribute to the good of the family. Perhaps my main concern, both then and now, years later, is that I had no real voice or choice in what I was being required to do.

Little did I realize then how much of my mother's sense of control was probably the result of her own upbringing. She was the oldest of five children. Her mother had been ill more than 10 years during my mother's growing up years. By the time mother was 10 years old, she was the manager of the family household. With that history, her outlining of tasks for me to do would come naturally to her, I'm sure.

Since my own childhood, I have come to understand that there is a part of me that will always be the daughter, except, that is, when I am urgently needed. At those times, I become the mother of a 94-year-old woman. I become the provider, the shopper, the manager of financial affairs, and the encourager. My dilemma revolves around the question of when I should assume which role, mother or daughter.

If I give my elderly mother choices, she often turns to me and asks, "What do you think?" Other times, she reverts to her controlling ways such as insisting that I go with her into the doctor's office. I find that her time in the nursing home is causing her outlook on life to become so small and narrow and so very childlike that I cannot be sure just how I am to perform.

I have learned that adult children who live with older adults need much patience, prayer and understanding. Daughters of mothers who have had strong personalities will need to expect to be told what to do, while at the same time making decisions –

often of great magnitude. My prayer is that I will have the discernment and the grace to know which role each of us will be playing each day.

Is there a distinction between being just a good mother and being the *Queen of All Mothers*? **Dawn Deak Morehouse (1994)** thinks there is, and she tells us how she arrived at her opinion.

Like most mothers, I wanted to be a *good* mother. From the moment I found out I was pregnant with my first child, I started on my own pathway to being the best mother ever. Finding every resource I could, I began educating myself about everything from breast feeding to temper tantrums. With enough preparation, I was bound to be not only a *good* mother, but the *"Queen of All Mothers."*

But I was hardly into my pregnancy when I became suspicious. Already, I was beginning to fall short of my important ideals. For one thing, I was forgetting to consume extra folic acid. I was not avoiding caffeine as I promised myself I would do, nor was I following through with playing classical music to my belly.

When the day of delivery arrived, that too proved far from my ideal. Graciously, my delivery was induced six days after my due date, which was good for everyone because I was struggling to refrain from snapping at anybody who inquired as to why I had not had my baby yet. During labor, I blew it big-time. I couldn't believe I was hearing myself actually asking for a shot to reduce my pain. By so doing, I was saying goodbye to a completely natural delivery that I was committed to seeing through.

And breast feeding, which I read was such a wonderful bonding experience between mother and baby, consisted of the combined efforts of my husband, a nurse, and a lactation consultant, of all things. Talk about coaxing my newborn daughter to "latch on" – by committee – no less. For me, things were by no means off to the perfect start I had dreamed for myself. I had already failed too many of society's expectations for the *good* mother.

But none of my failings diminished the reality that the whole experience was perfectly incredible! Seeing this new life, born in God's image, was such a humbling experience. So precious, so pure and beautiful, and healthy – holding her in my arms only increased my initial desire to be the *best* mother I could be to her.

Still, as my daughter grew, so did my fears and anxieties. What does a good mother do? Or not do? When to give the baby the pacifier? When to dare to flick on the television? When to take a shower? Or allow myself some personal time?

Later, I tried to measure my success as a *good* mother by my daughter's achievements. Certainly, if I was a good mother, she would be reaching the normal baby milestones at an extraordinary pace. With this thinking, I was now increasing the pressure not only on myself, but on my little one as well.

And then came the time for major decision making. What is best for her? Should she take swimming lessons at age one? What library has the best story time? Which is better, gymnastics, or dance class? And how about discipline? Whose opinions should I pay attention to?

Finally, I arrived at the most important decision of all. Taking together all I had read, all the opinions I had garnered, and all the authorities to whom I listened – finally I knew what I must do, and that was . . . to give up. The conclusion I came to was that my goal to be the best of mothers was nothing short of a trap. Striving to answer to everyone only made my daughter and me miserable.

So, I changed my ambition. Instead of straining to be the *good* mother, I shifted my energies to trying to be a "Godly mother." By this, I mean I would search out Godly wisdom and relax into God to work through me and bring all the details together. This way, I wasn't doing it all alone. And besides, whatever success I might achieve, I could then bank on being a good mother where it *really* counted – in God's eyes.

Father/Daughter Relationships

Father-daughter relationships have the potential to influence many of the attitudes of the daughter, not only toward members of his gender, but toward many facets of life in general. With permission to reprint her article, which first appeared in *Parnassus* 2002,* **Kristen Prillwitz** describes positive, life-affirming memories that can contribute richly to her life.

The island bears the name Dry Lake for good reason: for spans of years at a time the lake will be transformed into a bowl of reeking muck several feet deep. I cannot remember how many times we have come, camping gear and canoe ready, only to find such a sight. Thankfully we are fortunate this time. As we glide over forests of lily pads, our paddles sink into the muck a mere three feet below the water's surface, seeking some conglomeration of lily pad roots for leverage. The shape of the island begins to distinguish itself from the far shore, and I cannot help but smile, feeling the influence of so many memories.

"Just past the big rock there."

"Here?"

"Yeah, but watch the log sticking out on the right."

Aluminum grates against the stone and muck mixture at the shoreline, and I slide my paddle under my seat and step out onto solid ground. I love the familiarity of this ritual; there may be a difference of thirteen years, but all the trappings of the adventure are the same: the Grumman canoe older than either of us, the wooden paddles whose ends are splintering from use, even the ugly yellow life preservers that preserve the smell of night crawlers and fish more than anything else. I hold the canoe steady as A.J. climbs out, and we both drag it up until there is no danger of it floating away – a lesson learned from experience. He leads up the steep but brief slope to the slightly domed top of the island. Here our steps are taken in absolute silence on a year's worth of orange needles fallen from the red pine canopy above.

In my memory, the island is much larger than what I now see before me; years ago it was a whole world of its own. Twice every summer from age three to age eight, A.J., both our dads, and I came to this little island in the northern woods of Wisconsin to camp, fish, and revel in the outdoors. The Dads, as we corporately referred to them, were at two extreme ends of the social ladder, A.J.'s being a successful lawyer and mine a carpenter and pastor who lived from one paycheck to the next. But none of that mattered on the island; there the possibilities of life were endless, and income did not count for anything compared to the ability to catch dinner.

Standing here now, I close my eyes. The ring of stones for the fire lies just to my left, the faded forest green tent with its triangular form faces me ten yards back, and the reddish-brown trunks of the pines create immense, straight poles for our larger tent made of trees. I inhale the earthy fragrance of smoke and damp soil with the slight acidity of pine needles – a scent which will forever define serenity to me. Sunlight sifts lazily through the gaps between the trees, and a little boy with a brown bowl-cut and a girl with whitish-blonde hair, both already covered in dirt and marshmallow residue, creep around the edge of the island, readying to make war on an invading army.

"Stay down lower."

"You're makin' too much noise!"

"Do you see them yet?"

"No, but I think they might be coming this way." I led us through clumps of tagalder bushes and over fallen logs, skirting the shoreline of the island. Peering across the lake, hand shielding my eyes from the sun, I whispered back to A.J., "There they are! There must be hundreds crossing in canoes!"

"There's nothing to do then but to keep them from landing," A.J. whispered back.

"Wait for my signal . . . Get ready . . . Charge!" and the quiet summer afternoon was shattered with an explosion of water. The armies clashed in a fierce battle, and I sensed my socks were suddenly wet. My feet struggled against the suction of muck, but I only started sinking faster. It was a well-known fact between A.J. and me that muck behaved much the same way as quicksand, and a kid of our size could be swallowed up in a matter of seconds. I pulled with all my might and, with the aid of A.J., tumbled up onto the shore with one boot on one foot. There was no longer any invading force of hundreds; the cries of battle melted into a cry of panic – my yellow Smurf boot stuck up in the muck just out of reach. The tattered warrior scrambled up the embankment, one sock squishing in the remaining boot and the other collecting dirt, crying for the Dads to rescue Papa Smurf from the muck. They were both willing sources of comfort and help, and the boot was retrieved easily. However, what remains clearly in my mind so many years later is the image of my yellow boot with Papa Smurf on the side, sticking up out of the dark brown muck, accompanied by the empty feeling of helplessness. Many of my experiences on the island invoked such a feeling, but perhaps that was an integral part of the island's magic for me. For every feeling of helplessness I experienced there, I had to but turn to Dad and everything would work out.

I remember some of the mishaps we could often count on the Dads to fix in the realm of Dry Lake. If a fish swallowed our hook, if we dropped a paddle into the lake, or if some other crisis existed, such as the day A.J. ran straight into a gigantic beehive and was stung from head to foot, the Dads were there to reassure us that all was not lost. Likewise, my other most vivid memory of the island involves a night of sheer terror for me. We ended up going camping for the second time that year in September, even though the wind already had a biting chill to it. Snuggled tightly in the little red sleeping bag my mom sewed for me, with hat and mittens on and sandwiched between Dad and A.J., I slept easily for the first part of the night. A soft scraping was coming from the fabric of the tent, and it sounded suspiciously like nails

being run down the side. Not only that, but something did not
look right about the little bit of light coming from outside the
tent; it wavered and danced in shadows, but I never could quite
make out a solid shape. Knowing the wildlife in the area fairly
well, I concluded a black bear cub was producing the noise as he
pawed at the tent. For a moment relief calmed me; cubs are small
and harmless. Then I remembered that essential advice of the
Northwoods: never get between a cub and its mother. I translated
this into a more general command: never be anywhere near a cub
because its angry mother is bound to be in the vicinity. Images of
massive claws and never seeing my seventh birthday flashed in
front of my eyes. Soon the tent seemed quite warm inside, and I
began to sweat under my winter hat. This initiated what seemed
like several hours of tortured inner debate over whether to wake
A.J. and the Dads to warn them or stay frozen in case making
any movement would provoke an attack by the mother bear.
Despairing of an answer to this question, I silently and cautiously
slid over in my sleeping bag until I was cuddled with Dad as
much as possible. The noise and flitting shadows persisted, but
my new position curled up with Dad provided me, I knew, with
complete safety and allowed me to trade my worried vigil for
sleep.

When Dad finally stirred in the morning, I told him about
my experience during the night and made him promise to look
around outside for any bears before I came out. Climbing out
of the tent, he whispered back for me to follow. With a smile,
he showed me my bear cub - it snowed during the night, and
the snow had fallen on our tent in clumps from the pine boughs
above us, creating the shadows and scraping noises. Over the
following years, Dad had the opportunity to explain away many
more such "bears" in my life, but not all were as easy as this one.

Shaking my head to clear my thoughts, I glance over at A.J.
to find him squatting next to the fire pit, playing with a few twigs
and his lighter. I sit down next to him, knowing what he is thinking. This island is a tangible representation of our childhood. The
problems we encountered here, the helplessness we felt, all had

their solutions in the Dads. It has not been so simple in recent years. When A.J. and I were eight years old, my family moved three hours away, and though we have come back every summer to go camping at various other locations, more has changed than has stayed the same. A.J. and I, once inseparable, now, after a year of college, barely even know each other, and what I do know of his life deeply saddens me. I want to make him understand how much I care about him and where I fear the road he is on will take him, but the reality is that we are two vastly different stories with only a common beginning. I know this is the last time we will visit our island – we have brought to it a helplessness the Dads are powerless to solve, thus the magic, at least in part, has been broken. But although it may be impossible to go back again, I will always visit in my memories – I know we both will.

I know this is the last time we will visit our island – we have brought to it a helplessness the Dads are powerless to solve, thus the magic, at least in part, has been broken.

**Parnassus*, Taylor University, 2002, pp. 52-54.

The manner in which we internalize and act on the unique quality of early family interactions has the power to influence and color future relationships. Studies of father/daughter dynamics have long suggested the father's potential for significant influence on his girl child. **Linda Carlson Bagshaw (1968)** illustrates this dynamic in the way she grew up accustomed to her role as her father's little princess, only to face head-on the realities of role reversal when confronted with the loss of this special status.

I stood in the kitchen one spring evening in 2000, the phone pressed tightly against my ear, and a chill in my heart. I'd been talking with my dad about my mother's recent health problems when his speech became confused and incoherent. I felt, with frustration, every one of the 670 miles between my parents and me as I quickly called one of their friends to check on them.

The evening ended calmly because of the friend's help, but early the next morning both my mother and my dad were rushed to the emergency room with medical crises; my mother with a severe reaction to medication, and my father at the point of exhaustion from his continual care of her to the neglect of his own health. Hurriedly, I packed a bag, made flight arrangements, and found myself in a motel room near my parents' home.

I was suddenly pushed into a role for which I was woefully unprepared, and one that I initially resisted. From early childhood into my adult years, I have always felt the warm cushion of love, of "daughterhood." After my sixth grade debut as the Princess in the play, *The Frog Prince*, my father always referred to me as his "Princess," which enhanced my role as the special daughter among three brothers. I was not exactly spoiled "rotten," since I clearly remember rules and punishments that applied to me as well as to my brothers, but perhaps a bit spoiled around the edges . . . .

I reveled in my role as daughter and relied on the love, security, and direction my parents consistently provided. Gradually, they prepared me for adulthood with the usual parental releases toward independence. Blithely, I traveled the fairly smooth road from the rules of the home, household chores, and curfews to the increased responsibilities and freedoms based on my parents' trust. I say, "blithely," because as I approached life on my own, I was a bit hesitant but was bolstered by the reassurance of their continued parental caring. The security of the parent/child relationship held me like a warm hug.

I can't say there were no warning signs before the traumatic event that spring, but as I look back now, I realize I did a careful job of ignoring them. Dad's bi-weekly letters slowed to one or two a year, and I saw with each visit that he was growing more and more feeble. The sparkle in his eyes and the familiar jokes easily distracted me from the reality of his health. The tradition of going out for special lunches that Mom and I had always enjoyed began to fade, as well as the fun-filled shopping trips. Even the year Mom and Dad almost forgot my birthday, I did not hear the alarm bells.

As Dad's treasured, newsy letters became infrequent and the idea of a jaunt out to lunch lost its appeal for my mother, I made vain attempts to re-establish the past. I bought Dad stationery, and when an occasional letter did arrive, with its telltale shaky scrawl, I would call to thank him sincerely and profusely, mentioning how much I had missed his letters. I repeatedly tried to plan visits to include the special lunches with Mother, arming myself with comebacks for every excuse of tiredness she gave. My pep talks to Mother and my psychological pressure applied to Dad changed nothing and simply frustrated me.

Now with this crisis staring me in the face, I could not ignore my new, and unwanted, status. My parents were in fragile health, thinking unclearly, and reacting negatively to the idea of moving from independent living to assisted living. I suddenly realized that I was now in the role of parent rather than the comfortable role of "child," and my reaction was resistance, even tears. I resisted by clinging to the emotional insistence that I was the *daughter* and they were the *parents* – and always had been. It didn't seem right that I suddenly had to be the parent to my parents. I resisted to the point of desperately trying to think of someone to whom I could delegate this unwanted responsibility. My longing for the simplicity of childhood again – or at least my adulthood with everything in its proper, and accustomed place – dissolved into hopeless tears. Of course, my tears and bewildered objections did nothing to change the reality that was fast enveloping me.

That night and the following weeks and months, I thought of

the Apostle Paul's statement that when he was a child, he spoke, thought, and reasoned as a child, but when he reached adulthood, he put away childish things.* I began to realize that it was time to put away my own childish attitudes, my childish expectations, and to accept not only a new relationship before me, but a new ministry as well. At my age of 54, I began to realize the need to "grow up."

I began to relate to my parents in a different way, one characterized by acceptance of their frailty and their needs. I continued to honor them with respect, recognizing their dignity, their God-given place as my parents, but also to lovingly suggest and encourage them in directions they needed to take. The path has not been easy, but I've grown through this time of change, and somewhere along the way the Princess put away her crown.

* I Cor. 13:11

Considering the inherent positive qualities to be found in a healthy, father-daughter relationship, when any of those characteristics are – for whatever reasons – absent, considerable frustration on the part of the parties involved will likely ensue. The writer of the following vignette, who graduated in the mid-1990s, elects to remain anonymous. She describes her emotional response to an unfulfilling paternal relationship.

My father sat at my dining room table, his voice choked with emotion. "Do not make the mistakes I did," he said, tears rolling down his face. "Don't let 20 years pass without spending time on things that really matter. Invest in your child. Know each one as a person. Do not repeat my mistakes."

A few weeks earlier, my husband and I had shared that we were expecting our first child, my parents' first grandchild. I listened to my father's words, but he need not have said them. I had already learned the lesson he was finally trying to share.

My father is a minister. He went into the ministry for all the right reasons: a love for God and a desire to lead others to Him. He has served passionately his whole life. He visits the sick, comforts the hurting, rejoices with the joyful, and buries their dead. He performs the day-to-day functions of a pastor in a small congregation. He serves with a quiet spirit and a true faith. But, for him, ministry has been a consuming fire. There was seldom time for family.

As I grew up, I clearly remember feeling as if I needed to earn his love through my performance. As each progressive success failed to attract his attention, I felt that what I had achieved must surely not have been good enough. Then I would feel compelled to try even harder, and to be better.

I can easily remember my sense of competition with parishioners, and even with God, for that matter. But somehow it seemed "they" would always win. How could my selfish needs ever hope to compete with someone else's crisis, or others' ultimate needs?

I've carried these feelings throughout my life. It was only after I was married and beginning a family of my own that I was able to begin to realize my own sense of worthiness apart from my performance. My husband's commitment to me and our marriage slowly began to undo the years of hurt and frustration.

As we begin the next generation, I am committed to making motherhood a significant priority while needing the intellectual stimulation and challenge of a full-time career. I am thankful to be working for a company where I have a unique position, delivering unique skills to the workplace. I work for people who understand the value of family and understand that this season of my life will not last forever. They also understand that if my career interferes with my commitment to my family, I will walk away. I have found a solution that meets everyone's needs. I continue to work full-time, but on a flextime schedule. My day begins at seven a.m. and ends at three in the afternoon. Although most in my field spend several days a month on the road and log many evening hours, I am committed to investing quality time in the lives of my children. Rightly or wrongly, I do not work overtime and I seldom travel. I am determined not to repeat the mistakes of my father. My children will not be sacrificed on the altar of my career.

My children will be small for such a short time. I learned well that I am given only one chance to raise my children. When that opportunity has passed, it will never return. This, I experienced firsthand. When this time of my life is over, and my children are pursuing careers of their own, I will have time to invest more deeply in my career again. And, I will pursue my passions knowing that I enjoyed many of life's sweetest moments.

Thirty years from now, no one will remember my on-the-job successes, but my children and I will never forget the moments we shared together.

When, owing to any number of personality deficiencies on the part of a parent, the offspring feels obliged to assume parental responsibilities, the essential structure of the family unit may be severely threatened. The writer of the following vignette, who graduated in the mid-1990s, elects to remain anonymous. She shares her account of an emotionally charged challenge that arose within her family.

I never knew anything different growing up; it was just the way that he was. I was eight when the liquid indulgence became a hardened habit. Something broke inside him when he felt like God had let him down. And so he drank. He drank to forget. He drank to cope. He drank to escape.

It changed him. It changed us.

My dad's scent was a mixture of *Old Spice*, red wine, and

Halls cough drops. We always thought the cough drops were meant to disguise the lingering acrid, stale smell of cigarette smoke. He never smoked in front of us. His hidden secrets. He never drank excessively in front of us. More hidden secrets.

Angels held our car on the road when, as it often did, it swerved at his hand. His liquid vice often lulled him to sleep early in the evening. And yet, through all, he was amazingly high functioning, high parenting, and high loving. He was a dad of care and nurture, yet corrupted by a hidden obsession.

Later, a jolting reality. Finally I understood. That scent of my dad . . . he was an alcoholic. The only family I knew was a system that had learned the twists and turns of a demon dance. This liquid indulgence was robbing a man of his life, his faith, and his family. I wondered what my dad was like without alcohol flowing through his blood. I couldn't remember.

The day before the intervention, all of us were scared. We feared it would be the hardest thing we'd ever done. Confrontation. Exposure. Then perhaps, honesty.

Finally, the time came. Dad was irritable, argumentative, and aggravating. Still, we had the confidence to persevere. Cautiously, with heartfelt sincerity and care, we tiptoed our honest words into his heart. Surrounded by the ones who loved him, this sensitive man did not, at first, shed a tear. I participated with fear that we might hit a brick wall. But then, slowly, the tears began to fall. It was as though God took his broken heart and poured in the love of our family. Although the process was difficult, Dad did the work. Detox. Therapy. And, spiritual renewal.

A family system altered. A faith restored. Reorientation. Health. Sobriety.

It changed him. It changed us.

Grandparents

Heady, feisty, challenging, adoring – all these and more

Eleanor Radtke Key (1956) reveals in this charmingly zestful interaction between grandmother and granddaughter.

Let me begin by saying that I am not an overly indulgent grandmother. Having had five kids myself, as well as having taught elementary age youngsters, I kind of take it all in stride. I could have taken care of my darling little granddaughter early on while her mother worked. At that time her mother was owner of a children's consignment shop. I admit I felt some pressure to give up my newly-earned retirement. But then, I feel pretty strongly about mother and baby bonding so I let things ride and, for those very important first two years, my granddaughter accompanied her mom to work every day. She was nursed there and she was socialized there. My daughter's staff proved wonderfully helpful during that time.

In my house, Dear,
I am the Queen of Everything!

Now, the little lady is nearly five years old, well-adjusted, and supremely independent with a mind of her own. When she visits me, I set all my projects aside. She's my first and only granddaughter. I make my time hers. I know it won't last long. I become her playmate. At tea time, she lets me pour. When we chat, she suggests what we can play next. Oftentimes it's, "You be the baby, Grammy, and I'll be the Mommy." And so go the magic times spent with this special little person.

One evening she wanted to do something to which I objected. She stood her ground and challenged me. So, using Mary Engelbreit's famous line, I said, "In my house, Dear, I am Queen of Everything."

Not to be outdone, she replied, "No, I am Queen of Everything."

"Darling," I said, "not in my house."

"Well, then I'm the Queen of Everything in *my house!*"

At that, I let the issue drop, but inwardly, I chuckled. *Not a problem. Let her mother handle that one!*

And what does this beautiful, feisty, yet charming little lady mean to me? She fills a void in my life that I didn't know I had. She's loving and affectionate, boastful and bossy – and even at times – a pain. But what I know without a doubt is that just as she brings so many important things into my life, so I do likewise to hers. She's my reminder; she's my reality check on what's really important in life.

"Look everyday for the exciting, the joyful, and certainly the romantic," we are encouraged by **Sara Sigworth Nader**, who unfolds an incident of sorrow and loss that turned into their bold opposites.

Life is, to me, a journey – a wonderful journey. One divided by segments and phases, but also with a common denominator that runs throughout. This is not to say that less than wonderful things have not happened in my life, or that my life was like a straight, upward line with no difficult places. When I look back over my 81 years and think of it in terms of the music I so loved to play as a pianist, there have been times when my life seemed to have the richness of a symphony, with strains nearly ethereal. But there have also been the discordant times, events cacophonous like a bow being pulled over an out-of-tune violin string.

But, through it all, what impresses me is that just as I came into life nurtured by ideas and behaviors meant to teach me love for God, so I prepare to depart from life in the same wondrous manner. So that I may live a fulfilled life, my aim, even at my age, is to live a full life.

And this is the reason that, now in my eighties, I sense a fresh calling on my life. The calling is urging me to make myself available to offer to others what I call, "Grandma Talk." Certainly, I am available to my own 10 biological grandchildren and my 3 great grandchildren, but what is nudging me forward is an inner desire to be accessible to young people who, in these times of broken marriages and disjointed families, have a soul-cry for a stable contact point, a candle in their storm, a warm and accepting Grandma.

During others' times of insecurity, I will share my story of loving, consistent parents, of the importance to us of the family altar, and routine family prayer.

During their times of indecision, I will tell them how I wavered and nearly faltered in my own teen years – not knowing exactly how to assess relationship or ways to comprehend God's will in those very personal, and very important times.

I will be open about life's stresses and demands, and I will remind them again and again that we make our own memories every day of our lives – memories that can heal, or memories that can haunt.

I will even allow myself – when called for – to tell the account of the time the light went out of my life. When everything that seemed bright with promise, turned abruptly grayish-black. It was the evening of that particular day, now four years ago. I noticed my husband of 53 years had developed difficulty breathing. Then later, he described a sensation in his chest like an explosion. Hastily, he was taken to the hospital and directly into surgery. From surgery, he did not return. Oh, how the darkness fell around all of us at that time. It seemed heavy and suffocating. Then, I happened to remember how that very morning before he went to the hospital we had devotions together. We had prayed together and his voice was still clear in my ear. And I recalled how, when he was carried from the house to the hospital, his words were gentle praises to the Lord, and his face seemed, for a moment, to glow. And ever so tenderly came to my mind the way he had looked over at me and told me once more that I was the love of his life, and he touched my hand, then charmingly added, "You are so beautiful."

For three full years following this time, I was in transition and adjustment. Loving friends and advisors helped me with questions about finances and life plans – now that I was a single person, a widow.

In time, my life assumed a new sense of order, and even a new direction. And yet, through it all, I am reminded of the sustaining power of the love we had for each other. And to anyone who would ask, I would encourage them to look everyday for the exciting, the joyful, and certainly the romantic – to look for and be open to ways of showing love. This is not only the way my life began, but it is now the way it will be brought to completion.

And I will share this as a part of my "Grandma Talk."

Beverly Jacobus Brightly (1964) shares her personal reminiscences – shocking, poignant, and deeply life-influencing – and gives the past a heady, lively presence.

The path to Gram and Gramp's house followed the hill. It ran parallel to Jacobus Avenue, the street that proudly bore our family name and ran through the town settled by the Jacobuses who came from Holland years before.

We children, my younger brothers and I, would skip along that path in great anticipation. Sometimes it was cherry-picking time, which meant climbing the trees with Gramp, or just standing at the bottom looking high into the branches, or helping Gram pit the cherries in a big pail for delicious pies or maybe for canning. Or we would be greeted with the surprise of Gramp's new puppy. Or the day Gram's new stove arrived and Gramp was setting out the old one for trash pickup – one that would be

a prize antique today. Or the day we all said good-bye to the old
Model-T Ford.

And, always there was the air of hospitality. Anyone could
drop in anytime and be assured a place at the family dinner table
and enjoy a hearty home-cooked meal. There would never fail to
be enough to go around. Always on the stove would be a pot of
homemade soup, or lying nearby, freshly baked cookies.

Or there would be spring cleaning, or fall cleaning, or time
to sow the seeds in the garden, or harvest the vegetables, or plant
the flowers, or bring up more water from the well, or build a new
garage, or install a bathroom, or paint a bedroom, or wallpaper
the bathroom, or have the first bite of the apple pie taken hot
from the oven. In the summer, we sprayed each other with the
water from the garden hoses; in winter, we went sledding down
the hill nearby.

Sometimes I'd come upon Gram's quilting bee, with all the
women sitting around the dining room table, busy making quilts
for the foreign missionaries from our church, or I'd watch Gram
tying a new quilt made for one of us, stretched out across the
frame mounted in the closed-in porch at the front of their house.
If not a quilt, I'd watch Gram's fingers fly, working on her latest
embroidery project.

I'd run up to Gram's house to practice on their piano, or
to get a piano lesson, or watch while the piano tuner worked
his skill. The path also led regularly to Gram and Gramp's top
drawer in their dining room buffet. It was there they kept all
those candy surprises and packages of Wrigley's Spearmint gum
– all available to us when we were careful to use those powerful
little words, *please* and *thank you.*

And, I'd listen to Gramp rave about our wonderful country,
"America, the land of the free," he'd say. And I'd take note of
the anxiety he expressed about the new liberal teachers in our
schools back then. Or he'd talk about our family heritage, his
courtship of my Gram, who as a teenager visited the States from
Nova Scotia. I'd learn about how our family history was tied
to the history of our town – how the Jacobus family was one of

five families that migrated from the Peter Stuvesyant Colony in Manhattan to settle in Wayne, New Jersey. And how the land was divided into their five farms. I was told how the rules of land descendancy would apply in our family and others and how, generation-to-generation, the land became divided repeatedly among later children. That's how I learned how the original farms grew smaller and smaller, and today of course, the town of Wayne is an affluent, fairly dense bedroom community for New York City. But back then, listening to gramp's stories, I'd also hear about the family births and deaths, and accounts about Little Gramma, Gramp's mother, whom we all adored. I'd hear about his milk route, and the cows he called by their own names. Eagerly I listened as he shared his precious bits of wisdom.

"Your smile is worth a million dollars," Gramp would say to me. And sometimes I'd see tears in that sweet man's eyes when we stopped by on special holidays. Like the times we delivered a flowered plant, then would see it later, proudly planted in their yard.

There was Thanksgiving and Christmas and turkey, home-baked bread, and pumpkin pie.

And then there was *that* Christmas afternoon – the afternoon my life would change forever. In high excitement, I had run to my grandparents with my cousin so we could show each other our presents only to scurry back along that path to the shrill sound of sirens. Never for one moment did I think that I had kissed my mother good-bye for the last time.

My cousin's mom and my mother had driven to pick up some things for dinner, but on their way back, the brakes failed and they crashed into a tree at the foot of the hill nearby.

"Mommie is in heaven," whispered my Dad when he returned from the hospital. It was there, at Gram and Gramp's house, that I found myself motherless at the age of 12, and about to learn from that day forward that my life belonged to everyone else, and especially to my younger brothers for years to come, and to God on whom I learned to lean heavily.

It was at my grandparents' house that I learned what it was to be crushed by grief. And there, too, I first learned that one's capacity to love can go to the very depths of one's pain.

That path of my childhood is long gone now. The weeds have grown and new houses are built on the wide, adjacent fields where we once played. Those last years up and down the path found Gram growing more and more weary. The afghan remained on the couch for taking frequent naps. The pillow, no longer put away. But in spite of the changes time inevitably brought, there, waiting for us, would be a newly baked pie or plate of cookies.

In truth, my Gram and Grampa were my greatest role models in life. I am sure they had no idea of the esteem in which I held them. They understood family. They lived constancy. They breathed duty and commitment. They knew about love, like that time that remains clear in my mind's eye to this very day. They were nearing their 70th wedding anniversary. I happened to be at their home that night. Sometime after we had all been tucked in, I got up to go to the bathroom. As I was returning to my room, I passed by my grandparents' open bedroom door. For the barest moment, what I saw was an image I took away with me – one that has become a precious and profound part of my life ever since. There, I saw them in bed, wrapped in each other's arms as they slept. My heart nearly skipped a beat. Forever impressed upon me is the memory of a man and a woman who, in all those years of marriage, had never spent a single night away from each other's embrace.

These two dear people are real to me to this day. They lived simply and naturally. They worked hard. No nonsense. No pretense. No doubts. Never deception. They lived their faith. They lived their love. They lived all I hold dear and that formed my character as a child and fills my heart as an adult, and that provides my roots and my destiny. They, and the path to their home, taught me all the things about life that matter the most.

Jessica St. Clair (2006) takes us on a weekend trip of great anticipation only to encounter what she comes to know she should have attended to earlier.

My boyfriend and I take the three-hour drive home just for the weekend, the odometer turns over to zero on the way, and I visit my grandparents. They no longer live in the two-story, yellow house on Laurel Road with its built-in garage large enough for a semi-truck, but as I remind my boyfriend what direction to turn out of my driveway, I forget this.

"Which way?"

"Turn right, and then we'll get on the bypass. I'm still not used to this corner not having any trees. There, you'll go west on the bypass, now."

But he remembers what my mind has chosen to forget.

"Honey, don't your grandparents live next to your aunt and uncle now?"

"Oh . . ."

"You forgot? How could you forget that your grandparents moved to the other side of town?"

"I just did. I've been going to see them at the same place all my life and, in a month, everything has changed. I think that maybe I'm allowed to forget that, okay?"

"I'm sorry."

"You can turn around in that parking lot. We'll go east on the bypass now. To Main Street. Then to Grape."

"I know. It's okay."

There are tall bushes on the front edge of the lawn. They form a barrier against the sound of the busy road, and they block vision of their new driveway as we miss our turn and, after turning around, nearly miss it again. The house itself is small, with a small yard made of small patches of pale green grass. When I last saw this house, I was inside helping clean out the remaining possessions of the last elderly person who lived here. The siding had been yellow, like their old house. Since then it had been scraped and patched – the beginnings of a tan paint showing up at the roughest edges, the same paint my uncle's house had recently received. A small, hand-written sign hung in the window of the front door, reads, "Please use other door." I know this means there is a fear that the cat will sneak out the front door and into the road or will be lost forever in the great wilderness of this new neighborhood. This same fear placed a sign in the garage window of their old house, "Beware of cat." Anyone who has seen my grandma's cat may believe the sign more as a warning about the cat's twenty pounds, seven-inch-wide chest, and four extra claws – one to each foot.

The flower bed along the driveway had long since been given over to weeds and the driveway is now full of things moved out of the garage for a good, thorough cleaning. My grandparents' new neighbors, my uncle's family, are doing the cleaning today and Rob and I give them a quick hello as we walk past them, carrying a dozen doughnuts and four bananas.

When we walk into the back door and past the retro avocado washer and dryer, we enter into confusion. My aunt is searching for something in the newly green kitchen and pauses briefly to greet us.

"Hi, there. Did you have a nice trip back?"

"Pretty good," Rob answers, "It rained quite a bit, but we made it back alright."

I wish I felt up to the kind of lighthearted conversation we had had with my parents about how Rob's turned-over odometer reminded us of leveling up in a video game, but something holds me to only necessary conversation for the moment. As I make my aunt pause again to give her a slight hug and a quick peck on the cheek, I ask her what she is looking for.

"I'm helping your grandma clean out the kitty's box. I'm trying to find a baggie." She finds one that is acceptable and briskly returns to the room in the back of the house where my grand-mother waits in worried confusion.

Three moderate steps from the middle of the kitchen is the living room, where I find Grandpa standing, somewhat unstable. His sea legs, which were always steady, have recently been affected by the cruelty of a stroke. A stroke, by definition, is a lack of oxygen to the brain, which is often caused by a blood clot. His steady legs have had clots before, and he has been on blood thinners, to avoid this more critical clotting, but some things cannot be avoided. There are, of all things, lighthouses on the curtains my aunt chose for the living room, and I notice that there is a sheer section in the middle of the large picture window. Grandpa likes to be able to shut heavy draperies tight across the windows of his house so that no one may look in from the outside. I know these new and fanciful sheers must be a bother, though he doesn't mention a word about them. The hall tree stands guard next to the front door; still bearing Grandpa's walking hats. He will wear these less often with no park across the street and a right leg that drags behind him. Before the stroke he had a particular sort of dignified and gentlemanly shuffle, and a bit of a stoop caused by a fall from a tree stand when he was 78, but now he has this dragging gait and this new, hunched posture. As I hug him and plant a kiss on each cheek and his forehead, and as he returns these, I smell that he is old and that he no longer bothers to wear aftershave or cologne. The few hairs on his head are more haphazard as of late, and his skin more tender, but his eyes are still bright and his smile still says, "So, what do you know?" in that old British way I always tried to fully understand. My left hand receives a warm and reassuring squeeze from his left hand, as if to tell me that it will be alright, and he turns to Rob to say hello with a nod.

The room where Grandma is receiving instruction from my aunt on how to clean a litter box – something she has done most of her life – is literally stuffed from wall to wall. A moose head once hung in the corner of their spacious living room, almost unnoticed, and as a child I always begged to be lifted up so that I could pet his nose. This moose is now taking up nearly all of one wall in this overly small room and standing guard, ridiculously, over the cat's litter box, and end table, and a love seat. On the opposite wall, or, rather shrouding the opposite wall is my grandfather's gun cabinet and a closet that his good friend, now dead, whom we all called Uncle Reginald, made for him many years ago. The gun cabinet is used to hold important family papers and his always well-kept hunting guns, and the closet now holds all of their warmest winter clothing and two of his many pairs of boots. The other 50-odd pairs of boots still remain at their old house, waiting for a time when someone can bring them all up for him to choose which pairs to keep. My grandmother does not greet me with the usual elated grin and calling of "Jessie Jayne," she greets me with the same confusion that can be felt throughout the house.

"Hi, Grandma. It's good to see you. I'm home from college for the weekend."

She needs this prior warning so that when I am gone again she knows, or at least someone else can remind her, that I have not abandoned her for more important things. This was always a danger over the summer when we often visited Grandpa on the physical therapy wing of the hospital, and she did not often understand that we would be coming back, and that we had obligations and not preferences of other things to do.

"Hi, Jessie. I don't remember what I'm doing in this room," she tells me, the litter scooper still in her right hand and a plastic baggie in her left.

My aunt continues the step-by-step instruction that is so easy to become impatient with. When this task is completed, we move to the kitchen to wash our hands and to see that my grandfather has made a fresh pot of coffee of which he is very proud. His face reminds me of a small child and I feel inappropriate giving reinforcing praise of his efforts. I want to be home so that I can escort them through this part of their lives, but I also want them to be able to comfort me and hold me the way they did when I was very young and needed careful instruction and tender comfort.

"Grandma," I say, "we have doughnuts and bananas and Grandpa made coffee and there is apple juice and grape juice and milk and water. What kind of doughnut do you want?" And I realize that I have presented too many confusing options for any of it to sound appealing.

"No, thank you. I'm not very hungry. I have a tummy ache." But I know from experience and the way she holds her hand inside her brown sweater, against her 90 pounds, that she must be hungry and is mistaking this pain as having eaten too much or as feeling nauseated.

I pull four white plates from the cupboard and a couple of very stained coffee mugs from the dish strainer next to the sink, and place them near the box of various doughnuts on the very small laminate table against the very bare, green kitchen wall. I offer grandpa the powdered doughnut, a guess – but he takes the raspberry-filled instead. I take a blueberry and Rob takes a sprinkled doughnut. As I turn my back and walk to get juice from the refrigerator, I hear grandma asking Rob if there is a plain doughnut, which she takes and eats happily.

While we are sitting, making small talk, and trying to catch up with how we have been doing, grandma inserts something that I cannot get out of my mind.

"It's terrible losing your memories, losing your mind. It's a terrible feeling."

No one said a word until I made some stupid comment about where the cat might be hiding, or about the weather, and again about the weather, or about the ceramic triceratops on the table. Triceratops had been Grandma's favorite dinosaur for as long as I could remember, but she didn't remember that anymore.

I hadn't a clue what to say to fill the deafening silence.

I could only think: I want to talk to the grandfather and grandmother I knew before. The grandparents I knew before their falls, before their forgetfulness, before their strokes, before they got old faster than I could realize. I want to sit with them and ask them all the questions I should have asked them. The

ride back to my house seemed long while I stared out the window, Grandma's words stuck deep in my mind.

Other Family Relationships

Even the slightest gesture of recognition or affirmation can
carry great power for healing within the life of another. **Mary
Ellen Gudeman (1964)** tells about a small act that reaped
large benefits in her life as an insecure child.

You're my little sweet potato . . .
I read and reread these words. The postcard, featuring
a large, sweet potato in the center, was worn and frayed
from handling. My young Aunt Esther had drawn tiny x's
all around the perimeter of the card. Her note said these
kisses were all for me. Then she drew five small x's in the corner
of the card with a note that they were for my brothers and sisters.
Only one kiss for each of them and loads of kisses for me! And .
. . she called me her little sweet potato! For me, this simple card
represented total love from my dear aunt.

One summer, Mama let me and my older brother, Milton,
spend some time with Aunt Esther and Uncle John in Eureka, a
small town in central Illinois. Used to sharing things with five
other siblings, I enjoyed all the undivided attention I received
from my devoted aunt and uncle, especially on Sundays. The
long sermons at church seemed to shorten in length as I stared
at a whole roll of mints Uncle John had given to me . . . just for
me!

Not being the oldest or the youngest in a large family, I often
felt my personal insignificance. Being called Skinny didn't help.
My poor appetite left me less robust than the rest in the family,
and the nickname only added to my poor self-image. At Aunt

Esther's, I did not need to share my mints, and no one reminded me of my skinny body.

Toward the end of summer, Mama telephoned Aunt Esther from our farm in Indiana. Two of our near neighbors, teenage boys, had been suddenly killed in a motorcycle accident. Although they were older than Milton, they were his buddies, and Mama felt we should come home for the funeral. With our things packed in the rumble seat, Aunt Esther, Milton, and I climbed into Uncle John's Ford coupe and started out on Route 24 from Eureka en route to Indiana.

A few months later, Aunt Esther sent me this special "sweet potato" postcard. I read and reread the card. On Sundays, I slid it into my little purse along with my hanky. During the long, boring sermons, I would periodically take out the postcard and reread the message. I counted and recounted the number of kisses allotted to me and compared them to only one for each of my brothers and sisters. Somehow, my personal worth seemed to increase each time I read the card.

Not too long after our stay with Aunt Esther, she had a baby girl. Although little Luann was born alive, Aunt Esther never saw her. The baby died soon after. Too young to know how to express my sympathy, I just peeked up, silently, at her little coffin in quiet grief.

At home on the farm, where each of my sisters and I were allotted one dresser drawer for our own personal treasures, I sadly took the worn postcard from my little handbag and slipped it into the back of my dresser drawer. I don't remember ever throwing the card away, but somehow in time it disappeared.

Whenever I recall my beloved Aunt Esther, I feel thankful to her that, even in the face of her own great loss of her baby daughter, she could give "worth" to this little girl so long ago when she took the time to send a sweet potato card framed in kisses . . . all for me.

Siblings

Taking a loved one for granted, or perhaps feeling a touch competitive – whatever the emotion, it can serve to restrain us from expressing the true depth of our admiration. **Shirley Holmgren Sheard (1949)** writes about just such a poignant revelation.

❧   ❧   ❧

Sometimes I wish I could have mustered up more of an appreciation for my sisters and their talents, especially my eldest sister who happened to sing like an angel. Actually, harmonizing vocally was a delight for all four of us sisters. But, added to that, the sister next to my eldest sister was an accomplished pianist. And, my younger sister would occasionally add to our music sessions with her talented flute playing. When my sisters would perform separately and I would hear the enthusiastic applause from an audience, my tendency was to think there was no need for *my* admiration as well.

It is true that we'd sometimes mention something to one another about how helpful it was when we sang with the flute because her playing kept the others of us in tune. Or, with the piano, we'd enjoy the additional accompaniment. But then, there were those other times – those casual, at-home times – when my eldest sister added her voice, singing the melody for our three-part harmony. That was always a special occasion – one of great beauty. But what I didn't do was mention it. There was no doubt about it, music was the joy of our souls when we four girls were growing up together. We'd sing while we did the dishes, while we cleaned house, and we soon learned that music offered a cohesive quality when things got rough.

Grant you, my memory becomes a bit jaded as time goes on; but I declare, my eldest sister really did sing like an angel. She'd hit each note as clear as a bell. At the time, back then, little thought was given to the quality of our renditions. Maybe that was because I was so young. When we sang together, we all seemed the same age but in reality my eldest sister was actually seven years my senior.

Recently, while reflecting, I seemed to stir up some very clear memories. Again I could hear my eldest sister's solos in church. I recall how beautifully and clearly she sang the words, and yet I never mentioned this to her.

I wish I could bring back those days and let her know how truly superb a singer she really was, and that I held her and her talent in such high respect. But, far too much time has intervened.

My sister realized she was dying. I hope she also knew that it was I who was holding her hand – there, during her final moments.

I bent over and, close to her ear, I began to sing, "Under His wings, I am safely abiding." This was our signature song when we sisters sang together. Sometime during that chorus, my sister opened her eyes wide. Then, her lids closed. My husband, standing by my side, gave me a knowing look. His eyes said, "She is gone." My hand went to her wrist. I felt no pulse. We did not want to turn away, but we knew we must call for the nurse.

Maybe I don't need to be so hard on myself, but most certainly there has been much within this experience that spoke to me. What I have taken from this very personal and very moving time is that I was privileged to be with my sister in the final moments of her life. And, whether or not she was fully aware of it, still, I had the opportunity to give her the gift of what we both loved best and that was to sing words we both loved. Hopefully, through it all, she somehow knew just how very much I appreciated her and her exquisite talent.

I only wish I had told her earlier.

Friendship

In our fast-paced lives, friendship can be short-lived and su-
perficial. To go through a lifetime knowing your childhood friend
is just a few miles or a phone call away is a treasure, indeed. It is
just such a treasure that **Heather Gladhill Kehr (1995)** describes
for us.

My third-grade class was full of festive bulletin boards, a
coat rack, a big window overlooking the playground and lots of
energetic eight-year-olds. It was here that I met the best friend of my life! Imagine that – two little eight-year-old girls starting a friendship that has already lasted over 22 years!

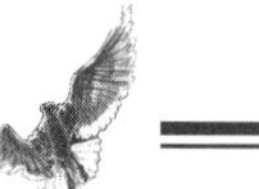

*We saw each other through our first boy-
friends, "break-ups," braces, and first jobs.*

It *is* possible to find a "kindred spirit," – that's been my firsthand experience. And what is so curious about it is that she and I are so very
different, and yet in many ways very much alike.

We have been there for each other through many of the most
challenging and exciting times of our lives. We saw each other
through our first boyfriends, "break-ups," braces, and first jobs.
We've giggled late during many a sleepover, shared tears, and
even managed to stay close during college with my friend on one
campus, and I on another.

We were each other's bride of honor. We held each other's
newborns.

We have said the hard things to each other, and we followed
with the soft. We have contacted each other to talk through our
frustrations; we have listened to each other – really listened.
We've offered one another our views and support. When we've

phone.

Distance, we have learned, seems to make little difference. Changes in life circumstances seem to matter very little. What does matter is the bond that we share. My friend is more like a sister than a friend. I have the sense that she wants what is good for me. She has let me be me, and yet she encourages my best. We both have many friends, and yet we have each other, too. There's a loyalty. A trust. A "comfortableness" that has formed over the years.

I look around at others, and it is easy to see how rare it is to have a friend so true. Even now, we work together on our scrapbooks, and watch our children at play. And it's not at all difficult to see into the future – still keeping in touch. Laying plans for our monthly lunch together. Laughing. Remembering. And, as much then, as now, we will be there for one another – just like we were when we were little eight-year-olds.

While in conversation one day with a young woman graduate student, I was the fortunate recipient of her story relating to the value of peopling one's life with "intent" – or, as she went on to explain, the intentional introduction into her life of certain types of personalities, each with the potential to represent a certain set of qualities to challenge her. And, each would be selected to offer her unique growth opportunities – experiences that might easily be overlooked were she to ease herself through life aligned only with those persons she found pleasant and most compatible. With her permission to recount our conversation, she went on to explain to me how she first heard of this idea and made the conscious decision to implement it into her life.

"First of all," the earnest young woman said to me as we sat at a desk across from each other, "in my quest for friendship with intent, I set out to look for a Paul. What I mean by this is that I would actively look for someone older and wiser than I. For me, this would be a woman who had lived longer and had experienced far more in life than I had. To me, it is important to find someone who could help me stay grounded while I undertake this particular journey. And, although I use male names, what I really mean by the name are the attributes of the personality as they are revealed in the New Testament rather than the person's gender."

Then she went on to tell me, "After I found my Paul and I came to know her well, then I set about to find a Barnabas. From this new friend, I would take encouragement and find companionship. And, in return, I would offer her the same. Both of these intentional friendships would prepare me for my third encounter. Next," she explained, "I was to look for a Timothy – someone who would stretch me, challenge my thinking, take nothing for granted, ask the hard questions, and make my life uncomfortable."

When I asked her if she thought she had succeeded in her plan, her response was enthusiastically positive.

"For one thing," she said, "if I hadn't searched out a Paul, I'd be far less wiser than I am. My Paul brought me a longer view of life. She challenged my inclination to see only what surrounds me and makes up my private world. And from my Paul, I learned ways to be a mentor to others as well."

"And, from your Barnabas?" I asked.

"From my Barnabas," she replied, "I learned the two-way power of loyal friendship, of being there for another, of the value of supporting one another through the tough times, of helping one another keep our focus and go for the goal."

"And, what about your Timothy?"

At this, she unfolded a sprightly account of her third new friend who came from a vastly different background than she.

And, sure enough, as she described her interactions with this friend, she said she was repeatedly set back on her heels by her. "And here I was," she continued, "thinking I was the educated one with my two college diplomas on my wall, and going for still another, and this young woman I came to know had hardly finished high school. And yet, she was well read. She thought deeply. She observed people. She studied their interactions. In short, she was the very challenge I had hoped to meet. And, you know something more," she said with a wistful tone to her voice, "this young woman is becoming a very good friend."

"So, you would assess this approach to 'intentional friendship' as valuable to you?" I asked.

"Not only valuable," she replied, "but, I'd say, almost essential. If I want to make a difference in the lives of others, it's for sure I need to be open to many different people with many different characteristics and views."

"Do you give considerable thought to the kind of difference you want to make in other's lives?"

To this, the young woman said something not completely expected. Certainly, I thought to myself as I listened to her, *many young people are driven by compassion and a desire to serve others, and to share their faith and the Christian message. How might this young graduate student be different?* I had wondered. Then, she responded.

"It's what I can learn from others, too," she replied.

I was moved by her enthusiasm, her compassion, and very much so by her insight and balanced perspective.

Mentoring

Taking part in a "Big Brother/Big Sister" program can offer many valuable experiences. **Heather Gladhill Kehr (1995)** tells

us about a special relationship that went beyond casual friendship.

Here I was sitting in a trailer full of soybeans with my
nine-year-old "Little Sister." I didn't even know what soybeans
were, let alone think I would ever be on a farm where they were
grown. Through my four years as a "Big Sister," I learned much
about farm life, about my "Little Sister," and about myself.

As a college freshman, I thought being part of the "Big
Brother/Big Sister" program would be an interesting ministry. I
was soon assigned a nine-year-old girl. We had many fun experiences. She spent several nights at the dorm with me. She didn't
like to eat at the dining commons, but was just happy to hang
out with me. I have so many fun memories of her. I have vivid
images in my mind of sledding at her home, sharing shakes at
the local ice cream shop, playing in the hay with new kittens,
and carving pumpkins from the local farm. As I became more
involved with my studies and new friendships, I found myself

saying to her that I was busy, more and more often.

But still, I regarded her and her family as special blessings in my life. Yet it wasn't until I received a letter from
her grandma in July 1995, that I began to realize how
important our relationship was to be. The letter said that
my little sister was in the children's hospital with a heart
problem. The doctors had to take a biopsy. By August, she
was diagnosed with cancer. We talked on the phone and we
continued to write to each other during this time. Finally, I
was able to visit with her in October. It was then that I was
able to see how cancer had affected her life . . . her leg broke
with a simple move and she was having radiation and shots. In
January, I got a call from her mom that the cancer had spread to
her brain, and this was to be the last time I was able to talk with
her.

When I came home from work one day in February 1996, I
learned that my little friend had died. I had such a hard time that

night. This wasn't supposed to happen to someone so young. I
still remembered her as a vibrant young girl, not a cancer patient.
I drove back to Indiana through a snowstorm to get to her funeral. Her family gave me the honor of sitting with them during
the service. I just couldn't believe this was happening.
As I reflect on my time with my "Little Sister," I have become
a better person for having known her and her family. I learned
the importance of not becoming "too busy" with life that I miss
out on important relationships. I have gained a deep love for her
family and continue in a wonderful relationship with her mother.
I believe my little sister would laugh if she knew that, years later,
I married a farmer . . . she really thought I was a lost cause when
it came to the things of farm life.

I write this in memory of my very special "Little Sister,"
Staci Elaine Dollar.

A latch-key youngster, **Tamara Hittle Germain (1990)**
tells us about her long hours at home alone and what she learned
about the benefits of having and becoming a caring, creative
mentor.

The very best mentor, to me, is someone who shares from
the richness of her own life experience, someone who teaches by
example. Certainly, it is not about someone saying what should
or ought to be done, how to, or not to do something, or how to
use the most perfect means to achieve my greatest desires. To
me, the best mentoring is about relationship. In my own case, it
is about two women, one very much older than the other.
    I was very young when my parents divorced. After my much
older siblings moved away, I was left with great quantities of
time on my hands. While my mother was at work, I spent many

hours home alone after school. My school didn't have after-school care and there was no money for either a summertime or after-school sitter.

Fortunately, or unfortunately, I was a voracious reader. The unfortunate part of this was that I chose to fill my time by reading romance novels that seriously influenced my ideas of relationships between men and women, as though they offered accurate descriptions of the way life really was and thus could be expected to be. There was no one in my life to suggest otherwise or discuss these matters with me.

Thus entered my first mentor outside of my family. This woman was a neighbor, old enough to be my grandmother. She really didn't take on the actual grandmother role in my life because I already had a grandmother. Instead, she became more of a wise and wonderful friend to me.

I remember many summer days spent with her in her garden, or in her kitchen while she prepared meals, or sitting with her on her patio eating the fresh chives she grew just outside her back door. Some days, she just chatted as though to a little girl starved for conversation while she went about her household duties. I don't remember much of what we talked about, I just remember being there and how much I enjoyed her company.

She was an avid seamstress, always working on some craft project or another. Often, she made toy animals, or dolls, or doll clothes. Occasionally, she would give me one of her creations. But, the one project I remember most was a pillow with a girl's profile stitched onto the fabric. She handed the pillow to me before it was completed, then helped me finish the project. If I had been alone, I'm not sure I would have completed a project quite that demanding. But after we were done, I felt encouraged to look for more craft ideas, ones I could do on my own. All in all, I think I completed about 50 latch-hook projects, many, many cross-stitch pieces, and even tried my hand at knitting and crocheting.

Since that time, I now have three children of my own. When I have the opportunity, I speak to my children about this wonder-

He leads me to take on. I feel strongly that it isn't
me with Him that I am ready.
document this account, I am a second-year
t. It is three and a half years after that perceptive
Since that event, I felt the inner nudge to consider
education. It came through the encouragement of
me randomly through my life, one of whom was
tor himself. I was resistant at first because I had
with my station and enjoyed my time to pursue
h, but when I finally felt what I discerned to be the
ing, I knew I would be given the strength to un-
ponsibility and not lose myself, or God, in it. No
torate a plaque to hang on my wall but a privilege
h the responsibility to use my education to benefit
uccess, to me, is to sit at the feet of Jesus and listen
still small voice that whispers wisdom, and that
to offer healing and freedom to others just as one
ise man, in one pointed conversation, freed me.

F.A., *No Little People*, InterVarsity Press, Illinois,

is written in honor of the gift of wisdom given to me
bell, Dean of Students, Taylor University, Upland,

Friendship and mentorship can have profound, positive effects in our lives. Sometimes the very message we sorely need
comes by a casual word or off-hand comment. Or, conversely,
the very wisdom needed may be the result of studied counsel
as another offers us fresh insights into our lives and crowns our
understandings with valuable and compelling self-knowledge.
Caryn Grimstead (1996) tells us of an encounter that served to
change her life-perspective in a highly significant way.

❦   ❦   ❦

In the fall of 1999, I began my five-year tenure as a university residence hall director. I had just earned my master's
degree the preceding spring, and was eager to begin climbing
the ladder of success. The moment I was seated after receiving
my diploma, I began to think about pursuing a doctorate. Being
a residence hall director was going to be an interim step on my
upward climb toward senior level administration. Looking back,
I was a rather ambitious young woman who would learn that my
striving was motivated by a discontent with myself. A desire to
be respected pedaled me forward with the rationale that "when
I have attained (you fill in the blank), *then* I will be respected,
influential, and worthy." On the surface, I felt I was pressing on
sincerely because I wanted to fulfill the potential God had given
me, and to make a positive difference in the lives of others. I
feel it was God, in His loving wisdom that exposed a selfish root
in me and taught me an important lesson that I will take with me
for the rest of my life. It came in the form of a humbling and
somewhat embarrassing rebuke, and how thankful I am today for
that brief, yet deeply felt, pain.

My first semester of work was very busy and somewhat challenging because my new responsibilities had an obvious learning

curve. Assuming the position with little previous leadership
experience inspired my prayer life and had me pouring over the
book of Proverbs at night. In my attempt to respond to the needs
of the students, I found I had little free time for myself. It is no
exaggeration to say that I soon became overwhelmed, falling into
bed every night and spending less and less quality time with the
Lord. In the face of this, when I heard about a position opening
for a research assignment that could have provided wonderful
material for my future Ph.D. dissertation, I leaped at the opportunity. Despite the inner promptings to resist adding one more
thing to my already full plate, I scheduled a meeting with those
responsible for filling the position. I distinctly remember telling God, as I laid in my bed one night, "This seems like a good
opportunity, and if You don't want me to do it, You will have to
stop me." The day before the meeting, I received a phone call
from a secretary who told me the meeting had been cancelled.
When I asked who had cancelled it, she gave me the name. This
gentleman was not actually a participant in the meeting, but he
was my supervisor's supervisor and therefore had the authority to prevent me from pursuing this particular position. I had
known this man to be a humble and fatherly person, and I trusted
him, so I scheduled an appointment to ask him about his decision.

A day later, I sat across from him in his office. In a kindly
manner, he said he thought I was taking on more than I could
handle with my new position. In my heart, I knew he was right.
However, I contemplated whether God would not give me the
strength to do another good thing for Him. I would learn that
this was the wrong question, especially as I began to understand
that this "good thing" was not really for Him. It was for me.
Already I felt the affirmation from having the letters Ph.D. next
to my name. Most certainly this kind advisor sensed my longing.

And yet, in his God-given
condemnation but rather sw
proceeded to pull a book of
People by Francis Schaeffe

"All of us . . . are tempt
because it will give me more
according to the Scriptures
sciously take the lowest plac
us to a greater one. . . . To b
pressure into a desired shape
metal at high pressure throug
in a certain shape. This is th
choose the lesser place until
more responsibility and autho

The Truth pierced me wh
suddenly able to see the root
tivation it was. The striving v
and as such would likely not b
enable me to attain the peace I
on is about persevering in my
adding more and more to my s
the very real possibility of "bu

The embarrassment of the
cause he communicated concer
ing a stark judgment. His hum
to hear this criticism and let it s
The conversation was a turning
a practical, real-life way the sin
relationship with us far more th
Him. I came to understand that
good will flow naturally from m
quiet before Him. It is in this sta

whatever roles
until I prefer ti

Today, as
doctoral studer
conversation.
furthering my
people who ca
the gentle men
grown content
spiritual grow
Lord's prompt
dertake the re
longer is a do
associated wi
others. True
quietly for the
empowers me
very gentle, w

* Schaeffer,
1947, p.22

This account
by Walt Cam
Indiana

ful woman who helped me so very much when I was young.

My children will learn from her as well, but indirectly. They will learn lessons from my mentor lived out through me. My children will learn the importance of organization, and the value of a consistent routine. They will learn the many skills my mentor so graciously taught me.

Perhaps what my mentor impressed upon me the most is the importance and value of responding to opportunities wherein I could become a mentor to others - maybe to a young woman or a new mother. And when that time comes, I will remember that being a mentor *doesn't* mean I have all the answers, or that I do everything well, or that my life must look perfect. Rather, it's more about being available, being genuine, and showing a Christ-like love in relationship. That is what the very best of mentoring means to me.

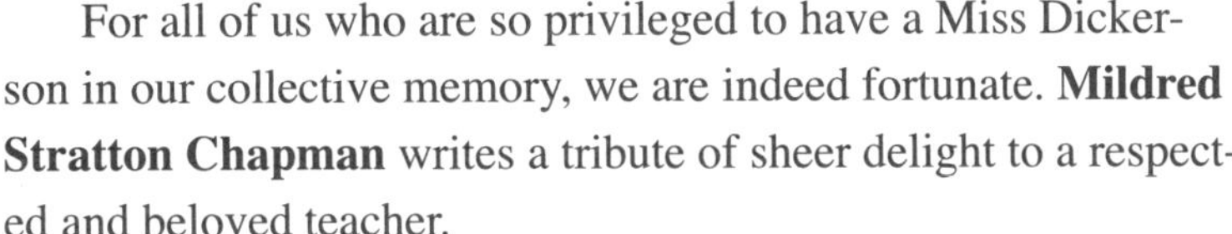

For all of us who are so privileged to have a Miss Dickerson in our collective memory, we are indeed fortunate. **Mildred Stratton Chapman** writes a tribute of sheer delight to a respected and beloved teacher.

The year was 1940, and I was a sophomore in a small central Kentucky high school. Relief from the loneliness I knew as the only child in a farm family came from incessant chatter at school, submergence in almost every book our small library afforded, and forging my dreams into school essays highly complimented by my teachers of previous years.

That was the year Irene Dickerson came to the Fairview High School English Department. My extraneous classroom chatter ceased as classmates and I became well-behaved ladies and gentlemen on whom Miss Dickerson sprinkled massive doses of the cultural erudition she brought from one of the

South's leading colleges; my beloved reading became directed
and patterned and variously reported according to a world view
of which I had no previous concept. Most shattering of all was
her red-pencil onslaught on compositions. Seemingly unaware
that I was a good writer, she transformed my first paper into a
vivid red inferno, which became an indelible memory.

I had neither social nor financial prestige in our country
kingdom, but I had gained identity in academics. Miss Dickerson was crushing my world. Usually loving parents offered
no sympathy saying only, "You're there to learn." My father's
authoritarianism was the final blow to my faltering self-concept.
He issued an ultimatum that never in our home could I discuss
the crimes of Miss Dickerson.

Meanwhile, Miss Dickerson moved the world of our youth
into an arena of previously unexamined superlatives. A gifted
musician, she also directed the glee club and chose a repertoire
that had never before penetrated our hills and hollows. Those of
us who didn't sing well must at least learn about the great music
of the ages if we were going to be somebodies.

Classmates and I found the desire to be somebodies wag-
ing rampant battle with our rebellion at forced departure from
the comforts of mental laziness. Miss Dickerson inferred that as
somebodies we practiced prescribed social amenities. We knew
that for her these extended beyond good classroom behavior, and
when she was not looking (or maybe she was), we hurried to dust
and read the previously neglected copy of Emily Post's <u>Etiquette</u>
on the top shelf of the library. We read with awe. We found
Emily quite fascinating, but translating her instructions to the
limited resources of our homes was a major intellectual exercise.

Truthfully, we soon learned how really nice Miss Dickerson
was. Spending numerous hours beyond the classroom for our
welfare, she deluged us with endless supportive commentary.
She told us we were intelligent, and we believed her. We knew
she was interested in every facet of our lives, and we wanted to
prove worthy of that interest.

Miss Dickerson personified style in so many ways. We

especially delighted in her wardrobe. I have never determined how it evolved from the salary she earned. Every girl wanted to look and be like her. We practiced and practiced tying scarfs and twisting belts to parrot her wardrobe distinctives.

Most important of all, she convinced us that learning was to be used, not just regurgitated on test papers. I don't think we ever told her of the many lunch hours when we hurried to eat in order to write letters to military service boyfriends and relatives, joyfully incorporating the vocabulary words she had written on the board for our consumption that day. These men were learning much on World War II battlefields; we were learning much from Miss Dickerson.

She moved my world for three crucial years. I was determined to write a paper that would completely survive her red pencil. In the spring of my senior year, there was one having only one red mark for a slightly misaligned margin.

How she carefully evaluated so much, making the always appropriately incisive commentary and yet remained so vibrant and alive I have not ascertained. Although I am enveloped in her inspiration, discovery of her fountain of youth and strength is seemingly elusive.

Since Miss Dickerson impacted my life, I have known the challenges of my own college and graduate school and the guidance of many influential, effective teachers. It has been my privilege to teach with inspirational colleagues in three high schools and three colleges and to be national coordinator for a Writing Across the Curriculum program operative in thirteen colleges. Through all of these experiences, I still consider Miss Dickerson my foremost mentor. I continue to proofread all that I write with her surrogate eyes, and I have aspired to kindle for my students the spirit of learning she kindled for my generation at Fairview High.

Today a retired and still very intellectually alive Irene Dickerson Knight lives near a long-demised Fairview. She continues to be a beacon to the community she loves and to those of us

scattered everywhere for whom she so ably built the fires of
learning.

Eldercare

Born to perseverance, to sacrifice, to doggedly toughing out
life's hard stuff, while all of this may build character, one can
still know the pangs of loneliness. **Lois Haycock McKuhen
(1968)** shows us how important it is to be sensitive to those who
never think to ask for help – and yet, a helping hand is exactly
the angel-touch to change their lives.

On that particular Christmas Eve, there arrived outside our
door a small group of carolers. I was only a teenager at the time.
Mom and I went to the door and she identified them to me as
people from our church. This surprised me at first and, for an
instant, I thought . . . perhaps someone did know what we were
compelled to live with. Perhaps someone even cared a little
about us. But the thought passed quickly. Most likely they had
never come to our house before, and they would probably never
come again.

In the three years we were confined to the care of my Grandmother, I cannot recall anyone ever coming to our home in
sympathy or to extend any form of compassion. No one offered
to stay with Grandma. No one brought us any food. No one
asked what they could do to help. But then, perhaps that was
partly our fault. Mom was not a complainer. She protected her
privacy. That was the old German way, stoically accepting life as
it presented itself. It was our place, or so we were conditioned to
think, to tough out our lives no matter what we faced. And surely
this must have been God's plan as well, or so that logic would
suggest. In fact, it was quite likely that no one knew that we

had never been out of the house together for that full, three-year period.

What had happened was that three years earlier it fell to my Mom to take over Gram's care. She had turned 90 and was unable to take care of herself. It was now Nurse Mom's turn to be Gram's caregiver. I, at 14, was Mom's only backup. We were a good team, having just nursed my stepfather through his final illness - through the hallucinations and through the addiction to morphine that was his only refuge from pain and that sent him shuffling wildly from room to room in search of the most recent hiding place for his drugs. Such was the state of oncology 45 years ago. Now, a year later, I wondered what new nightmares awaited us. I no longer expected life to be pleasant or simple, but I would learn that I was being given strength to survive the unthinkable.

We quickly discovered that Grandma's atherosclerosis had progressed. When she arrived, she had no idea who we were and could barely see us anyway. She called for "Hannah" whenever she had a need. Mom had no idea who "Hannah" might have been. She would complain loudly that no one had fed her all day, so we would hurry to fix toast and soup. By the time we got it to her, she would politely refuse, "No, thank you. I just ate." Her routine was simple: rise early, grope her way to the bathroom next to her room, then ask to be dressed, always including the stiff, whalebone corsets she had worn for many years. With a little luck, she would choose to eat, then settle into her chair to fade off into some distant memory.

Our shouted conversations with Grandma resulted in either very short responses or opening a floodgate of reminiscences. She actually recalled men coming home from the war (Civil War, that is) and resettling in her small Pennsylvania town. Or she would tell us she could see the ladies in bell skirts making their way down the hills to meet the soldiers. Grandma was concerned that they would maintain appropriate modesty in maneuvering their skirt hoops as they rushed to the wagons and carriages.

Snippets of history from the late 1800s and early 1900s would occasionally return to her. When she first came to live with us, she still recalled Arthur, her oldest, as just a boy. A year later, she could remember none in her family. I learned from my mother that it was okay to laugh gently, in a loving way, at the foibles of aging brains.

Mom and I were alone. There was no family within hundreds of miles of us and none were sufficiently endowed to visit. Whatever Grandma needed, we must supply. In those days, as an "out-of-stater," Grandma had no resident rights to medical care choices. Mom simply understood that we must care for our aging parents in a loving way . . . no matter what. So Mom stayed home day after day caring for a woman who no longer knew her.

Grandma couldn't be taken to church, nor could she be left alone. Mom drove to an early church service (not the one of her choice, but the one at the right time) and returned in time for me to walk to another nearby church for a late service. We accomplished all necessary tasks in the same way. I left for the school bus before 7 a.m. and returned around 4 p.m. Then Mom would run to the grocery, or take care of whatever she had to do.

For three years, until Grandma died peacefully in her sleep late in my senior year of high school, this was our life. I was not free to be involved in church or school activities. My whole world consisted of academics and caretaking. I felt tired most of the time, often sleeping only five hours a night. At 17, I already felt worn down from years of watching old folks die in slow motion.

In the years since then, the needs of caretakers have been identified and much discussed. Support groups, senior day care, home nursing, various levels of independent and assisted living, skilled nursing, and hospice all combine to ease us from stage to stage, often absolving relatives from any regular involvement or responsibility. Forty-five years ago, for the common folk there was only family or the "poor home." Years ago, women stayed home if someone needed care, and that usually meant they moved from caring for a household with multiple children to caring for ailing aunts, uncles, parents, siblings, or spouse. Now, women work outside the home and struggle to find time to so much as schedule a visit with sick relatives. In my childhood, people got old and died; we didn't always know why. Now, people get old but no one wants to let them die. Their death is burdened and prolonged by attempts to delay the inevitable.

Certainly today's aging process has much to recommend it over the wearing isolation of caregiving decades ago. But the years of my life that were "shortchanged" by these experiences were also greatly enriched in ways I could not recognize until much later. In young adulthood, I observed friends become intolerant of their spouse's behavior and walk away. I saw children abused because of the day-after-day-after-day demands of parenting. I observed co-workers being fired for not having the perseverance or discipline to do the work properly.

It was not an epiphany, just a gradual dawning. Yes, God had used those years of stress and deprivation to build into me the qualities that would later help me to cope without buckling. I had learned that eight hours of sleep is a luxury. Having enough money meant only that the electric and telephone bills were paid and anything else one needed could be grown, bartered for, or made by hand. I had learned to keep on doing the right things day after day: studying, attending church, staying in Scripture and prayer, caring for my body, cleaning my environment, but never neglecting the care and well-being of others.

Ultimately, I had learned to rely on God's omniscience, omnipotence, and omnipresence because I had no other to lean on. After Grandma's passing, life was full of promise. All the things I had never been able to do I could now attempt. Nothing ever seemed hard again compared to the life I had lived growing up. And always I have remembered the plight of the caretaker, the prison that no one can comprehend until they live in it.

Alzheimer's disease, dubbed the "long goodbye," is what

Linda Wade faces with wide ranging emotions as she tells of her care for her failing mother.

❦ ❦ ❦

"I can't do this anymore," I literally sobbed as I drove home. Yet, I knew that I not only could, but that I would. Over and over again, I would. "Oh, God," I cried out. "This is too much." I circled the block again to make sure my mother was back inside the house. She insists on stepping out on the porch to see me leave. And I drive on, watching her through my rear-view mirror, standing there, waving in my direction, and guilt cascades over me once more.

Four years ago my mother was diagnosed with Alzheimer's disease. At first, we only saw the memory lapse. We began the nightly Aricept medication, but with her age we could soon see the disease beginning to take its toll. Ever so slowly, and yet consistently, it began to steal her away. I guess it wouldn't be so hard if she wasn't so healthy otherwise. Her blood pressure and heart are perfect.

I watched and knew Mom would become more and more my responsibility. My younger sister shares the home my mother inherited in 1951, when my grandmother died. She works a full-time job, and thus I am the daytime caregiver. For me, this responsibility not only requires all my waking hours but extends into the night as well. My middle sister wants nothing to do with the whole situation and refuses to help us.

I think the struggle goes back to my early years. I was a care-giver even then. As the oldest of three girls, I took care of my sisters. When Mom developed varicose veins, I did the cooking, cleaning, and laundry. It seemed natural, actually, but then I had always helped out. In many ways, I think I rather enjoyed the responsibility back then and, in retrospect, I think it taught me how to be a leader and organizer. However, I also began to see how I was being used. Mom would tell me stories of how her mother had treated her. Because of what I was told, I came to see my maternal grandmother as a sort of tyrant. Mom had lived with a devoted grandmother, but when her mother came on weekends she was always in for a spanking – *just for good measure,* she would be told – and based only on her mother's comment, *I know you did bad things*. When her grandmother died, Mom had to return to her mother's home and life was not at all easy. She married as soon as she could. I was born 11 months later.

Now, looking back over the years, we believe that my grandmother was a very sad and lonely woman, but I, an insecure girl growing up in the '50s, knew her only as a woman who would lecture me about being good until I cried sorrowful tears. I told my mother about these lectures, but she seemed unable to help me. I was on my own. I finally realized that if I cried sooner, the lectures would be shorter.

My mother seemed to see me as the child she had longed to be. As I became a teenager and then began dating, she waited up for me and wanted all the details of every date. When I didn't reveal a kiss, I felt guilty. She told me how men would take advantage of me if I didn't follow her instructions. I was under her spell. When I spoke up, I received a slap in the face. I developed a very healthy respect for that right hand of hers. I promised myself that I would never slap my children, and I've kept that promise.

Over the past few weeks, Mom has lashed out at me. I tell her "no," and she doesn't like that. One time she brought her hand back and, suddenly, I was a child again feeling the sting of her slap. But this time, I grabbed both of her wrists and looked her directly in the eyes. "Mom." I said, *"You will never do that to me again."*

My Dad was a factor, but Mom seemed to "rule the roost." He longed for a son, and only had three daughters. I knew I had disappointed him, too. I tried to be the son he wanted and did the tasks I hated, like holding the dead squirrels and rabbits for him to skin after he brought them home from his hunting trips.

When he died of a sudden heart attack (while hunting), I was once again thrown into the position of caregiver. I felt I had to be strong for my mother as well as for his parents and my two sisters. I was particularly sad because, at that time, I had married and therefore had given him a son-in-law, and a granddaughter, and then his pride and joy, a grandson. I was finally feeling accepted by my father and it felt so good.

Mom was devastated by my Dad's sudden death. Although she complained about him constantly, I believe she loved him very much. His death shocked her and I think she felt a lot of guilt because of the way she had treated him. In time, she was able to find a job, and began life again, and even remarried. For several years, life was good for all of us. Later, in the aftermath of a serious automobile accident, my stepfather turned from her and went to live with his daughter many miles away. Mom was alone again. My sister in Georgia lost her husband in death and moved into Mom's house in 1994. It was so good to have her "back home" and we became a loving and caring family, often eating together and sharing evenings.

My mother seemed to see me as the child she had longed to be.

Today, as I care for my mother, I find that I have become the mother. Sometimes, I hold her as I would a small child. We cry together as she tells me she knows that things are not right. I try to make everything right, but I can't. I tell her I love her and she tells me she loves me, and I know she does.

Then, sometimes, when she is so rebellious I get upset and the guilt pours in again. The suppressed resentment bubbles to the surface, but I have never slapped her. Instead, I've walked away from her to avoid her. Then the guilt chokes me. I was a child when she abused me, but I cannot retaliate now that the roles are reversed. She didn't know how to get help then, and often the only way I know how to deal with the situation is to leave.

The way Mom dresses is odd sometimes, and we laugh when she wears two or even three dresses at once. I'll say, "Mom, you must be cold today." She replies, "I couldn't find a sweater." (But all the while, I knew her sweater was there on the hanger with the last dress she put on.) When we go outside, she gathers pretty leaves and takes them inside. They become a mess as they dry, but seem to make her happy. Often, she sits with her cats gathered around her and I watch as she dozes off. But soon she's up again, shuffling her many papers. Then she's back to the rocking chair. As long as she's in her home she's happy, even though she's up and down like popcorn in the cooker.

But, I can't be with her all the time. I, too, have a job although my hours vary. Even her cats are too much for me. The house is depressing. I want to be in my own home. I want to go to the lake and spend time doing my crafts. Mom doesn't want to come to my house and she hates my place at the lake. I resent the feeling that I must take my spare time and go where I am uncomfortable and unhappy. Then guilt returns, and I agonize about how selfish I am.

I know my mother will not live much longer. She is 87 years old. She knows my face, but often forgets my name. She knows my love and my touch, too. Of this, I feel sure, but I wonder if she knows the resentment that I sometimes feel in having to take care of her, of always having to be the caregiver.

Surely, mother doesn't know that the guilt I feel for never being able to fulfill her dreams has nearly crushed me for many years. The adult in me says that I've done my best, but the child in me is still trying to please and make everything right. If there is anything I am genuinely guilty of, it is for not accepting the reality that I am unable to make this disease go away. I can't put a bandage on the boo-boo and say it will get better, because I know it won't. Her condition will only get worse and worse and soon she won't know me. Soon she will forget that I am her first born, her only little redhead; but still, she will have need of my care.

And I go on living with the guilt.

Yet, while writing this I realize I have done my best for her. I cannot change what was. I cannot change her feelings. I cannot change the disease. I cannot change anyone or anything, but myself. Perhaps coming to this realization will help me deal with my demons of guilt.

This has been a lesson about patience as well as love. Even when I'm sad I know that God is near. His love often floods over me and comforts me in the darkest part of the night. Over and over again, I feel I hear Him say, "Linda, you are my child and I love you." So, yes, I am thankful that my mother taught me about God's love, the One I could turn to when I was lonely, or feeling guilty about something over which I had no control. That gift has carried me through the "guilty" times, and is a gift that will remain long after mother is gone.

Neighborliness

A kind gesture can be like a stone dropped in a quiet pool. The rings can grow wider and wider. **Kayleen Brewer Reusser (1982)** describes an event that has this quality – the ability to magnify goodness.

One day, several years ago, my husband got a serious case of the flu only a few hours before milking time. I was frantic. Our hired helper had the night off and I had not been in the barn since our baby was born. My husband thought he could sit and give me instructions during the milking process, so I phoned our teenage baby-sitter to ask if she could care for our little one while we worked.

Her mother answered the phone. When I explained the situation and asked if her daughter would be available, she surprised me by her proposal. She said that her entire family of five would be over to help us.

I hesitated. It was Wednesday and I knew the family always attended mid-week church services.

But our neighbor sounded eager to help. I told her what time chores should begin and she assured me they would be there at that time.

Promptly at the appointed time, the family arrived. My husband, balancing himself against the milk tank for support, assigned jobs to all of us. Two of the men helped my husband by lifting milking machines and washing the cows. Two girls fed buckets of milk to the calves. I fed the cows in the barn and, from where I stood, I could hear my baby's squeals of delight as she was being cared for in the yard. I relaxed, knowing everything was going well.

Light chatter and serious work filled the next three hours. Finally, my husband turned off the milk house lights and everyone met in the barnyard. Every job had been completed without mishap! Our friends offered to return for the next morning's milking, but we assured them we could take over. Had this precious family not given us their help, my husband and I would have been working deep into the night.

That incident took place over 15 years ago, yet it is still fresh in my mind. When our friends chose to get their hands dirty for our sake, they showed the meaning of *I Samuel 15:22: Behold, to obey is better than sacrifice*. What they did was a living lesson in love to me.

Since then, I try to emulate their example, and in the process I have learned many more ways God can love others through me.

Taking stock of the attitudes we have internalized from our childhood can be a valuable exercise in forming new levels of honesty and compassion where old prejudices may have taken root. **Marilyn Willet Heavilin (1959)** takes us on her own journey begun with an early childhood impression.

❦   ❦   ❦

"Yup, they're gone alright." I was about five or six years old, standing at the kitchen door, listening to our milkman talk with my mother. The milkman continued, . . . "We just made sure no one would give them service, and we hoped they wouldn't stay long where they weren't welcome. We have to make sure this community stays white."

At that time in my life, I was barely aware there were people in the world who weren't white, but I remember feeling sorry for the family who was being driven out of our community. Even in my five-year-old mind, I questioned whether color should dictate how we treated people.

Later, as a Christian motivational speaker, I had the opportunity to speak to people of every color, and loved doing so. On one occasion I traveled to a southern state to speak to a group of women.

After the session, a group of us gathered, chatting near the entrance to our meeting room. The hostess gestured to me and made her way through the cluster of women. "Marilyn," she called out, "did everyone treat you well?"

I told her I hadn't noticed any problems. Everyone seemed warm and friendly to me, when suddenly the hostess looked beyond me to the next woman. "Why Jean," the hostess spoke up to her, "you're black!"

I was aware that this church was in a very strongly segregated community but I was unprepared for this. The hostess went on, "Apparently, the committee didn't realize you were black until they saw you in person."

Suddenly, the milkman's words came back to me: "We have to make sure this community stays white."

As for myself, I had completely overlooked the fact that Jean was black. To me, her color simply didn't matter. Then I got to wondering, *Have I taught my children to be prejudiced against those of a different color?*

I recalled an incident when my son was in kindergarten. One morning he started to tell me about his friend Willie. I thought I remembered seeing him playing with this little boy, and I recall asking him if Willie was black? I can remember it even to this day. My son paused, then he squinted his eyes and gave me a very thoughtful look. Finally he replied, "I don't know, Mom. I don't think so."

Later, when I met my son's little friend there was no question about it, Willie was definitely black.

I suppose we all walk through life with some prejudices that have been etched into our minds from when we were children. The milkman's statement could have formed a prejudice in my mind, but my parents had taught me God's love is all-encompassing. Their teaching superseded the milkman's.

Much later, when our son was an offensive guard on the high school football team, our home became a meeting place for the team. One evening a tall, handsome black team member said to me, "Do you know what I like about your kids? They're color blind!"

And as circumstances would have it, this same young man served as a groomsman in our son's wedding, and our son did the same for him. At the ceremony, this young man said to me, "You have always acted like a mother to me; you might as well be my mother now." I proudly sat in the spot for the mother of the groom. There were many raised eyebrows among the wedding guests, but Jerome said, "We'll just let them wonder. Do you think they will see a family resemblance?"

I learned something as a little child listening to the milkman's comments. I determined I never wanted to see anyone deliberately hurt or left out, regardless of their color or any other characteristics that might cause them to appear different from us, for that matter.

Love Relationships

As with any number of unexamined assumptions about life, there just may be far more facets to them than one might, at first, presume. One such assumption, widely held, is the notion that love is only for the young.

Hazel Butz Carruth Anderson (1938) offers an opposing point of view. With delight and charm, Dr. Hazel's life challenges the supposition that with advanced age, the capacity for deep and romantic love is somehow beyond the realm of the possible.

❦   ❦   ❦

My life had an orderliness to it. It had a certain degree of predictability, and a pleasing serenity. The pressures of my professional life as Chairman of the English Department and the broader responsibilities as Chair of the Division of Language Arts at the university level were now far in the past. I had been retired, sold my house, and moved into a retirement facility. My retirement income, while by no means sumptuous, was adequate and the security of my senior years seemed in place. I was gifted with good friends, fine intellectual opportunities by living not far from the university campus, and I could still drive and live independently. I thought I would live out my days there, but I was wrong.

The most unlikely incident occurred when I was 86 years old. I was visiting my brother and his wife in another state. One day she answered the telephone and it was her brother, Park. I overheard her ask if he'd like to talk with Hazel. Surprised at first, I felt a little uneasy about how to respond to him. We had not spoken to each other since the few dates we had enjoyed all the way back in 1937 when we were both college students.

At the time, I thought little of our conversation but was surprised when he phoned again, and later, after I had returned to my retirement home, a cordial note arrived. Again, I took little notice thinking my brief response to him would end the communication. It didn't.

In very little time, what had started as a casual reacquaintance through friendly letters, became more personal and loving. At that time, I was 86 and Park was 85 years of age. After a silence of 62 years, we literally fell in love with each other. We found we each watched the mailbox for daily letters, berated the postal system when the box was empty, and rejoiced when two or three letters arrived in the same mail.

Within three months, by that November, Park began expressing his desire to see me. Making arrangements to accommodate his medical needs and entertain him in the retirement complex was not feasible. So I finally offered to fly to the west coast where he arranged a guest room for me in his retirement facility.

With a rose in his hand, he awaited me at the airplane ramp. Instantly, we felt completely comfortable with each other. During a week of conversation and activities, our spirits wedded. But should we risk marriage? Both of us were struggling with health problems. During that week together, I confirmed what I had already sensed – that Park was a thoughtful, considerate, generous, lovable Christian gentleman. I knew that I could marry him, yes, wanted to, but very practical matters had to be considered.

Through my joy over the commitment to marry, I did not struggle overmuch about what was entailed in my move all the way across the country, although we did some careful planning. Leaving loving and supporting step-family members and close friends did give me pause. They, I'm sure, questioned my judgment. Nonetheless, they graciously sent me off with parties and gifts.

By making this move, I was eager to live in a larger and better retirement home in a beautiful, scenic location. But above all else, the prospect of living with my soul's mate outweighed all other considerations.

On April 10, 1999, we were joyfully married in the presence of his and my family in our new apartment.

Our courtship was from August of 1998 to April, 1999. Our

marriage lasted just 20 months, from April, 1999, until February 9, 2001 - the date Park passed away. If I knew then what I have experienced since that day in that August, would I have done anything differently? Made other decisions? Opted for some other alternative?

Most certainly I gave considerable thought to a life change as significant as this one. It was important that I consider the long move away from my loving relationship with my step family. I knew I would miss the church in which I had been an active member for many years. Missing my friends and colleagues, plus participation in women's monthly groups such as the Reading Club and Bible Study would be significant. We discussed our finances and found ourselves capable of meeting both our maintenance and personal expenses. We laid plans, and together, we found we could make our lives work, even to the enlargement of Park's apartment. I found it feasible to contribute my furniture and have it shipped to the new accommodation. I was comforted to learn that the new retirement facility had apartments for assisted living, plus a rehabilitation center that was well staffed with medical personnel. Throughout this time, we were both mentally alert, spiritually alive, and physically and emotionally sensitive.

I have no idea why these events occurred. I was content where I was and envisioned living in the retirement facility the rest of my life. Furthermore, Park had been dismissed from my thoughts many years ago. Perhaps the Lord was quietly active in

the events as they unfolded, just as it is my opinion that He has been active in *many* critical periods of my life.

Making changes has been the pattern of my life from one level of education to another, from one professional level to another, from one residence to another. However, I was not one to make decisions on the spur of the moment. My practice was to allow circumstances to open up and then respond with anticipation and satisfaction, trusting the Lord for the outcome.

I had never been a risk taker. However, this time, both because of our ages and health problems, I assumed the risk of being left alone again, this time in a "strange" part of the country. However, considering how much Park and I had in common and how deep was our love, I made the conscious choice to let our love overcome any fear of another change.

To those who would ask if I would do it all again, my reply is yes, I am sure I would. As with most significant shifts in one's life, there are both losses and gains. But, despite the losses, I gained a wondrous dimension to my life. Marriage brought a joyful completeness and spiritual companionship to my life. It opened my way to fine new acquaintances. I have gained a loving and accepting new stepfamily. And I am left with the fullness of memories I might not otherwise have had. And now in my 90s, I rejoice in my thoughts of a unique and special person and a movingly profound "late-in-life love."

Just as young love can have its magic, so too can "later-in-life" love, when two people find they possess qualities so harmonious, so complementary that together they weave a new fabric of shimmering delight. **Jessica Rousselow-Winquist** describes a love you will not soon forget.

I was awakened early by a thunderstorm rumbling overhead on the morning of June 2, 2001. I was momentarily disappointed by the prospect of rain because this was to be a pivotal day in my life. After going through my fifties as a single, professional woman I was about to marry my best friend. The rain only temporarily dampened my spirits, and by 8:30, the sun was shining brightly on the newly washed world. This perfect day made us believe that God was smiling on our decision to join our lives.

During the previous spring break we had been in New York City and attended the morning service at Fifth Avenue Presbyterian Church. In the afternoon we went to an organ recital at St.

Thomas Episcopal. During a Bach piece, one of his favorites, I felt his arm around me drawing me closer to him – an unusual gesture because, in public, we normally limited ourselves to hand-holding. When the concert was finished, he turned to me and said, "So, shall we start planning the rest of our lives together?" I responded affirmatively and we began to make plans. The first thing we agreed on was that we did not want a big, expensive wedding. We wanted a simple ceremony where we would exchange vows in the presence of a few close friends.

As we faced each other that June morning and promised to love and to cherish till death do us part, I was grateful that we had known each other for a long time and had built a strong friendship over the years. We already had considerable understanding of each other's idiosyncratic behavior. For example, we have different approaches to time. I am a by-the-clock, on time individual. If I say I will be there at 5:00, you can count on it. If he says 5:00 it may be 5:15 or even 5:30 before he appears. I had long since learned not to start cooking until he walked in the door! We shared a deep respect and appreciation for each other's gifts. We had written one book together and were deeply involved in writing the second one. He is by far the better editor and the better historian, but I am the creative writer. He makes sure we get the facts right, and I add the description and drama. We hold many interests in common including music, drama and the visual arts. We both like to travel and we both are avid readers. Because mutual supportiveness was a habit with us, the transition from single to married was almost seamless. We gave up two houses for one and began the process of building a home together. We also set about the process of synchronizing our professional and domestic lives.

Two years have passed, and as I reflect back over my life and the influences that shaped my thinking I realize what a miracle my marriage is. I grew up in a home fraught with tension. The dinner table frequently became a battleground for my parents with my mother screaming and crying and my father retreating into stoic silence before throwing back his chair and striding out of the house. As a result, I vowed never to marry.

This resolve to remain independent was deepened when I went to high school and college. I discovered fairly early in my educational experience that God had gifted me with a good intellect and that this intimidated people, particularly males.

I recall vividly a conversation with a male classmate during the first week of college. The subject turned to future plans and I said I intended to pursue a graduate degree eventually, whereupon he adamantly asserted, "no man would ever marry a woman with a master's degree." I exclaimed, "if that is true, I will never marry!"

After graduating from college, I plunged almost immediately into a graduate program at the University of Minnesota. I loved the challenge and was rewarded by receiving a contract to teach speech at my alma mater the year I received the M.A. degree. I was terrified the first time I stepped in front of a classroom full of undergraduates, but I warmed to the task and began to find real joy in teaching.

In 1967, I took a position teaching at Taylor University and began work on the Ph.D. I did it the hard way – during summers. I would pack my belongings into the back of my turquoise Rambler and head to Minnesota where I would take up my place on the other side of the desk. My future husband had come to teach in the history department in 1974. A few

I had long since learned not to start cooking until he walked in the door!

years later he invited me to go with him to a play in Indianapolis. We had such a good time together that we continued doing things together over the years.

Finally, I had passed my qualifying examinations, had my dissertation topic approved and had completed most of the research. Then I got bogged down. Writer's block hit me in a big way. I could not imagine how to convert thousands of note cards and hundreds of bibliography entries into a readable study. When I communicated to my friend that I was so discouraged with the process I was ready to quit, he responded as I knew he would. "Of course you are not going to quit! You are almost finished and this is no time to give up! You are going to be Dr. Rousselow by next year. When you complete a section, we will read it together and I will give you feedback. We can do it together!"

As an editor, he was a stickler! I would work through the material repeatedly correcting errors and refining ideas until I  was confident it was perfect, and each time he would find a problem in the first paragraph! Although this was a painful process, it paid off in the end. The dissertation was accepted with no revisions required, and when I came home triumphantly having passed the final oral examination, he threw a party for me.

My husband constantly communicates to me that I am special. He never fails to tell me that dinner is great even if it is a simple casserole or salad. He tells everyone how proud he is of the things I do at home and at work. He knows how to make me laugh and can even cajole me out of a major funk! Whenever I think I cannot do something, he is there to tell me I can do it and he walks beside me easing my fears and instilling confidence. I look into the mirror and see a rather ordinary woman who is beginning to develop a few wrinkles here and there. He looks at me and sees his gorgeous wife!

We know that we are still novices when it comes to marriage, but the habits of friendship developed over the years are helping us each day as we negotiate our personal relationship and our professional lives. Balancing our demanding jobs with life as a couple is not always easy, but we are committed to each other and we both know that our life together must take precedence over anything else.

Separation/Divorce

Barbara E. Davenport (1988) takes us into one of life's most difficult times. She shares with us the descent into her dark night of the soul and her re-emergence into the sunlight of powerful, new understandings.

I pondered the words of Psalm 73, " . . . and the earth has nothing I desire besides You," and I wondered how a person could plan the events of her life in such a manner as to bring herself to a point in life when she can say with honesty and sincerity that her Lord God is truly all she needs or even desires in this world?

For 26 years, I had been quite happily married. The normal ups and downs were present, but they had presented no major problems. Then, my husband began going through some changes that dramatically affected our relationship.

At first I thought it would just take some counseling and some serious talking, and all would be well. To me, marriage was a sacred trust and one that should last *til death do us part*. But a problem with unfaithfulness persisted.

During this time, I began to experience panic attacks. At times, I felt I was literally falling apart. I could sense I was losing a grip on my identity and my life. *Who was I anyway? Why was this happening?* My heart was crying out to God for help and understanding. *Did He know what was happening? Did He even care?* I wondered. *Couldn't He, Who holds the stars in their places, hold our marriage together?* My faith was being greatly challenged, but I knew that if I wanted to be a person of faith, I had to hold fast even though it was a time that was darker, more confusing, and more painful than I had ever experienced before.

For exercise, I had been jogging each day for several years by this time, and I found it a great opportunity to get off alone to pray and to think. Then those times became valuable for me to talk out this dilemma with the Lord and try to listen to Him about who I was, and what I was to do. Sometimes my heart was so heavy that all I could do was jog a while then cry a while, and run some more, then weep again. One day while running, a thought came to me with great force: before I was anyone's wife or mom, I was, first of all, God's child. That's who I was; that was my first identity in life and my truest identity!

I treasured this thought. I focused tightly on it. I knew I had to let my relationship with God grow and enlarge. The prayer that Jesus taught His disciples to pray came to mind because He had taught them to address God as Father. I started to pray this prayer daily, but I could only pray it as "my" Father, not "our" Father, as it appears in Scripture, because I felt so very alone and I needed to feel an intensely personal sense of God's nearness.

Each day that I prayed this prayer every sentence of it became meaningful to me, especially "Your will be done on earth as it is in heaven." I began to pray for God's will about my marriage. "Forgive us our sins as we forgive those who sin against us" became "forgive me my sins . . . ." Slowly, and with time, I felt a sense of healing begin to take place deep within my soul and spirit, and I viewed this as directly from God to my wounded, broken heart. I began to use the gift of praise to God. By so doing, I was saving me from myself because this practice turned my mind from myself to Him. This gift also gave me the assurance that I am His child, first and foremost in this life.

I have read many wonderful stories of "saved" marriages by God's interventions. But mine is not one of those stories. Did the Lord fail me? I don't see it that way. Instead, I see my basic and most fulfilling relationship – the one that will last long after all my earthly hurt – to be my deep, heart-filling closeness to God. For this, I am able to lift my thankful heart. He is God no matter what, and worthy of all my praise, no matter the outcome.

Do I still love my ex-husband? Yes. Do I miss the connectedness of marriage? Yes. Is it awkward sharing the same children and grandchildren? Yes. But I know to Whom I really belong. My confusion and turmoil can be shared with the one who has given me the power to live outside myself. Now, I can honestly say ... *earth has nothing I desire besides Him.*

❦ ❦ ❦

Beverly Jacobus Brightly (1964) takes us deep into the caverns of a broken heart and shares insights that inspire compassion and serious reflection.

❦ ❦ ❦

On Halloween 1991, I finally drew the strength to cast aside the "demons" that had been seeking to infiltrate my home for 28 years. How subtle had been their influence. I couldn't see them – in fact, I denied their occupation. But they were there. They had been gnawing away at the foundation of my marriage and my home. They sought to devour my ideas and my ideals. They had taken them and trampled on them – they had smeared my commitments and stolen all my money.

From where had they come? How did they get in? When did I acknowledge them? Finally recognize their power?

My innocence and naiveté were fertile ground for the Deceiver. Growing up in a totally loving and protected environment, my life had been surrounded by family members and friends who lived and cared for me, each in his/her own way, a church community that nourished and instructed me, a school setting that encouraged my learning and recognized my achievement. As a personality that trusted thoroughly, I believed the best in everyone, and gave freely to all. I had a head-knowledge that "man is basically evil," but never consciously had any personal confrontation with anyone or anything that I considered downright evil – not until I became an adult.

The philosophies of the '60s were masked in flowers, and freedom, and openness, and were referred to as the "higher" laws. "Free love," "liberation," and "situational ethics" – all meshed well with the basic lack of discipline, discretion and moderation I was observing. They opened up a whole new playing field and smorgasbord for mind, body, and soul.

I listened and watched (and entered into denial about) what was really happening. These new ideas and experiences were

twisting the values I had thought we shared. New behaviors and
rationalizations became the man to whom I had committed my
life "until death do us part." While I was caught up with working
hard to build my marriage and family and home, my partner was
captivated by the new "modern" mind-set that came along. "So
many women, so little time." "Lying is the most loving thing to
do." "Eat, drink, and be merry for tomorrow we die." These were
the new mantras of the times. I was in disbelief. How could I
compete? Surely this wasn't really happening.

After dozens of years of watching the "playboy" style
magazines, sex journals and trash novels pile up in my home,
after returning the articles he shared with me about "group sex,"
"wife-swapping," the "liberated woman," "open marriage,"
"nude parties," after being dragged along to striptease shows and
topless bars, after watching my bank account regularly dwindle
below zero, after working to pay off his debts and spending
sprees, after supporting him during periods of unemployment,
after losing everything, after dealing with his extended absences,
feelings of rejection and pain, the intense loneliness – I finally

confronted the reality that I couldn't "fix" what was happening. I faced the hypocrisy and the "demons," and drew
the strength to say, ENOUGH!

What is this? Why am I in this marriage? Is this any
kind of "covenant"? The nights alone, the long days and
weeks, the rationalizations, the lies, the lack of fidelity and
commitment, the financial responsibility, the PAIN! It was
time. Even my children were telling me it was time. I had
tried hard to cover it all up, hide it from not only myself,
but from my children, my family, friends. Everyone saw me
working hard to hold my family together, attending church
with my children, devoting myself to my children's endeavors and achievements, paying bills.

But that Halloween I knew it was finally over . . . realized
there would be no turning back. I flew my weekly commuter
flight from my Washington, D.C. job, called ahead to get the
door locks changed, and met my "husband" at the airport for din-

ner. He had paid no bills in six months, saying he had no salary (yet he always had money for his dates, managed to eat, have fun, and buy whatever). I simply told him he couldn't live in my house anymore. At that, he left. I returned home, went into the bedroom and experienced the wrenching of my entire body as I sat on my bed and sobbed. Letting go of 28 years - it felt like an EXORCISM!

Now the masks were off both of us. But, curiously, no one seemed surprised about what I thought were well-hidden, secret behaviors. As for me, I cried and cried, packed and cried, moved and cried, worked and cried, cried and sought to pay my children's college bills, worked and worked, and cried and cried. It is no small thing to give up a 28-year investment.

I knew I would have to put together a new life, a new identify, a new SELF. I knew I had to save my children. Thank goodness I could still be a mother. I surely didn't know how to be anything else but a married woman and a mother. My family was my whole life, all of my identity, as a Christian and otherwise. My children and my faith were all that mattered to me. They were the core of my being, the inspiration that kept me going.

Years have passed. I have learned that the only way *over* pain is *through* it. I have learned when all is gone, GOD IS. I held fast to the words, *I am the Lord your God, who takes hold of your right hand and says to you, "Do not fear; I will help you."* And I witnessed His miracles in my life. I experienced the severe physical illness that results from a "broken heart," and the healing power of trusting God for life itself. I have loved and supported my children through their respective college and graduate school programs. I have completed another advanced degree of my own, and I have built a new home. Through all of this, I have continued my professional work and have rebuilt my life as well, enjoying my children and the blessing of grandchildren - all the things that matter most, including my true identity before the Lord.

Missy Nieveen-Phegley (1991), when faced with unworkable circumstances, dared to ask the "hard questions." Missy shares with us the major steps she took to address a highly challenging dilemma.

Exactly six years ago I made a monumental decision in my life. I finally came to the realization that divorce was a possibility and probably should be a reality for me. This was a difficult decision for me for three reasons: I still held to the idealistic and childlike notion of "happily ever after," I had grown up in a strict Christian home that did not approve of the notion of divorce, and I had (and probably still have) an almost obscene sense of pride that will not allow me to acknowledge failure.

Just as every child my age, I was inundated with romantic themes of Disney movies and the bliss of Prince Charming and his beautiful princess while I was growing up. I dreamed of the perfect prince, the perfect wedding, and the "happily ever after" as we rode off into the sunset together. As I grew older, I planned my life according to a very specific timeline: after I graduated from college at 21, I would marry; at 24 I would have my first child; at 27 I would have my second child; I would not work while my children were young, but I would go to school to get my master's and my doctorate. Once both children were of school age (I would be 33), I would get a teaching job at a university; my children would grow up while my loving husband and I looked on and, of course, grew old together – happy and fulfilled. Nowhere in this plan, of course, was there even a minute's consideration of divorce. Well, reality set in and it certainly was not aware, or considerate, of my timeline. Still, I clung to my dream of Prince Charming and my "happily ever after." Unfortunately, when I did finally marry, my prince turned out to be Not-So-Charming and my "happily ever after" was looking to be an eternity of "I'll grit my teeth and pretend I'm happy." Aside from my childhood fantasies of an idyllic marriage, I had certain expectations for how the marriage of two people was supposed to work. I believed that for a marriage to be successful, each partner needed to contribute equally – emotionally, intellectually, spiritually, and financially. Eventually, I became exhausted – exhausted from trying to keep our relationship both emotionally and financially stable – from keeping up our home – from taking on part-time jobs to try to provide for many things we really could not afford – and from being the strong one when problems arose. But, even though I knew the marriage wasn't at all like those childhood fairy tales I had dreamed of, nor was it near what I believed a marriage should be, still I did not want to consider divorce because I did not want to give up those sweet dreams from my childhood.

My religious upbringing also had a strong influence on me. The church in which I grew up was terribly unfriendly to the divorced, at times even condemning them to hell, and consistently excluding them from church privileges and responsibilities. According to my church, even the mere consideration of divorce was a sin, so obviously this became quite a struggle for me when I knew my marriage was not working out. Although my mother had divorced long before she married my father and before I was born, this fact was seldom spoken of in my household and rarely spoken of, if at all, in my church. However, despite her "evil deed," she was pardoned for her sin because she divorced for unfaithfulness on the part of her husband, which is acceptable according to the Bible. Unfortunately, I did not have this as an "out" for my marriage. To my knowledge, my husband was faithful throughout our entire marriage. So, not only was I unwilling to give up my fairy tale dreams, I was also tormented by the possibility I would burn in hell, a belief I still carried from the teachings of my church.

Finally, the biggest obstacle I had to overcome was my refusal to admit failure. Six months into my marriage, I realized I had made a grave mistake, yet I felt I must make the best of the situation I had gotten myself into, and it simply did not matter that I wasn't happy. I was going to do everything I could to make the marriage work, and I tried very hard to pretend it did work and that I was happy, but when I was by myself I knew I was lying to everyone around me and, most of all, to myself. When my friends asked me how married life was, I could hear my own empty voice mocking me as if it was somehow detached from me when I replied that married life was great. However, those words, "Till death do us part," kept running through my head, and I knew divorce would mean going back on my word, breaking a vow I had taken before both God and man, and admitting I had failed to make this marriage work.

Coming to the realization that divorce was a viable option and could very possibly become the best choice in my particular situation was not easy. In actuality, the process of arriving at that realization took a full two years. There were many facets of this issue I wanted to consider, to think through with utmost care. It was important to me that I arrive at whatever decision I was to make by the most rational thought possible, without letting emotions lead my decision-making process, and especially by my most honest understanding of myself. What I wanted to avoid was an unthinking acceptance of others' views. I wanted to release myself from concepts and ideals that, while I would not dispute their appeal and purpose, still, for me they simply were unreal and unworkable. I felt the importance of unburdening myself of "oughts" and "shoulds." I became focused on finding my authentic self and in separating that "self" from those forces that would detract from my genuine integrity.

Soon after I was married, I made a major career change that was an extreme confidence booster. I began diligently to pursue my master's degree; although I was only able to take one class per semester due to working full time. The continuation of my education was also a confidence builder because as I fed my mind, I began to realize my potential – not to mention that the gap was beginning to widen between my husband and me at an ever-increasing pace emotionally, academically, and career-wise.

The more I realized my potential, the more I realized that I had certain rights in my relationship, the most important being a level of stability in my home that gave me strength to face the inconsistencies of life. This stability was necessary in order for me to be genuine with myself, to be true to the calling of my own spirit rather than simply performing a role that others expected of me. Added to this realization, long discussions with my mother, who had somewhat mellowed in the strict adherence to her beliefs as she aged, made me recognize that my marriage was not consistent with the biblical marriage described in the Gospels (a model that I aspired to emulate), in that there did not exist a mutuality of respect and commitment to those principles. I began to feel that perhaps divorce was a strong possibility.

I became focused on finding my authentic self and in separating that "self" from those forces that would detract from my genuine integrity.

Discussing my situation with my parents' pastor at their current church and also another pastor in my town, I was told that sometimes, even though they seldom recommend it, divorce is the best option. Finally, after a failed attempt at marital counseling, I realized that this relationship would never be that "happily ever after" dream I had wanted. I figured that the longer I stayed in this marriage, the less chance I would have to pursue other dreams I had for my life, which meant I would continue to fail. By admitting this one failure, I could open myself up to many more successes that were extremely important to me. And that is exactly what I did.

Once I made the decision to file for divorce, I was extremely confident in my choice. Although my marriage did not succeed, I don't regret it because I feel that I would not have become the person I am today if I had not been through this particular experience. Even though my outlook on life has changed quite a bit from what it once was I still find myself clinging to that childhood notion of "happily ever after." But there is an important difference now. That notion has expanded from the concept of a simple relationship to the broader expanse of my entire life.

I have become a strong and happy woman, confident in myself and confident in my faith. Albeit I made a decision that, at first glance, seemed to erode the very foundations of my values and beliefs. But this decision has actually worked to strengthen me because I now understand the significance of why I have chosen to embrace those particular values and beliefs.

Divorce: A Child's Perspective

What can be the impact on the mind and heart of a child when her world is turned upside down and her essential security threatened? From her own personal experience, **Dawn Deak Morehouse (1994)** explores these powerful emotions.

I am sitting in the recliner in our living room and my mother is crouched down in front of me explaining to me how it isn't my fault that Daddy doesn't love her. Daddy is leaving, but not because he doesn't love me. He doesn't love Mom, and now that my brother and sisters have grown up and left home and I am full grown at 12 years old, he is leaving.

Confusion and pain flood me. If he loves me, why is he going? And how can he not love Mom? Did he ever love her? I thought I was special, I thought I was important to him. How can he leave?

Mom gets up to leave for the grocery and I stare at the television. What is going to happen to us? After Mom leaves, my Dad, who is sitting on the couch out of my view, asks me to come and hug him. As I get up, I hear a noise that I think is him laughing, but when I look at him, I realize he is crying. He's crying? My Dad doesn't cry. He is big, strong, and a firm disciplinarian. Tears are uncommon.

Why is he crying? Does he feel bad? Does he really want to

go? I thought he loved me. Where will he live? I can't stop crying and I am choking on the sobs. I don't want him to go. I want him to love me. I want him to love me enough to stay. I don't know what to say to him. I don't want to make him feel bad. I want him to be happy. I love him so much. I want him to love me. I don't want him to go.

When my Mom returns, she and I go to her sister's house. She is working out details for when Dad leaves. I sit in a swivel chair and turn round and round. I am trying not to cry. My aunt asks me if I am okay. I am not okay. Daddy is leaving and I thought he loved me. But, since I don't want to be any trouble, I tell her I am fine.

Back at home, trying to sleep, I can't stop crying. Will I run out of tears? Was there a time when I would laugh and smile? I am having trouble remembering. How will I ever get rid of this suffocating sadness? My prayers consist of "God help me," and "Why?" Although my grief is heavy, I feel God is with me. In the middle of this chaos, I find two things that will be my tools for survival in the weeks and months to come. First, I found my heavenly Father was still there. My world had turned upside down, but my God had not changed. This stability was crucial. Secondly, I found hope. Even though this time was difficult and dark, there would be better days. Hope would get me out of bed each day.

My Dad moved out about a week later. When I got home from school he was gone, but he had left me a note saying he would contact me as soon as possible and that he loved me. I kept the note for a long time and would read it over and over. I think it is possible he loves me. I think it is possible his leaving and his loving were not connected. I just wish there was no doubt about his love. I wish, for Dad's sake also, that it was a love without condition. A love that can endure much, never fails, but most of all, never leaves.

Forgiveness

To forgive is no easy feat, not when hurts run deep and over a prolonged period of time. **Linda Wade** takes us into her world of betrayal and abandonment and, with her, we experience the depth of her pain and the manner in which she copes with the challenges before her.

I walked out to the porch with my friends and my new landlord, and I waved goodbye, thanking them again for letting me rent this very nice apartment. Then one looked back at me from the sidewalk and said, "You know if you hadn't divorced none of the others would have either." My already bleeding heart received another stab.

My minister husband had decided a few months earlier that I was not the right wife for him. He left me with four small children, ages three to eight. I moved back to my hometown and tried to begin life again. My husband was actually a ministerial student and we came home one Sunday a month so he could preach and go calling with the pastor. Other Sundays found us in various churches doing weekend meetings. We always sang together and he often drew a chalk picture, since he was also an artist. When the break came, I refused to give details and would not damage the influence he had on the youth or any of the church members. In the ministry I dared not share these things. Besides, I loved him and felt that surely he would be back when "he straightened out his priorities."

When that remark was made to me about others getting a divorce because of what I had done, my heart and spirit were crushed. All I could do was manage a smile and give the feeble excuse, "I better check on the children," in order to free myself from the pain of it all. Yes, I knew two other marriages had fallen apart, but I had nothing to do with their split. How could I be blamed? Nevertheless, I accepted the guilt, thinking that our influence had not been positive.

After several more unpleasant encounters, I withdrew.

From then on I stayed away from everyone I could. I stopped going to church. I went to work, picked my children up from my mother's home, and took them to our home. I told myself that people did not understand, and even if they did it wouldn't make a difference. I was an outcast. I often cried long after the children were tucked in for the night. I was so lonely. The phone seldom rang and I was afraid to call anyone. During the day I managed to bury my pain, but the long nights were terrible. The weekends when the children went with their dad became times when I only worked and slept.

I finally pulled out of my malaise. Instead of continuing to feel sorry for myself, I decided to try to make something good come out of this hard time. We had a little "family conference." In reality, I think I began the forgiveness process that evening. I confessed to my children that I realized I had been so involved in my own pain that I had failed to listen and understand their pain. I told them that we were going to make some good changes in our family, and I promised them that we were going to be happy again.

So I made the shift. I began to live entirely for my children. We played more games, spent more hours in the park, and even took some vacations. I worked an extra job on the weekends, but every minute that I was not working we were doing things together. We even cooked and cleaned together. And yes, sometimes we still cried together, but those tearful times ended with hugs and a wonderful bonding that still carries on even today.

Forgiveness was not yet possible toward the people who had hurt me so much. I was still convinced that only by avoiding those people could I protect my children and myself.

Then one Friday evening a year or so later, we went to a family roller-skating party. Suddenly, I lost my balance and fell. I shattered my wrist. As a result, I spent 10 days in the hospital – not because of my wrist only, but because I had a nervous breakdown. From all I was dealing with, including total exhaustion, stress finally won.

Soon after returning home from the hospital, I woke up one morning to find that I could not see out of my right eye. After extensive tests by the eye doctor, I was finally sent to a nearby university medical center. Injections were put directly into my eyeball for two years. Although the disease was stopped, the sight in that eye never returned. Stress had played an important role in the loss of the eye, my doctor told me.

Finally, the doctor suggested that I see a counselor – someone who would listen and not sit in judgment, not blame me or stab me again – a safe place to cry or even scream – a place to release my heavy load of pain and stress.

In those sessions, we did a lot of role-playing. So, naturally, the people of the church came into the discussions. Slowly, I began to realize that to find peace I needed to return to church. I must learn how to forgive the people who had wronged me. I began to understand that they had said things out of their own hurt and frustration and anger. In reality, we were all victims.

Forgiveness is hard. So many things get in the way: hurt, anger, pride, injustice, and resentment. But still, forgiveness is worth striving toward. It's freeing. And it's healing. The sacred writings of all religious traditions speak of it as essential to spiritual wholeness. Rather than being some kind of a "favor" to the person who wronged us, it is a key to unlocking our own

closed hearts. It frees us from being stuck in a past moment and in old feelings. It relieves us of the burdens of anger and resentment. Forgiveness makes good "soul sense." It is a personal decision, and one I wanted to make.

Someone said that the sins of all humanity are but a single hot coal in the ocean of God's mercy. I often think how wonderful it would be if my own quality of mercy were so deep and vast that an injury against me would just make a tiny kerplunk in my soul.

It had to be God who helped me forgive those who had wronged me. I couldn't do it alone and it didn't happen overnight; in fact, it took years. God gave me a greater understanding because of these experiences. I learned firsthand how a few words can penetrate deeply into an already wounded spirit and crush a hurting heart.

Since those past incidents of some years ago, two ladies are now in Heaven. A few years after I remarried, I saw my old friends. We rekindled our lost friendship. Even my ex-husband and I have remained friends. There are dynamics here that I never want to forget.

Living Single

Sara Oyer Hall (1996) minces no words when she describes the intellectual and emotional confusion one can experience when attempting to sort out the dynamics of a love relationship. From Sara, we can learn that we are not alone when faced with this important life dilemma.

I am 30 years old and single. My parents met in college and were married shortly after graduating. My 33-year-old brother has been married for 13 years and has two children and a house. I have all of his hand-me-down furniture in my apartment. I have had the hopes of a new boyfriend, the ending of hopes with others, the late-night pow-wows trying to figure out how men think, and thinking I knew exactly what I wanted in a man. I've made my lists of non-negotiables and negotiables. There have been false starts, the quick endings, the stupid phases, the times absent of trust in the Lord, then, conversely, the periods of complete trust, the phone calls to my parents, the bridesmaids dresses, the inner struggles to gain contentment, the moments of achieved contentment, the good advice received, the biting of my tongue while hearing bad advice, the over-analyzing, the crying, the

laughter. Then the hopes of having children and the ticking of
the biological clock. I have had dreams of sharing and growing,
of companionship on lonely Saturday nights, yet the desire for
freedom to move and travel. I've watched far too many romantic
movies, the dreams of what a wedding and marriage would be
like, the realities of seeing other couples struggle in their relationships, the anxiety about remaining single, the days when that
doesn't seem so terrible. The question of "When will it be my
turn, Lord?" The sensation of "Thank you, Lord, for sparing me
from him." I have been, at times, both cool and logical, and hot
and emotional. I have known exactly what I wanted and needed,
while at the same time having no idea at all.

Relationships that work are, to me, truly a miracle!

I wish I knew the answers to all my questions, but I don't.
I wish I knew which things are deal-breakers, and which things
I can deal with. Some perspectives seem so clear, while others
just spawn more questions. Although I may seek advice, who can
have the answers that are right for me, or that only I can find appropriate for me? I have to figure all this out for myself. Where
is it wise to compromise? Or not? What is settling for less than
what my God desires, and what is it to be realistic? Are these the
same, or different? I wish I knew, but right now, I don't. I guess
all I can do is be patient and willing to learn through them. But
still, I say, relationships that happen, and that work out - no matter how they begin or end - to me, they are a miracle.

An issue common to many of us pertains to the subject of
living in relationship or remaining single. **Joan Haaland Britton
(1960)** relates her struggle as she attempts to come to terms with
this question.

Does God care about my singleness? Certainly the desire to

love and be loved is normal. I felt no different. My life's plan included a loving husband and a family.

In high school, I had a steady Christian boyfriend. We broke up because he decided he was not called to be a missionary. I felt I could not be anything else. During my senior year of college, I found myself facing graduation with no "special" man in my life. I had not planned to go to the mission field alone.

During the next three years, I taught school, completed my Master's degree, and prayed for direction in my life. When it became clear that I would be going to the mission field alone, I changed my prayer: now I asked, *"Please, Lord, if I am to be single, don't let me become overly concerned about myself, bossy or boring."*

In January, 1964, I began my first term with a mission program in Europe as a journalist. I was excited and challenged. During the next four years, I lived and worked with other single women, as well as married couples. Although my colleagues were helpful and accepting, I found myself gradually returning to my previous condition - lonely and frustrated about being single.

To cover the way I was feeling, I came up with a pat answer when asked if it bothered me to be getting older, and still be single. "No," I'd say, with some bravado, "not really because the older I get the sooner will be my wedding day." That usually brought a few laughs, but what it really meant was that I had still not become reconciled to the idea of living my life single. On one occasion, I believed I had found my man. I prayed and "put out the fleece"* with the conditions that if this were true, my friend would write or phone me by a certain date. I now wonder about the wisdom of that gesture, but it none-the-less brought an answer: no letter and no phone call.

Soon after, I came upon the Bible verse that says, *My grace is sufficient for you.*** For me, this meant even in my singleness. I interpreted this as meaning that I was being asked to trust the Lord in this matter just as I had trusted Him for salvation.

Miserable, I finally yielded to the trust I had in God. Certainly this could mean I could have a meaningful life even living singly. What I knew I had to do was to let go of the assumption that to be happy I had to be married. Once I dealt head-on with this notion, my singleness ceased to hang over my head. Soon my ministry took on new joy and excitement. I wrote an article urging Christians not to stand in the way of single women following God's leading to the mission field. My own experience had shown me it was the obeying of God's call that counted. At the end of the article, I wrote, "If God has a husband for me, He can bring him where I am in Timbuktu, Chicago, Rome, Peru,

South Africa, or even Monte Carlo. The ratio of Christian men to the nearby population does not matter. After all I only need one. If I am in God's will, He will do what is best for me in His time."

Two months later, a young man visited our offices. We met on that December 11 and were engaged on December 31. He was 33 and I was 29. The article was published in spring of 1968. We felt deeply that we had been brought together.

What has spoken to me through this experience is that I did not realize the extent to which I had bought into the notion that if I was married, then I would be happy. As it happened, it was not until I let go of that assumption and yielded completely the issue of my singleness that I was able to serve the Lord effectively and joyfully. I have come to have a deep appreciation for the Bible verse that says, *Cast all your anxiety on Him because He cares for you.****

   * Judges 6:37-40
  ** II Colossians 2:12
*** I Peter 5:7 NIV

Marion Brown (1946) takes us into her thinking as she came to terms with living single and making it work positively for her.

❦   ❦   ❦

On a nightly game show, when the contestants are introduced, they invariably say they are married and have three beautiful children.

In listening to this program for years, I don't remember hearing anyone say s/he was single with no children. I wonder why? Does the executive director screen the contestants and just feature married people? Or is it a coincidence? Of course, I would take note of this situation because I am single and grew up in the '40s and '50s. That was an era when being married was the expected lifestyle.

In college I had, I thought, a great relationship with an upper classman. He graduated and went on to Seminary and I had two more years of college. In those days, of course, most everyone was married either before graduation or surely right after the event. I was maid of honor for three weddings.

Between my sophomore and junior years of college I had an operation that resulted in my inability to have children. I had not given the surgeon a written permission to proceed that far without my consent, but in those days the laws were sparse and unprotective of women.

When I was told of my plight, I knew I had to tell my friend; which I did. I made a special trip to the Seminary he was attending in order to plan our future. In discussing the matter I introduced the possibility of adoption. Without giving any thought or prayer to the situation, he broke off the relationship that moment. I was shocked as I perceived him to be a thoughtful, prayerful person. After distancing myself from this ordeal, I had to evaluate my situation to discover new options. The process was gradual. In my journal of those days, I remember confessing to myself that I didn't want to be hurt again, thus I sought male companionship less. Friends, yes, anything more serious, not then.

My "turn-around-Christian-experience" seven months before

entering college, gave me no rest. I had to give great consideration to this experience as it was dictating new directions for my life. Going against the tides of the culture in the late '40s and '50s was difficult. A woman's role was to get married, have children and serve her husband in his endeavors. Circumstances, I have found, are ways God provides directions. As time moved on, I became singleminded regarding the mission God had given me.

There have been advantages and some disadvantages as I have experienced my pilgrimage working in the institutional church and in society generally. A single person received less pay as supposedly s/he had less family responsibility. I was supporting my aged parents, so this wasn't true for me.

There were times when I was brought face to face with my single life style. One time, in particular, was when I bought my house. When I began to sign the loan papers the banker said "Are you going to have your husband come here to sign with you?" My reply to the question was, "No, I am buying this house, and no one else is involved. It will be *my* house."

In less significant ways I was reminded of my singleness when I went into a restaurant or attended a concert and the hostess/host would ask, "Just one?" or "Are you by yourself?" The "Just One" reply was so consistent that one time I replied "Yes, but I am one." When I was called "Mrs." I would reply, "You can call me by my first name or by my professional name."

Other aspects of society that are geared to the marriage relationship concern income tax rates. They are different for single persons than for married filers. Some special rates, when traveling by air, allow the spouse to fly without cost or at a lesser cost. A spouse's second income enhances one's borrowing power when applying for a loan or purchasing a home or automobile. Some auto rental agencies require the renter to pay extra if the second driver is not a spouse.

Even today, in my own local Church, the pastors use illustrations highlighting parents, children, and families, with no mention of persons who are single. It does give one a feeling of being left out, even within God's family.

It is wonderful, however, how resilient one can be. One Valentine's Day, it just so happened there was no one with whom to celebrate the day, so I went to a pricey restaurant, ordered a steak dinner and enjoyed it thoroughly. I celebrated February 14th and the love of God, who had given me a joyful heart and a mission in life.

I have, however, gleaned multiple advantages as a single person. I am free to make my own decisions regarding finances, where I live, and what kind of car I drive. I don't have to negotiate plans, but I can act independently. This allows me to make decisions according to my values and expectations.

I am free of resorting to incompatibilities that result in laying aside my dreams for the expectations and dreams of another. I have freedom to choose my own friends, ways of worshipping, ways of spending leisure time, and most of all, choosing the lifestyle my heart and inner sense leads.

The cultural expectations of the 21st century are more open and accepting now. The October 20, 2003, cover of <u>Business Week</u> said, in large print, "Unmarried America." Nearly half of all households are headed by people who are unmarried. It is obvious that society is changing.

Whatever the determining factors, life, I have found, can be fulfilling and challenging.

Single – yes – regrets – no.

Gender Tensions

Lisa Huber Toney (1997) tells it like it was . . . .

To me, it seemed just one more day. An ordinary day. Nothing particularly different from any other one. A day of high school classes, one leading into another, each keying off the day before.

I entered the crowded halls, weaving my way through the crush of bodies, and making my way to my locker. Suddenly, something caught my attention. Nothing big, just a hint of differentness.

I picked up on glances being thrown over shoulders. Eyes that were ordinarily focused elsewhere seemed to be turning in my direction. Nothing was obvious. Just subtle.

Rounding the corner of the hallway, I approached the corridor where my locker stood. Now, it became more obvious. Students, their books in hand, their backs up against their lockers, followed me with their eyes. I continued walking although my steps began to grow less sure, less confident.

Right then he came out of nowhere. I didn't see him coming. Instantly he was in my space. Then it happened. He grabbed my butt – full on.

Things seemed surreal. Like I was part of a movie. Then reality broke through. So that was it? The eyes were on me because they knew it was coming. It had been a bet. A wager at my expense. He bet on my body.

He ran.

Shock, then humiliation. Then anger. Then revenge.

I ran . . .

    after him.

He ducked into the boy's room.

This gender stuff – so difficult. Communication conflicts. Subtle competitions. Sexual tension. Discrimination. Condescension. Glass ceilings. Abuse. Adam and Eve. The male image of God.

I followed him . . .

    right into his bathroom

        and slapped him across the face.

Looking back over a lifetime of excelling within culturally prescribed circumstances, **Hazel Butz Carruth Anderson (1938)** tells of impositions that she felt obliged to work and live within.

❦   ❦   ❦

I entered high school as a shy, South Dakota farm girl feeling inferior to the town students. Gradually, performing leading roles in plays, earning good grades, and playing on the girls' basketball team helped me to overcome my shyness and make friends. The school offered a good college preparatory curriculum.

I entered Taylor University as a sophomore, having taught for three years in the same rural school that I had attended. As a college student, I was not aware of any gender bias, probably because I did not question the status quo. I do recall that class presidents were always men and secretaries were always women. College administrators were men – except for the Dean of Women.

Later, in graduate school at Indiana University, I was usually the only woman in the seminars and I was treated with respect by my male classmates and teachers. I ran head-on into the gender issue when the chairman of the English Department advised me not to try for a teaching position in a large university because a woman would not be hired. He also told me the English Department at Indiana U. did not hire its own graduates. Was he protecting me, or suggesting I was not qualified?

The hurt would have been worse had I not already planned to follow his advice: "Teach in a small college and get involved in the community." He probably did not know I had already taught English for four years at Taylor University in the small community of Upland, Indiana.

As a professor of English for 30 years until my retirement in 1978, I was one of very few women to head a department. Later, I headed a division, which included three departments: English, Speech, and Modern Languages. I enjoyed the courtesy and respect of both men and women in the division. But what was true then and is still true, women were paid less than men for equivalent work. That injustice *bothered me*, but I worked hard anyway and was able to live comfortably, though surely not luxuriantly.

Marion Brown (1946) recounts a sense of feeling "transparent" within situations in which her gender proved problematic.

Years ago, and now in re-runs, there was a television show, <u>Bewitched</u>, where the lead character, a woman, could become transparent or disappear and then return to her bodily form when it was necessary. When we refer to transparency related to the role women have had, it has often been the result of the place women have had in society. It was expected that a woman was the helpmate to a man, to care for the home and family, while the man earned the living. She was there when needed and ignored or appreciated less than the male. The national economy of the late 1900s and into the 2000s, however, changed this situation as women have gone into the workplace because two salaries were needed for the family. Transparency has become more subtle and consequently changed the role of women.

It wasn't until I began my professional career in the late '50s that I became so aware of being ignored, passed by or, in other words, being transparent in situation after situation. Being young and before the rise of the concept of sexism, I wasn't aware of the treatment women experienced. It was when I was the only woman on a Conference Staff that I realized discrimination was rampant and sometimes very subtle. I discovered I was paid less than my male counterparts, I had no benefits as I wasn't clergy, and in staff meetings my contributions were overshadowed by the men. Decisions were made to fit the schedules and lifestyles of my colleagues.

In 1967, I made a major shift. I was invited to teach one year in a Seminary as an interim lecturer. After being there several months I was invited to be interviewed and was hired for a full-time faculty position with the status of Lecturer, which was the lowest position on the Faculty. I was excited and challenged as I became involved in the teaching role. I quickly learned, however, I was in the midst of a group of professors with strong egos struggling to be favorites to students. Some had their Ph.D. and others were writing their dissertations for their advanced degree.

After three years of teaching and reflection, I knew I had to resume my studies if I continued to teach at the Seminary. I had been going to summer school during the three years, so I had begun my Doctoral Studies. The President was generous to me and gave me time to pursue and complete my doctorate.

Ironically, when I returned to teach in 1972, transparency was still an issue. In a classroom setting when we were team-teaching, my male colleague would add to or contradict my input with his "more profound" statements. It was as if I were there, but I wasn't there; in other words I was transparent and feeling ineffective.

This was a time when Betty Friedan's book, *Feminine Mystique* (1963) made its appearance. It stirred great controversy within the male climate, which caused situations to worsen. One particular incident was during a planning session when we were brain-storming possible directions for a Continuing Education month. I made one suggestion after another and it was as if I were not there. I was transparent, present, but not present as the group planning continued. Finally, in desperation, I slammed down my fist and said "I have made many, many suggestions. Some of my suggestions were later used by one of you. What is going on here?" I made my point and I passed the "initiation" of my right of passage. Transparent, and for then, transformed.

Sexism in the Seminary and in society in general was becoming a hot issue. The Seminary President decided to have a Seminar on Sexism for the Faculty and Administration. During the seminar, the issue was confronted with heated debate. Being

such an integral part of the issue, I was again painfully aware
of how, all during my career, I experienced transparency; I had
fewer opportunities as a professional person, I was not on influential committees, wasn't the chair of any committee, and made
less money than my male colleagues with the same credentials.

The seminar had unearthed numerous situations in which I
was "dumped on." The next morning after the seminar, I knew
I had to team-teach with a man with whom I had had serious
confrontations. My self-esteem had been injured, and for survival I had to seek a way of dealing with the hurt. Interestingly, I
reverted to an incident about which my mother had told me years
before. When I was about five years old, we were having company and my mother had dressed me in my very best. While she
was getting dressed, I discovered a bowl of whipping cream on
the kitchen table, which I pulled over and spilled it on my head
and all over my beautiful dress. In reflecting on this catastrophe
in later life, I decided that when I was dumped upon, I would
take a hot bath, wash away the encounters of the day, put on
clean clothes, and enjoy the party.

Other women have found successful ways of confront-
ing transparency. I received a note from a friend who knew
I was writing this vignette. She shared an incident in her
life that had recently dramatized the issue. She had had a
routine visit to her physician and during the brief time with
him, he visibly yawned three times in her presence. He
refused to address her as Doctor (she has her Ph.D.) and
continued talking to her as he turned his back and walked
out. This caused her to have to follow him into the corridor
to receive answers to her questions. She said she found
herself laughing right at him. "I held up three fingers the third
time he yawned - which sent him into spasms of self-justifica-
tion." Sometimes humor is the only way one can dismiss the
experience of being transparent.

For my own survival, I confronted my early Christian upbringing of "God is first, my neighbor is second, and I am third."
I decided I had to be first sometimes, with God always pres-

ent, in order to care for my body and be healthy. Stress-induced weight gain became a severe problem, so again I had to be first enough to regain healthfulness. I gave myself permission to take time for a massage, a reflexology treatment, and exercising.

When I became a full professor in 1977, after 10 years of teaching in the Seminary, there was a major transition. My transparency was transformed and I began chairing prestigious committees, experiencing less confrontation, the "yes, but" became "yes and" and life, though very demanding, felt fruitful and productive. My reputation of doing my homework, of caring for the students, of providing substantive content and standing firm for my values and convictions was known. There were some reinforcing words of commendation. In reflection, I realize over and again how much my faith meant to me. I prayed much and there were situations when I felt that God gave me patience and endurance when the physical, emotional and mental resources were tested greatly. I had a mission and I knew I was in the right place.

During my 20 years of teaching at the Seminary, I had managed, with God's help, to keep my sense of humor, develop lasting relationships, work through the stages of anger, hurt, feeling unworthy, and seeing society, in general, change. We now have two women on the Supreme Court, women governors, more women in Congress, and there is even talk of a woman President of the United States someday. I hope to celebrate that.

I retired as Professor Emerita in 1987, which marked a long pilgrimage through the desert and thick brush of life and I experienced continuing transformation. The struggle has not ended either for me or for women in general. There is hope, however, and we look for a new day when transformation will be the norm and all people will prevail in God's love.

QUESTIONS TO PONDER

1)   Reflect on a specific person or persons highly influential in
your life. What was their primary message for you? Explain why
you felt that what they offered to your life was especially timely.
Is their wisdom appropriate even today?

2)   Recall a person or persons who caused you great pain. Now,
years later, do you still experience negative emotions when you
remember this person(s)?

3)   Have the influences (positive and/or negative) of these relationships colored your relating to others?

4)   If you feel it is your duty, your destiny to carry hurt throughout your life, where do you think this perception has its roots in
your thinking?

5)   If you feel it is your heritage to be free of negative emotions,
what means can effectively remove them and heal your emotions?

6)   What role in the healing process is played by the dynamics of (a) forgiving God, (b) forgiving yourself, (c) retrieving to
yourself the energy and spirit invested in the burden of carrying
unresolved emotions?

MY COMPANION JOURNAL

Because our lives are largely made up of relationships, all the while living in a culture characterized by individualism and competition, we are asked to function in diversity while respecting the sanctity of unity with our fellow man.

1)   In what ways has your personal life demonstrated sensitivity to relational tensions with the following: Family? Community? Church? School? Business? Politics?

2)   Return to the graph you developed for chapter one. Trace significant relationships throughout their existence. Do you detect patterns and/or similarities in your interaction with others? Do your relationships tend to be short term? Long term? Characterized by inter-supportiveness? Caring? Competition? Dependence? Other?

3)   A popular expression states that if someone wrongs you once, that can be overlooked as a coincidence. If that person wrongs you a second time, the fault is with that person, but if you are wronged yet a third time by the person, the fault is your own. How does this square with the scriptural admonition to forgive an offending person seventy times seven times?* What is the distinction between *forgiving*, *overlooking*, and *contributing* to a co-dependent relationship?

4)   Setting relational boundaries is a difficult task for caring, giving people. Reflect on relationships that have disrespected your need for boundaries and consider loving ways to express your personal needs.

*Matthew 18:22

REFLECTIONS

The following ruled pages are provided for you to record your thoughts on the subjects presented in the first two chapters. You may wish to enter a sketch of your life-graph so it will be readily available to you as you work through each chapter. Or, you may prefer to use these pages to develop a list of personal incidents you have been prompted to remember. Reflect on both people and events that have been a part of your life and from which you gain insight and new understanding

MY BODY / MY MIND / MY SPIRIT / MYSELF
Transitioning, Transforming, Transcending

For we are God's workmanship, created in Christ Jesus to do good works, which God prepared in advance for us to do –
Ephesians 2:10 NIV

Exhilaration. Curiosity. Wonder. Timidity, even shame and fear. These, and many more, are emotions known to present themselves at major stages of a woman's life. Owing to conditioning as well as the multitude of ways we have come to view ourselves and our bodies, our minds, and even our spirits, we all have our very own stories about our experiences with puberty, with young adulthood, with marriage and birthing, with menopause, plus our encounters with an array of traumas both physical and emotional, as well as our ultimate experience – the death we all face.

The conflicted feelings that inevitably arise from contradictory pressures are not trivial, nor are they necessarily transitory, and certainly not without the potential for very real impact on our body, mind, emotions, and spirit. Sorting out and thus arriving at balanced, integrated, satisfyingly workable perspectives is, for many of us, no small challenge.

Consider, for example, the uncertain norms regarding such preeminent female issues as body image, individual identity, relationship issues, domestic and professional roles, as well as those more ambiguous questions regarding duty, loyalty, place, sexuality and commitment. Or consider the many issues related to conditioned concepts of right thinking, proper demeanor, and appropriate feminine behaviors. The dominant character of our gender, together with our socialization, results in a spectrum of responses to life phenomena.

Knowing that we are not alone in facing challenging life events is highly significant for each of us.

From our first sensations of body consciousness, through the many phases of our lives, the reader will encounter the firsthand experiences of women who held opposing views about the role of childbearing in their lives, about the advancement of age, the struggles with depression, inclination to perfectionism, and all the way to the planning of one's own funeral.

The women whose stories appear in this chapter are to be applauded for their open and straightforward considerations of deeply challenging circumstances. From these accounts, we can take information and inspiration. Knowing that we are not alone in facing challenging life events is highly significant for each of us.

When the world is so much with us, it can be difficult to hear the still, small voice deep within. **Elizabeth Waldrop McLaughlin (1978)** portrays this dilemma so common to each of us at one time or another, no matter what our age or position in life. Desirous, as most of us are, to look our best, Beth reveals just how consuming such a concern can be.

Steam from the shower covers the mirror. I wipe it away with my towel.

There, in reflection ... the lines around my eyes, my mouth.

The steam clears. The image ... sharper. My imperfections ... in stark relief.

Hey there, can you hear me?

First, makeup. Then to the closet.

Where are those pants that don't stick to my thighs?

I grab the "evil twin" at my waist. I'll do more crunches, I vow.

Do you dare ...

There they are, the bright colored ones. Hopefully they'll distract.

... to live ...

Throughout the day, I reapply. Daub over lines. Add the gloss.

Lips. Eyes. Anything to cover the relentless course of time.

... as one who is beautiful ...

Then at night, comfortable, old jeans. The warmth of family. The embrace of dear friends.

In their love, it's easy to let go ...

... to God?

... and remember who I am.

Jessica Rousselow-Winquist shows us firsthand what it is like to grow up short in height. As with any condition that causes us to appear different and somehow less capable than others, we are challenged to explore compensative methods. Jessica informs and delights us concerning the creative measures she developed to meet her challenges.

It was a beautiful autumn afternoon in rural Wisconsin during the late '40s. A bevy of first, second, and third grad-ers erupted onto the playground followed by their young teacher. For the first time that year, they were all going to play an organized game rather than having an unstructured recess.

The game chosen was Red Rover, Red Rover. It required two teams to line up, grasp hands, and face each other across the playing field. The object of the game was to capture as many members of the opposing team as possible. Two third graders were designated team captains, and the process of choosing up sides began. The third graders and the larger, stronger boys were the first to be chosen. Two little first-grade girls were shunted to the side amid cries of "Don't choose them. They're too little. They'll make us lose for sure." Finally, the teacher assigned one little girl to each team.

I was one of the little girls that neither team wanted. The captain of my team won the coin toss and called out, "Red Rover, Red Rover, send Billy right over." Billy was a larger boy who ran as fast as he could directly at my arm. I tried with all my might to hang on and keep him from breaking through, but it was no use. My excessively slender arms were an easy target.

Billy broke through and I fell to the ground from the force of the impact. By the end of recess, both of my wrists were red and painfully sore.

I came to understand that my lack of size – I weighed 33 pounds in first grade – made me a liability in any game requiring physical strength. Not only was I an abysmal failure in the Red Rover line, but I was also an inept runner and was usually caught first in games of tag and Pom-Pom-Pole-Away. I was hopeless in softball and basketball. The bat was taller than I was and too heavy for me to hold properly. The basketball hoop might as well have been suspended from a star as far as I was concerned!

I began to dread recess, and searched for ways to avoid its myriad humiliations. One day I accidentally discovered that if I stayed in the restroom until everyone else was gone, I would probably not be missed. After that I made it a fairly regular practice to hide in a stall until all was quiet. Then I would slip back to the classroom and lose myself in a new library book.

Fortunately for my self-esteem, I made a second discovery during my first-grade year. I learned to read quickly and easily. Before the year was over, I realized I could read better than my classmates, better than many second graders, and even better than some third graders. It began to dawn on me that there were competitive arenas in which I had a better-than-even chance to win.

In junior high, I suddenly stopped growing and was devastated to realize that I was not going to reach five feet. I was still considerably underweight. My feet were not large enough to wear even the smallest women's size shoes, and shopping forays to find school clothes were disastrous because nothing that I wanted to wear fit me.

Mercifully, I accidentally stumbled upon another discovery that served to save my battered ego. I rode the bus to school, and there was one particular high school boy who delighted in tormenting me. He would grab my bag, hold it out of my reach, rifle through it, hold up objects and make sneering comments to the delight of the other passengers. One afternoon he began taunting

me about something he found in my book bag. "Where'd you get
this dumb thing?" he demanded. I retorted, "I manufactured it!"
"Manufactured it! Can't you use a simple word like 'made' the
way everyone else does? Why do you always talk so big?" Light
bulbs flashed in my head. There was power in words. Words
could intimidate one's tormenters and perhaps even silence them.

Since I had stopped growing, I learned more and more to
compensate for this physical deficiency by honing my intellectual skills. In college, I joined the debate team and had the heady
experience of winning more than my share of competitions. The
experience of intercollegiate debate was nearly immediately
positive, but it also led me to understand that the power of words
was a two-edged sword.

During my junior year, I took a class in advanced platform
speaking taught by my debate coach. The class was structured
so that we were either presenting a prepared speech or giving
an extended extemporaneous critique of a classmate's speech. I
vividly recall one day when I was assigned to critique a shy male
student's speech. The speech was weak in reasoning and evidence, and I approached the critique as a seasoned debater tear-
ing his argument to shreds. When I had finished my demolition,
he was in tears. I left class that day vaguely unsettled. I knew
I had performed well and won praise from my debate coach. I
had functioned as a debater was supposed to. But I had also hurt
someone the way Red Rover games hurt me. This experience
caused me to think about the power I had been developing and to
evaluate more carefully how to use it without being unnecessar-
ily hurtful to others.

In 1965, I completed my M.A. and began applying for a
college teaching position. One of the first applications resulted in
some encouraging interactions. However, incredible as it sounds,
I was eventually told that, though they were very interested in
me and believed I was qualified for the job, they could not extend a contract. Their reason was that no one who was 4'10" tall
could possibly command a college classroom! Fortunately, there
were a number of college positions open that year, and I soon

signed a contract with a less short-sighted institution. I have been teaching college students ever since.

I still do not like games. I am still intimidated by large animals, heavy traffic, and large crowds. I still know that words have power and I still work to use the power I have in a positive manner, opting to empower others and avoid intimidating them. I still wish I were closer to average, but I have come to terms with the world structured by an upward gaze.

Robust health and a strong, resilient body are not necessarily givens, as **Roselyn Baugh Kerlin (1955)** discovers. She takes us beyond assumptions about physical stamina and into her world where to ignore the body's signals can prove highly problematic.

I have always taken my body for granted. "And why not? It's always served me well," I would think to myself.

I was a tomboy when I was a kid. Keeping up with my boy cousins whom I greatly admired was never a problem for me. I was right with them playing cowboys and climbing trees. So what if I scraped a knee or banged an elbow? Everything always healed and healed fast, and probably always would – or so I thought.

Later, in the '50s when it became the vogue to wear those spike-heel shoes with the pointy toes, I chose to wear them with no question on my part. I even taught school all day in them, never once thinking of their effect on my feet. Then I noticed I was developing bunions, but like always, I figured they'd heal in time. When my feet began to hurt really badly, I started to carry a larger-than-usual purse. That way I could have an extra pair of shoes ready to rotate and ease the pain.

Finally though, my foot condition worsened to the point I

knew I must go for a medical exam. Still, I protested inwardly that my "to-do" list was far too long to spare the time. "Surely," I thought, "in time, whatever the problem was, it would heal itself." But I was in for a shock.

"What I want to do is operate on your feet now, immediately, and on both at the same time," the doctor stated after his careful examination. But even with his serious demeanor, and although I agreed to his suggestion, still, my lifelong confidence in my body led me to feel that the surgery would heal quickly and I would, again, be without pain.

That operation behind me, I found my oversized purse taking on additional significance in my life. From toting in it extra pairs of shoes, my bag went on to serve as a portable office. Into it went books and notebooks. As my daughters grew, they found it handy that Mom had a carrying case that was available to them as well. Soon, I was also hoisting to my shoulder their school gear and supplies. I shouldn't have been surprised that, in time, I began to develop neck pain. And to compensate for that new symptom, I ended up with dangerously poor posture.

Later, when I worked in my oldest daughter's medical office, I spent hours at the computer. In time, the repetitive activity began to cause wrist pain. To address this condition, I was faithful to wear wrist braces. And I thought I was on top of the matter until I realized I didn't have feeling in three of my fingers. I couldn't believe I had a serious problem but, nevertheless, I made an appointment for an examination.

I was stunned. "Your Carpal Tunnel Syndrome has progressed to the point that it is now causing nerve damage that could be permanent," announced the doctor. And, as before, surgery was immediately scheduled. But still thinking my body was as it always had been in my youth, I didn't so much as wince when the surgery was scheduled so that both wrists would be operated on at the same time! Then, severely limited with two wrists incapacitated, and with unstructured time away from my fast-paced work schedule, I found I could do little but sit and reflect. "Could it be," I began to wonder, "that my body actually does have limits?"

But then, only two months after the wrist condition was declared healed, I was walking along a sidewalk in a nearby city. Without the slightest warning, my rubber-soled shoes caught on the edge of the walk. I lost my balance, fell off the curb, and broke both of my recently healed wrists. By then, it was late October. Thanksgiving and Christmas were coming up fast. The pain, this time, was the worst I had experienced. With both hands and both arms in casts up to my elbows, I finally began to listen more closely to what I was becoming sure my body was trying to tell me.

For example, later, when my doctor ordered cataract surgery because of my failing eyesight, the image immediately returned to me of the hours I had spent back in my youth out in the hot sun without wearing sunglasses, and believing all the while in the advantages of a glorious tan. Little thought was given, back then, to the sun's negative effects on our bodies.

Throughout my adult life, whenever I was engaged in a work project I found it was not difficult to push myself hard. Concentrating, studying, working for long periods of time, I found it relatively easy to block out distractions around me and push ahead. If I felt any discomfort, I would try to lessen it by ignoring it and intensifying my attention on what I was doing. To do this felt like a good thing to me at the time. But later, I would learn that to push myself so hard wasn't such a good idea. Pain developed in my neck. Then it shot down my back. It even went into my legs and all the way to my ankles. The neurologist exclaimed that I must surely have been in some terrible wreck, but I knew differently. The condition resulted in spinal surgery and still more downtime for me.

When the message of all these conditions finally came through to me, I felt humbled. I had taken the great gift of youthful health and strength for granted. When the Scripture says that my days are numbered, I have to conclude that my body is not designed to serve me forever. There is a limit to my days and there is a limit to my physical faculties. What I had overlooked in my strong, healthy youth was that pain can offer important signals from the body. What is the point of abusing my body as though aging were somehow not in the natural scheme of things, or that healing is a given? The way I see it now is that it took some strong lessons for me to come into the understanding that I am to be thankful for my body, to use it but also to nurture it, and to respect it as the very temple of the Spirit of God within me.

Living with the limitations life imposes on us, while at the same time courageously searching for methods to compensate, provides a measure of the resilience and perseverance of the human spirit. **Janet Berst (1959)** delights and inspires us as she addresses her challenge.

I started wearing thick, dark, rose-colored glasses at the age of 14 months. Not until my senior year in college did I change to contact lenses. From that time, my vision improved and stabilized somewhat for the next 18 years. The only thing I knew I could not do was drive a car. Everything else was seen as a possibility.

After graduating from college with high enthusiasm, I looked for my first job. "Ah, so you're a college graduate ... great, then you can type!" exclaimed my first interviewer. I could hardly believe my ears. It had to be a joke. But then, the year was 1959. I was well aware that most women were largely restricted to clerical positions like typing and filing – and with low salaries. Perhaps my youthful expectations allowed me to think otherwise.

Nonetheless, I worked up my courage and applied for Engineering Assistant positions. But no sooner was my first interview drawing to a close than I was informed that large manufacturing corporations with positions I aspired to had strict medical exams, and those included vision. At two companies, I passed a battery of timed tests, was interviewed, and approved by the manager, only to go on to the medical exam where I faced the eye chart and flunked flat. At another company, I was told that I could have a secretarial job, but then, what did I do but flunk their tests in shorthand and typing.

In most cases, the vision requirement was 20/20, but most firms would consider applicants with a range from 20/20 to 20/40. I could understand that requirement for someone who would be expected to drive as part of their job, but I was looking for a desk job. I was told that this particular requirement was made because of the issue of company-sponsored health insurance. Finally, after a long list of discouragements, I left the last firm's medical department, walked down the long hallway and tears literally streamed down my face. "What," I wondered desperately, "do I have to do to get a job?"

My family suggested I go to the Cincinnati Association for the Blind. I followed their advice but soon learned that in order for the personnel there to be of help to me in my job search, I would have to fill out an extensive application form. The personnel were kind. They offered to help me, but I took the form and mentioned off-handedly that I was able to fill it in on my own. When they saw the completed application, I could hardly believe their response. "We're sorry," they said. "We cannot help you. Your vision is too good!" Suddenly, I felt myself slipping helplessly into a gaping crack within the system.

At this low point in my life, a member of my church, who was Vice President of an insurance company, happened to tell me that she might be able to help me with a position at her company where the medical exam was, as she said, almost nothing. It turned out, subsequently, that my positions were indeed the typical female jobs, but I earned promotions and moved ahead – although slowly. Women's salaries were discouragingly low, I learned firsthand. But once I became more knowledgeable, I moved forward more steadily and found better jobs especially in the field of Information Systems, which I found satisfying. I am grateful to that church member for giving me the chance to prove myself.

The way I have seen things is that, in spite of some of the lower salaries I have had to settle for, as long as I stayed ahead of the family median income, I felt successful. From these experiences, I have taken a new meaning from the prayer, "God grant me the serenity to accept the things I cannot change, the courage to change the things I can, and the wisdom to know the difference." I have overcome my discouragements and have chosen to make my past life not an undertaker, but a valuable teacher.

Working our way through negative life experiences equips us to offer knowledgeable and insightful encouragement to others experiencing similar tragedies. **Heather Gladhill Kehr (1995)** tells her story of heartfelt emotion leading to a profound new calling.

After God blessed me with a wonderful husband, we began to pray for our future children. Over a year passed before we were blessed with a wonderful little son. Severe scar tissue from a ruptured appendix had made it look as if having children might be impossible. We felt our prayers had been answered. My pregnancy was wonderful and, despite a difficult delivery, we were blessed to hold our precious baby boy in our arms.

Imagine our joy a year later when we found out on Mother's Day weekend that we were to be blessed with a second baby. We had an early ultrasound, which showed our precious baby with a normal heart rate. All seemed to be going well. But, three weeks later we knew something wasn't right. I spent the entire night praying for this child. On a hot June day, I went to the obstetrician for another ultrasound. I was not prepared for the finality of his words. "I'm sorry," he said sympathetically, "but the baby hasn't grown since the last ultrasound and there is no heartbeat ...."

Whatever the doctor may have said after that came only as a blur as I tried to accept the death of this child we had prayed for and already loved. I wept with a grief I had never known possible. I thought my heart was literally going to crumble into pieces. I couldn't think. I couldn't talk. I couldn't even look my husband in the eyes. All we could do was hold each other and cry. Our baby was only with us for nine and a half weeks. All my excitement, and dreams, and hopes now dissolved into tears of mourning.

This grieving process took me on a road that I didn't want to travel. I cried out to God. I went to church and I couldn't get my voice to sing because I was choked by tears. I knew at one level that God was still lavishing His love on me,

I couldn't even look my husband in the eyes. All we could do was hold each other and cry.

offering me grace and mercy, and holding out peace and understanding for me throughout the ache of losing my child. Yet, for months I couldn't get through this heavy veil of grief. I struggled with anger towards other pregnant women. I feared that I might never have another baby, and I felt consumed by my feelings. Finally, the awful heaviness lifted. After a time, I felt able to praise God again.

Over the past year-and-a-half since we lost our little daughter, I have become so much more sensitive to the grieving of parents who have also lost infants. A new calling came to me through this very difficult time in my life. I now participate in a ministry for those who have experienced a miscarriage. To me, the hope of heaven is real. And, I look forward to praising the Lord and being with our precious daughter one day.

Working our way through the many emotions of a negative experience can equip us with deeper understanding and provide us with tools for knowledgeable encouragement of others suffering similar tragedies. **Lisa Moritz Miller (1990)** tells her story of heartfelt longing leading to profound new insights.

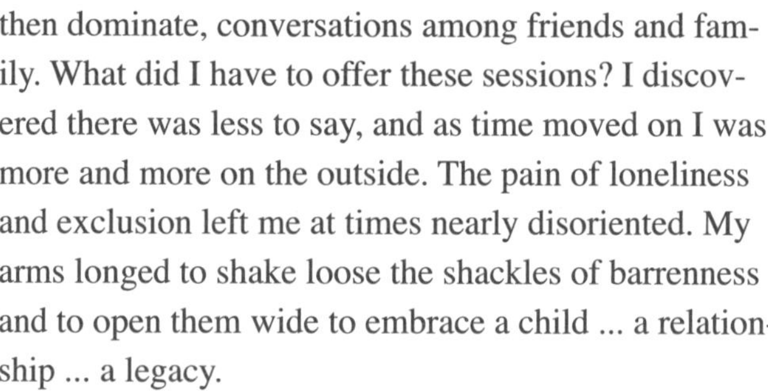

The community of motherhood, the universal club of life-givers and nurturers, was only a step away. This was a community I desperately wanted to join, but for me, it seemed just out of reach. It was but the simple difference between a negative and a positive indicator on a pregnancy test strip. Nothing more, and yet, the space between where I was and where I longed to be felt like a mile-wide canyon.

I recall vividly the familiar, knowing glances shared between women in the check-out lanes of grocery stores as their children begged for candy or a toy within reach of the cart. Or topics of childbirth and child rearing that would creep into, and

then dominate, conversations among friends and family. What did I have to offer these sessions? I discovered there was less to say, and as time moved on I was more and more on the outside. The pain of loneliness and exclusion left me at times nearly disoriented. My arms longed to shake loose the shackles of barrenness and to open them wide to embrace a child ... a relationship ... a legacy.

After four years of marriage to my college sweetheart, we felt the time was right to start a family. We were thrilled to entertain the hope of expanding our love. But hope turned on us as the months and years of waiting slid by. What seemed the ugly truth presented itself – the situation appeared out of our control. My barren womb seemed to poison my heart as well.

I found myself battling resentment, jealousy, and anger in my attempts to make sense of the grief I faced. I began to withdraw emotionally and conversationally from those who were parents, which obviously included many family members and friends. I felt too vulnerable to share my pain. And where Psalm 127 boldly proclaims that, "Children are a heritage from the Lord, children a reward from Him," what I wanted to know was, a reward for what? Why was I being denied this great gift?

Although I had not received the gift of a child, gradually, over time, I began to realize that I was receiving a new vision – as though I was gaining new eyes, and along with those, new ears, and a heart better attuned to the cries of others. When I would hear people sharing the pain in their lives, I began to realize the importance of responding to their hurt with tenderness and without spouting unsolicited advice.

I was learning more about what it was to need one another. I had kept my infertility largely a secret for years, but finally, I was realizing that I was someone who needed others to know me. When I felt it appropriate, I began to share my own pain, trusting that others would receive me tenderly. Gradually, I became more comfortable acknowledging my emptiness. I found myself becoming more honest in my conversations with others and with the Lord.

It was through my honesty and openness that I found myself desiring still greater intimacy with the Lord. I was coming to understand that God wanted me to want Him more than anything – more even, than a child. I found myself, for a time, teetering between hope and trust. I hoped that the agony of infertility would help me be a better mother should I have a child at some future time. And, I *trusted* that God did want His best for me – either with or without a little one to nurture.

And then it happened. One September evening in 1997, a test strip showed shift from negative to positive. It was as though I could almost audibly hear God proclaim, *Now is the time*. Joy exploded within us. We praised God and prepared to share the news with others. To this day I wonder if our little one was actually prayed into existence. I often joke that there must have been extra prayers left over because, not long after, another delightful surprise appeared! And one more joined the family four and a half years later."

I am now a member of the community of motherhood. Do I find myself revisiting the pain of those years of infertility, especially when I know of other couples facing the agony of childlessness? The way I want to respond is that it has become an honor to pray on their behalf – praying for little ones to cradle in their arms and for the Creator of Life to overwhelm them with His loving grace.

Tormented by the possibility of giving birth to an infant threatened with limitations imposed in utero, **Rosalyn Coburn Richmond (1956)** takes us into her time of agonizing decision.

The day presented itself like a blustery two-act performance with no advance billing. The subject was raw. The message, unpredicted.

That particular blizzard, back in the '60s, was called one of Minnesota's worst. Snow, already waist high, swirled upwards around the corners of the house and banked clear to the roof of the garage. My world was closed in. No one could venture out.

I felt comfort indoors from the raging storm outside, but no means presented itself for me to avoid what I would learn next. Both shivering and feverish, I woke up that morning to an angry rash that covered my entire body.

There was little guessing in my mind about the cause of this condition. And, I knew as I examined myself that what I was seeing could prove to be far worse than being closed in by treacherous weather for a few days. My fears suddenly stretched far beyond the whistling wind and the gusting snow.

I had been substitute teaching in our local school system. At the same time, I was in the first trimester of my second pregnancy. It had been only a rumor among the teachers, one I was too busy to take seriously at first. That morning, my thinking shifted. A student, so went the gossip, had been diagnosed with German measles.

I phoned the doctor immediately that morning. But no one could dig themselves out. "Could just be hives," was the doctor's response. "There's nothing we can do in either case," he added.

I made an appointment none-the-less, then waited restlessly for the weather and my rash to clear up. And, as predicted, in a few days things seemed to return to normal. That is, until I met with the doctor.

We agreed that my exposure to German measles was a viable reason for my rash, but at that time, during the early '60s, I was told there was no way to test for the accuracy of the diagnosis, nor was there any sure means to tell whether or not the fetus I was carrying had been affected by my condition.

I must have blocked out the grizzly prognosis the doctor described – the potential physical or mental mayhem to my unborn child from my exposure to German measles. What I do recall in stark specifics is the physician's consideration of the subject of aborting a baby. "It'd be kinder to drown the infant in a pail of water than subject it to the cruelty of abortion," I overheard him say to another patient on the phone. There was no question about the doctor's stand against terminating a pregnancy, no matter what the conditions.

Driving home from the medical office, the overheard words of the doctor replaying in my mind, I acknowledged to myself my own concerns about bringing unborn life to an end. I found myself looking once more at my own convictions. On the one hand, I felt that abortion was the taking of a life and for me, I felt it was not an option to do so. And yet, at the same time, I felt that it was not my place to harshly judge others in their decisions. I could not know what may have contributed to others' thinking. There was no avoiding it, this was an agonizing time for me.

But as I reflect on this moment, this critical time of emotional impact, I wonder at myself and my reactions to this dilemma. Where did my response come from? For one thing, it did not occur to me to lash out against God, to rail at Him for giving me a less than perfect married and family life. But then, it has never been a part of my belief system to expect a perfect God to bless me in special ways when certainly I have let Him down countless times. I'm not saying that what was happening was somehow a punishment. I did not see these events as coming from a vengeful God. No, I cannot reconcile a punishing God with a loving God. That doesn't compute in my thinking. But what does seem consistent with my concept of a loving, forgiving God is that, for whatever reasons, suffering tends to purify. I'm not talking about needless suffering. I'm talking about the kind of discomfort rendered when a loving parent must engage in acts of discipline toward a child who has much yet to learn.

What I saw myself facing was not how to escape this tormenting unknown, but how to accept it and cope with it. Maybe those words of wisdom I had tucked into my memory down

through the years also served to fortify me. *For all things work together for the good of them who love God and are called according to His purposes* – certainly this message worked mightily for my ruptured peace of mind. It's consoling to me to think there is someone in charge when things seem beyond my control.

When I think back over the many years since this event, although my winsome son was indeed born with a serious skin condition – which, incidentally, has never been medically and thus conclusively tied to my exposure to German measles – still, I feel a sense of peace that what happened, happened. For me and for my family, ours was to make the best of the situation, which I think we have.

And, once again, I saw that this does not mean that I am unequivocally and in all circumstances opposed to abortion. Certainly, taken case by case, there may be times when it is the greater act of grace to terminate a pregnancy in favor of the greater benefits to the greater numbers of others who could be seriously and negatively affected. Still, in my own case, although I felt deeply distressed by the magnitude of this grave dilemma, it was my reverence for life, no matter its condition, that shaped and justified my decision.

Certainly, the simplest observation of life has shown me that the rain will indeed fall on both the just and the unjust. And so, as it was when I was a young girl growing up on an isolated Iowa farm, it is the same now and I am a grandmother. I learned, back then, that I was to endure some things. And to this day, I see little reason for tantrums or hysterics when life doesn't go my way. What I have experienced is that life makes no promises. This doesn't mean I avoid using my education, my common sense, or the best of current knowledge. What it does mean to me is that when I accept an all-knowing, all-loving God as working to my best, I choose to consider that, no matter what the circumstances, there are good things in the works.

Standing aside in bold relief from commonly accepted societal norms, **Heather Myers Kittleman (1997)** offers a cogent explanation behind the personal life decision she has made, and which offers her a deep sense of inner peace.

You might find this incomprehensible, but I don't want children. At least, not right now – maybe not ever. Here's my perspective.

On the subject of children, there is a wide spectrum of thought with two strongly held views on opposing ends. On the "having kids" end, there are people who adore children and can't wait to be a parent while on the "having no kids" end, people don't like children and don't want anything to do with being a parent. Neither extreme is right or wrong. They just are. The decision to have or not have children is a choice, and like all choices, it is influenced by a myriad of factors.

One factor is simply how we were wired when we were born. Some people are born with the desire for children while others simply are not. I can no more explain why I don't have that desire just like I can't explain why I love broccoli. The desire for children has always been absent in my life, even back into childhood. I just have never felt the draw to have a child of my own and be a mother. Outside factors have only served to support and reinforce this. I have observed countless families and their interactions and have listened to parents express their joys and troubles. I have spent hours engaged in baby-sitting and childcare. What I have learned is that parenthood is a hard job, and quite honestly, the "perks" that they insist make parenthood worth it aren't all that attractive to me.

I know myself, and from what I know of my likes and dislikes, my needs, my personality, and my temperament, I am not one who would make a very good mother nor would I enjoy the job of being a mother. I like a peaceful, quiet atmosphere; I dislike complications and stress; I am independent and not a nurturer, and I am a very low-key, low-energy person. I can see that I would have difficulty in bringing these and other things that I know about myself together with what I know of what it takes to rear a child successfully to adulthood.

Not having children has its advantages. I have been married five years childfree and have loved it. In that time, my husband and I have been able to focus on each other, have a fun relationship, and built a wonderful closeness that would not have been possible if a child were involved. I have cherished and treasured this time we have had to focus on each other and to build memories together.

In this period of time I have also been able to explore and define who I am. At the local university I've taken classes to explore and develop my interests and talents. At home I've continued that as well as having completed personal projects that are important to me. This has been so vital because, even though

I'm 29, I still feel as though I am a child and have not figured out my place in this world. It is vital that I have had this opportunity for self-discovery because if I had not, I would have felt stifled, overwhelmed, and held-back.

I am thankful to live in the "post pill" era that has made this luxury of enrichment and self-discovery possible. Because I have a safe and effective means to control my reproduction, I don't live in fear of an unwanted pregnancy unlike women before me. How many of those women dreamed of the freedom I am living in now! My taking advantage of my birth control options honors those women and also those who sacrificed to bring options into existence.

Deciding not to have children is not easy, and I admit that I have not always been at peace about my decision. Even though I don't have the desire for children, the "what ifs" still parade through my mind: What if I have a child and I like it? What if I have a child and all of my fears are realized? What if I don't have a child and when I turn 50 I am hit by a pang of regret? Because of these

Deciding not to have children is not easy, and I admit that I have not always been at peace about my decision.

"what ifs," there was a point when I didn't think that just not wanting kids was a good enough reason not to have a child. One day I cried out to God to help me find an answer, and I feel He did. I came to understand that my heart wasn't in it and that that reason was good enough. How could I make myself go through with something as life altering as having a child if my heart wasn't in it? What I realized was that I simply could not do it.

After all of this, a child may still be a part of our future. I have felt my feelings and attitude shift over time in that I feel more satisfied with my life because of the time I have spent devoted to my needs and my marriage. Time has also brought a measure of maturity and "grown-up-ness" that I am easing into.

In a few years, I can see the possibility of myself being ready to take the step to having a child. In Ecclesiastes, God teaches that there is a time for everything, and I know that now is not the time for me to have a child, although there may yet be an appropriate time. God may or may not choose to bring a child into our lives someday. Whatever happens, I will accept it wholeheartedly. In the meantime, I can only trust Him and go from here.

Times have changed, and with the passing of time, many of the previously accepted notions about ways life is to be lived have also come up for review. **Rochelle Manor (1987)** dared to ask the hard questions of life. She takes us into her world, and we are the richer for it.

My heart was pounding. My breasts ached. I felt tears welling in my eyes. Once again – as I could count on them to appear at least a couple of times each month – I awakened from one more dream about birthing and breastfeeding a baby. It felt as though my very soul longed to be a mother. My biological clock was ticking. And, no pregnancy was in sight.

My husband and I had decided to put our careers first, but I always thought the family part of our lives would arrive by the time I was in my early 30s – after I had earned my Ph.D., and was in the first few years of my job. Instead, our lives grew more distant. We lived apart for five years while he completed his doctoral studies. With the passing of time, each conversation on the topic of parenting raised more of his concerns about having a child with me, such as possible genetic problems that might affect our offspring or back problems I had suffered earlier. All the while, my clock kept ticking.

My 35th birthday was one of the most difficult days of my life. My eggs are at risk, I grieved the whole day. Every Christmas was more difficult than the one before as my parents and I watched from a distance while my cousin's happy children unwrapped their gifts.

After two years of marital therapy, my husband and I were much better able to communicate. We spent hours in deep, emotional discussions about our hopes and dreams, fears, and disappointments. He was sure that his career would be fulfilling – once he got the perfect job. But I had the perfect job and I know I still wasn't fulfilled. I longed for a child and I felt strongly I'd never be able to forgive him if my opportunity slipped away. And, I know I'd never be able to forgive myself if I didn't at least try.

With anguish and heartache, we agreed that we loved each other enough to not hold the other back. So, in January of 2002, we went together to the attorney's office to file for divorce, went together to the bank to settle our assets, spent tearful hours dividing our belongings and separating out our memories.

The next two months were filled with healing my broken heart, building my new life, and redecorating my house into a comfortable home that I would come to love. Then came the months of blood work and hormone shots as I prepared for the next step in giving full expression to my deeply held desire to have a family. And finally, I was ready for the numerous attempts at artificial insemination through an anonymous sperm donor program.

It was July – the day before what would have been our 15th wedding anniversary. I headed to the clinic for my third attempt at insemination. My child, I felt myself calling to its spirit, I am finally ready for you.

After years of wishing for the perfect "All American Family," I had come to grips with the reality that it wouldn't be that way for me. So, I grieved for what wasn't to be and accepted this new challenge. I've done the intellectual work to educate myself about what I needed to know, and the emotional work to get to this place of peace and strength.

I'd find myself thinking, I feel ready to be a model for you,

My Dear Little One, of courage and stability. My heart is open to love you more deeply than either of us can imagine right now. I've done the physical work to prepare a beautiful home for us. There is a whole network of people who are waiting for your presence. Your grandparents, my circle of friends – they all know I'm longing for you and they are here to help make life as full as it can be. Now, My Dear One, it is time for your spirit to join me and for me to be your mother – forever.

March 27, 2003 – one year from the date the divorce became final, I gave birth to a healthy six-pound, four-ounce baby girl ... already named and planned for.

The irony of these dates is not lost on me. To conceive on what would have been our anniversary, to deliver my baby one year from the date of divorce ... it felt as though it was absolutely meant to be. But during the process of deciding to leave my marriage to pursue being an "only parent," the grief was indescribable. I had to let go of all the assumptions, expectations, and hopes for a "typical" family. I couldn't force things to be different than they were. And once I accepted that, and I let go of my assumptions, the dream of motherhood was given to me in a different way than I would ever have imagined.

Now, I find myself blessed with much more than I ever dreamed. I love being an "only parent." Each day, I get all the cuddles and smiles. My baby and I have a rhythm and synchronicity that is incredible. This is perhaps because – before getting pregnant – I was able to establish and organize so many of the peripheral, yet essential things of life such as my career, financial stability, and the developing of a support network. I've been able to enjoy fully each phase of the process, making my way through a myriad of unknowns to this place where I can love with a new love.

And from this journey, I have found courage. I have learned to step out in informed confidence, and I have found that the human heart has an infinite capacity to express love in new, uncharted ways.

Life's challenges do not always present themselves in single, neat, easy-to-handle form. There are times when we face multiple challenges, intersecting and overlaying one another, and competing for attention and resolution. **Angie Lyons Knight (1994)** minces no words in describing the profusion of crises converging in her life when least expected.

It seemed like a silly question, but at 19 weeks along, I was entitled to ask whatever I wished. So, at the end of my prenatal checkup, I asked the doctor, "By the way, is there any chance we could have twins?" The doctor looked surprised – a bit startled, actually.

"No," he informed me. And certainly my measurements were in line with a single pregnancy, he insisted. The very next week I was scheduled for an ultrasound. With that, all questions would be answered.

"Why did I ask?" The doctor was curious.

"Well," I explained, "my husband and I both dreamed that we were expecting twins, but then I dream a lot of things, so I hadn't really placed much stock in a mere ... dream." Not being a "baby person," the thought of two simultaneous infants, quite honestly, terrified me.

Fast forward one week: the ultrasound. My husband and I went to the medical office together. "Here is the baby's head," said the ultrasound technician. "And here is the other baby's head."

"The other baby ... twins?" my husband exclaimed. "You mean she is going to have twins?"

"No, you are both going to have twins," replied the wise technician. I was in a daze. But I have copies of the ultrasound to prove it.

It's funny how we make plans for our lives. At the start

of our marriage, my husband and I had decided that we would someday like to have two children; no more, no less. Then an unpredictable, chronic, neurological disorder entered the picture. Okay, so we could still have a child, but to keep from postponing the start of a medical regimen that would endanger an unborn child, we would have to settle for one child. Raising an only child would be fine. Do twins run in our families? No. Did I do anything scientific to encourage the development of multiple births? Absolutely not. Hadn't I always wanted twins? Quite the opposite, actually. But this is how life happens, isn't it?

So here I was, continuing to come to terms with both a diagnosis of multiple sclerosis, and also trying to prepare for not one, but two infants. I'm not naturally drawn to infants, and as I said, I am not what I would consider a "baby person." Sometimes, I think God looks down at us and chuckles. And I think this was one of those times. If God could bring two children into our lives, and those two would come at once to a very imperfect mother, then He could certainly help me find ways to make all this work. Reflecting back, I recall the shock I felt, but also a strange sort of peace. I thought I had been mentally prepared for a big life change: learning proper diapering techniques, losing a lot of sleep, learning how to nurse a child, cutting back from a full-time job to full-time motherhood, but hoping still to teach part-time. But after the ultrasound proof, these visions changed quite a bit. It was suddenly a fuzzier picture, one that my husband and I looked toward together with both fear and joy. And a lot of uncertainty too. But, as we figured, these babies would have two parents, each parent had two arms, and they would have a double dose of love.

And now, later, I can't imagine life with just one of these girls. Without them both, the picture would be, oh, so empty.

As we have approached the new millennium, we, as members of the human community, have been faced with lifestyle choices that represent a stepping aside from previous societal norms. All of us who think with seriousness about these issues, face considerable challenge. Do we hold fast to existing concepts and practices and view them as fixed and unalterable? If so, how do we express understanding, even empathy, toward those who follow a different path? Can judgment and compassion truly coexist? **Joyce Smith Helyer** struggles with this question as she takes us into her highly personal dilemma involving a beloved family member.

Christmas Eve, 1975 – the night my brother told me he was gay. Actually, he didn't come right out and say the words. He left that for me.

We were celebrating Christmas at my parents' home and my brother had flown in to be with us. It was about midnight and all the family had gone to bed, including my pastor husband and our two children.

My brother and I kept on talking and talking deep into the night. He was my baby brother and we had always been close. As we talked in my parents' living room with the colorful Christmas tree in the background, he would make comments like, "I have something to tell you, Joyce." But that is as far as he would go. I remember feeling very tense, and even suspicious. Thoughts raced wildly through my head. Is he trying to tell me he's gay? I wondered. Years earlier I had met some of his friends – handsome, beautiful men – but no girlfriends. We had even stayed in his apartment overnight on a trip near his home, but never met his roommate. "Working late," or "out-of-town," was what he would say. I was suspicious, but I never let those thoughts take shape. Surely he couldn't be gay, I thought. He didn't fit my stereotype. However, I was wrong.

I have blocked out of my memory much of the conversation of that Christmas Eve, except for his startling confession to me describing former relationships with priests and Methodist pastors. Finally, I asked outright, "Are you trying to tell me you're gay?" I remember his quiet response, "I thought you had it figured out." And at that, he seemed relieved ... someone else in the family knew. I felt sad and anxious. I called out to God for wisdom and the right words to say. I was not aware then how pivotal a turning point this moment was for him, or for me – this was just before the AIDS crisis hit America.

That conversation was followed by years of middle-of-the-night phone calls as my brother shared his fears, broken relationships, alcoholism, paranoia, and eventually AIDS. He experienced what seemed like all the highs and lows associated with living as a gay man. As AIDS came on the scene in the early '80s, he became terrified. What if he were HIV positive? There were many tearful conversations and I encouraged him to be tested so he would not have to live with the fear of not knowing. My brother had lived in San Francisco for three months and he deeply regretted his time there. It took two years for him to build up his courage to face the consequences of what an HIV test might tell him. And, all around him, his friends were dying.

He finally made the decision to be tested and soon after we received the word. "Joyce, I tested positive." That's when his alcoholism increased in his attempt to self-medicate and rid himself of his emotional pain.

Soon, he was on a variety of medications that totaled over $2,000 each month, and with each passing year his T-cell count became lower and lower. In 1992, he qualified for disability. The emotional trauma of AIDS together with his alcoholism affected his ability to remain employed.

One of the kindest things my brother said to me during all of these events occurred on a trip he made to our home. Even though short of breath, weak, and sweating profusely, he had insisted on helping me plant a privet hedge in our back yard. While we were working together, he told me, "I love being here. I feel a peace when I am here." Those were precious words to me.

When I first discovered my brother was gay, I sent him literature imploring him to turn away from his gay lifestyle and I quoted scripture to him – often. I came to a point when I finally had to release him to God. I had to let go of all that was happening to me as well in my attempt to figure everything out. I had written a Catholic priest who had a ministry to gays and he so kindly shared with me his godly wisdom about how to relate to my brother. "Just love him and let the Holy Spirit work in his heart. He's overwhelmed with guilt," he wrote. And then the priest laid out for me in his letter what would be a pattern in my brother's life. As I reflect on the priest's words, everything he wrote about in his letter happened to my brother – the addictions, the self-destructive behaviors, broken relationships, fears, and eventually death.

My brother died on November 14, 1995. He was only 43. Along with my parents who had spent several months with him, and my two sisters, we were all with him that last week. At first, it was devastating when I saw him. I remember walking into his room in the nursing home before he died and seeing him smile, but all I could do was cry. He looked like a holocaust victim. As the days passed, all I wanted was for him to be comfortable and to reassure him of God's love and my love for him. My heart was breaking as he became consumed by the word Why. He could not keep food down and was burning with fever, so I slowly fed him ice chips to help him feel cool. As the disease ravaged his mind and body, he was able to speak less and less.

At my brother's funeral, I gave a eulogy that focused on his life – the things he enjoyed. I spoke of his compassion for others and his love for the beautiful Northwest. Questions regarding his homosexuality and the dynamics that surround this controversy came and went during years of discussions with him. But instead of focusing on his homosexuality, I chose to focus on the fact that he was my brother and a person of dignity and worth even if I disagreed with his lifestyle. As I grieved over his death, I experienced peace when I reflected on God's character – His mercy and justice. With God, I could leave my doubts and "what ifs."

Do I have all the answers? Not at all, but I trust the One who
does.

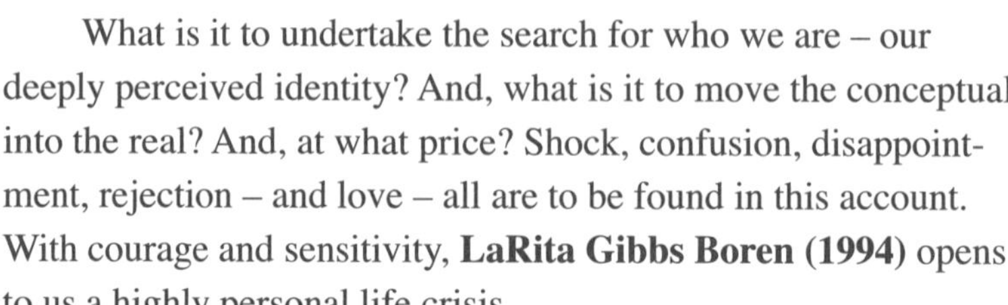

What is it to undertake the search for who we are – our
deeply perceived identity? And, what is it to move the conceptual
into the real? And, at what price? Shock, confusion, disappointment, rejection – and love – all are to be found in this account.
With courage and sensitivity, **LaRita Gibbs Boren (1994)** opens
to us a highly personal life crisis.

"Just relax and it will happen." That's what the doctors told
me after I had numerous tests, but despite all efforts there was
still no baby. That was back in 1963, and my longing for a child
had grown only more intense each year since my marriage in
1958.

Adoption, at first, did not seem to be an option. Family dif-
ferences of opinion discouraged our serious consideration of this
possibility. And then, intervention happened. A trusted employee
of my husband mentioned to him that she hoped we would not
make the mistake she and her husband had made. She explained
that, by the time doctors finally decided she could not have a
child, the adoption agency wouldn't accept their application
because of their age.

It worked. No sooner did she close the door behind her, I
learned later, than my husband phoned me. "Do you have the
number of that adoption agency in your wallet? Call them now
and make an appointment."

The following February our first baby was born and we
received her in March. Following her, we received our second
daughter. Then we rounded out our family by adopting our third
child, our infant son.

It was not until much later, after the children had become

adults, that we were, one day, vacationing in Florida. With us at that time were our young son and his wife, together with another young couple.

On the second night of our vacation, the phone rang. It was our youngest daughter. What she said to us came as a profound shock – followed by the most traumatically emotional experience of our lives. We were left numb. What she told us was that her name was no longer as we had known it. It was now in masculine form. The reason was that she was now a man.

We hardly slept that night. The next day, my husband wrote our adult child a very emotional and angry letter. This child had been very special to him. My husband was proud of her stamina and her abilities. We lived on a farm and she was always the one who could throw the most bales of hay, work the hardest, was the neatest, could fix any piece of machinery, and seemed always to have energy to spare. If she needed a sign painted for an activity, or an area organized artistically, or even the feedbags mended, she was the one who did it to perfection.

Now, he felt betrayed.

As a mother, my experience was almost immediately one of not wanting to reject, but of wanting to understand what had happened. She was, I reasoned to myself, after all is said and done, my child. Perhaps the hardest part for me was the sense that now, this young man – as yet unknown to me – somehow had killed my precious daughter and I hadn't been able to tell her goodbye.

Over time, when I'd sit quietly – trying to gather my anger and give it sense – I had to admit that my daughter had slowly become less my daughter and more my son. I used to cringe when we'd walk through the mall because people would literally turn and stare at her, and while she appeared oblivious to it all, surely she had to have felt very uncomfortable. She was physically very feminine, but she wore men's T-shirts and jeans and she moved like a man, so that one had to take a second look to actually determine whether she was male or female. Still, I never believed for a moment that she dressed and acted this way for any motive other than to release what she so strongly felt to be her genuine, inner self.

As our son, he began to make the transition from female, first, by wearing a loose shirt to the Bureau of Motor Vehicles and by telling them they had made a mistake on his driver's license and that it must be changed because he was male. Co-operatively, they changed the gender, asked no questions, and apologized profusely. Next, he changed his name, which I then learned anyone can do. And only a week later, on the recommendation of a psychiatrist, he began taking hormone injections.

I cannot say there weren't indicators along the way. I recall that her first-grade teacher had phoned to request that I come in for an unscheduled conference. It was then that the teacher told me she thought my daughter might be gay – a comment I thought so ludicrous at the time that I totally ignored it. But, with time, there did appear noticeable indications. Even I had to admit my daughter was demonstrating characteristics different from other girls her age.

As we flew home from that Florida vacation, my husband advised me that I would have to withdraw my membership from the board of the Christian university I served. "And, you'll have to resign all your positions in the church because of this," he added, to which our younger son, who was traveling with us, spoke up. "What's happening here?" he asked. "I think I'm having a crisis of faith. What is this? Mom holds a lot of secular positions, too, Dad, but you have mentioned only the Christian ones. Are you saying our secular friends will be more understanding than our Christian friends will be?" Suddenly, our focus began to shift.

I would like to say that I was accepting and supportive of my new son in all the surgeries and activities required by such a transition, but I was not. I did not see him for two years. During those two years, our youngest son's wife kept the lines of communication open. Our new son even visited our youngest son who lived across the street from us, but I could not bring myself to talk to him during much of this time period. Most of this time, we were separated by distance. He lived in the South; we lived in the Midwest. As soon as he saved enough money, he underwent a double mastectomy, the first of many surgeries. During this time, he was married to a wonderful girl whom our family adores. She has been supportive of him throughout his procedures.

Our new son was so sure he needed to become a man physically that he was willing to sacrifice his family, if that needed to happen, plus whatever money it would cost (because the surgeries were never covered by insurance), as well as endure both the physical and mental pain that can be enormous if not approached appropriately.

Through the years, a considerable amount of on-line information and support has developed and our new son has asked me to encourage parents and anyone considering this procedure to seek on-line help because it is now very available and tremendously helpful.

Until his surgery, he was struggling to deal with his own identity, and so to everyone he seemed very self-absorbed. Now, he has become involved in meeting with others who are considering this surgery, and will even meet with them as they tell their parents what they are considering, as well as offering to meet with their parents for them. He has been instrumental in starting a support group in Texas.

What I have learned is that the things I loved about my daughter still exist, but they now exist in my new son. Today, he is a handsome, loving, gifted, young man. It has been by no means a walk in the garden; rather, it has been more like wandering confused and blind through a desert. And yet, I would be less than honest if I did not admit that within this otherwise difficult – even at times torturous – journey, there exists much that is positive. I have gained a strength I never knew I had, and my understanding of life's surest virtues has expanded beyond measure. I have relinquished my tight hold on what is right and on what must be. Rather, I have learned that my life's journey may contain side paths, paths from which I now know I need never shrink. And, as my new son says, it may be bad at the beginning – but, with time, it definitely gets better.

Rosalyn Coburn Richmond (1956), together with her husband and daughter, endured a natural disaster of life-threatening and life-changing proportions. In detail, Rosalyn describes the terror she felt during the event, and the aftermath of serious emotional problems – part of a post-traumatic syndrome – that pervaded the later life of her then-infant daughter.

Late in the afternoon of that day, its memory permanently fixed in my mind, the local meterologist announced that a storm was approaching. "Conditions are ripe for a tornado," he warned. In no time, ominous clouds took shape. Dull thunder pounded and rolled in the distance. Then came the sound of splattering rain. Heavy, intermittent raindrops, carried on sidewise gusts of wind, hit hard at the windows. Lightening split the darkened sky. Then came the hailstones. Huge, marble-sized balls of ice bounced against the roof and began to whiten the ground.

"This is no ordinary storm," my husband and I remarked almost in unison. We gathered up our year-old daughter and ran down to the southwest corner of the basement where everyone was cautioned to go in this tornado-prone section of Minnesota. There, we huddled, taking refuge under a sturdy table. Sensing our tension, our child was terrified.

And then, in only a moment, everything strangely went calm. So did the pounding of the hail, even the wind. The atmosphere changed abruptly. The air pressure intensified, making our inner ears feel compressed and painful. Then, with a roar, the silence broke. With the sensation of a whole rail yard of freight trains passing over us, accompanied by a raging, whistling sound, the storm was upon us.

We were told that it takes about 30 seconds for a tornado to pass over a dwelling, but to us it was, of course, an eternity. The entire basement shook. Then came the ripping, pulling sound above us. We could literally sense the moment the entire house broke free from the foundation and sailed away.

Then the deafening roar diminished. The air pressure equalized. And, our shock was replaced by disbelief. We examined ourselves. We were alive.

Crawling from our corner in our refuge, through the darkness, we groped our way across the basement floor. The hissing of a ruptured gas main alerted us to the danger of lighting any matches. But our fears only intensified. We found we were trapped in our basement.

There was nothing we could do but wait for help and pray. And pray we did. We prayed hard that the Lord who calmed the storm for the disciples on the Sea of Galilee would calm the tempest raging around us. Suddenly, then, came the familiar voice of our next door neighbor calling down to us. He was able to remove debris above us and kick in the door. As we crawled out, flashes of lightening still pierced the sky and gave us a glimpse of the devastation around us.

The walls and roof of our house were gone. Plainly, they were no place to be seen. Later, we found that the cement blocks of the basement walls were separated seven layers down from the top row. Everywhere, broken glass, household goods, and personal items littered the ground. We ended up living in an apartment for four months during the rebuilding process.

Freakish things can happen during tornadoes. My husband's antique pocket watch, passed down to him from his grandfather, had been stored in a special box in a dresser drawer. We found it the next day out in the yard in a neighbor's high heeled shoe. Lying on what was once the living room floor, midst piles of refuse, there was a card, face up. On it were the bold letters that said simply, "Jesus is your truest friend."

And, along with these many ironies, there have been the more lasting impacts on my life. And perhaps the single most traumatic after-effect are the panic attacks suffered by our daughter well into young adulthood. Earlier on, the panic sensations were more clearly associated with the onset of adverse weather conditions. But, with the passing of years, the sensations have become extended even so far as to unknown provocations.

From this condition, I have learned more about panic attacks and the symptoms and treatment of post-traumatic syndrome. I am sobered by the emotional complexities that can arise from childhood experiences and even from adult trauma. Such conditions can remain troublesome to peace of mind throughout a lifetime.

I have learned from my current reading that few memories are as easily triggered and as hard to shake as those in which a person is confronted with an immediate threat. Certainly, this condition holds true in my case. I have learned that fear plays tricks with memory and with perceptions of reality. Fear systems in the brain have their own channels for storing traumatic memories, some conscious and rational and some unconscious and innate.

I have learned that emotional memories or sensations can be very difficult to eradicate. And, that effective treatment is not so much about eliminating the memories as a retraining to respond differently once the memory or sensation is triggered. With every step into and through an otherwise triggering event, I have learned the potential for rerouting the path of fear. Good therapy, perhaps together with medications, can aid in addressing otherwise debilitating panic sensations suffered by an estimated 5% of Americans – that is, I read, more than 13 million people in this country.

For me, and for my family, I have found I must address these issues head on. From this and other major catastrophes I have experienced, I could not help but learn a higher respect for the destructive quality of nature, as well as helpful survival techniques to employ. It had been further impressed upon my thinking that the uncertainties of life guarantee me neither freedom from negative experiences or sure delivery from them once they have presented themselves. Therefore, to walk in unending fear does not serve me. To do so would surely rob me of the peace of heart and mind that are a part of my healthy spiritual and emotional life as well as restrict me from living life fully. In my observation of life, there will always be storms of one kind or another. But what consoles and empowers me is the promise that, no matter what, God is always with me through the storm.

Paige Sheard Jaeger (1978) takes us into her world of chaos and hurry, and reveals profound lessons from a life too consumed by "busyness" to listen to the body's signals.

We didn't take my husband's complaint of chronic back pain too seriously. For three years he just pushed a few painkillers and it would go away. "Busyness" had consumed us, and painkillers assuaged any sense of urgency to see his condition other than something easily managed. In our hurried, over-committed world, we had no time for pain, check-ups, or warnings such as, "If pain persists, see a physician."

Then came the phone call. The day had started off like any other day. It was an ordinary morning of chaos, hurriedness, and morning good-byes. It was the doctor calling to ask that my husband return for additional images of his spine. My heart was knifed, and my stomach churned. That's when I knew the day would not be like all our others.

I could not help but learn a higher respect for the destructive quality of nature, as well as helpful survival techniques to employ.

That afternoon, the diagnosis came in: "There is a tumor inside the spine. It spans five vertebrae. We don't understand how the patient is even so much as standing up."

Five days later, my husband underwent neurosurgery – despite none of us having time for any such interruptions to our busy schedules.

And then, everything stopped. This wasn't the road we planned on taking, but there was nowhere to turn around. Suddenly, we had plenty of time: time to ponder, time to pray, time to regret, time to recover, time to plan, and time to talk.

My husband did recover, and his tumor, although huge and strategically located, was found to be benign. Through all of this, we have come to believe that life is like a long car ride. We're often traveling too fast to read the Surgeon General's warning on the billboards along the way, and much like our car engines, we're probably running most of the time low on fuel and in need of a good tune-up. What we found was that we had come to the place where only when our car needs repair, or hits a dead end, do we stop and take stock.

When this tragedy hit our life, we stopped. We took this time to do what would have been wise to have done all along. We re-evaluated, communicated, and purposed in our hearts to make some important changes in our life. We laid plans, received blessings from others we didn't have enough time to see before, and we had time to watch God at work. When life is too full, it's easy to say we trust the Almighty, but in reality, we found ourselves driving through life on cruise control, and what we called "trust" had become merely a noun. But when life takes an unexpected and tragic turn down a road like ours did, for us, "trust" suddenly became a verb and led us to important life changes.

Carole Ann Shoup Smith (1958) provides us with a clear, well-drawn and precise overview of her diagnosis of catastrophic proportions. Given only months to live, Carole makes a heroic decision relating to an alternative treatment regimen. She records her important findings in her book, *From Hopelessness to Hal-*

lelujahs: A Seventeen-Month Day-by-Day Diary of Trauma to Triumph.

*As of the printing of this book, Carole Ann Shoup Smith indicates that her medical oncology-examination results show her to be cancer-clear.

As I reflect on the summer of 1999, it seems like a nightmare. I can still recall my gynecologist's words, after an initial examination, saying that an internal tumor, which he found, almost surely confirmed a 75% chance of ovarian cancer. Following a second opinion, surgery was scheduled for mid-July with three specialists in attendance. Hours later, they fully agreed that the final decision was inoperable, Stage 4, gastric cancer with a hopeless diagnosis of a probable three-month survival. My husband almost fainted as he heard the piercing medical report, but told our grown, married children, with families of their own, to be strong as they awaited my arrival back to my room. It was there that medical science took a back seat, and faith in God's promises dominated as they had throughout my life after Christ entered my heart at age 9.

As months passed and my husband burned the midnight oil reading and exploring the internet on stomach cancer, I still appeared to be such an unlikely candidate. Yet, we were determined to find the answers, if not scientifically, then through searching for an alternative approach. My weakened condition gradually became stronger as the months passed and, as the next year approached, we learned more through constant research. We discovered that a Christian health workshop was being offered in North Carolina and that, through its teachings, scores had been healed of cancer and related diseases, while others were experiencing optimal health.

We immediately made plane and motel reservations. From the workshop we gained excellent information to put into practice. The major change involved a nutrition life-style turnaround eliminating all meat and dairy products plus sugary desserts. The former was fairly easy for me since I loved vegetables, but both they and fruit were to be eaten raw for maximum health. The dairy and dessert changes were more difficult, but my determination outweighed my desires. We had already purchased an expensive juicer for freshly extracted carrot juicing and learned that I was to consume many glasses daily in addition to a green barley product dissolved in distilled water.

With the support of family and friends, my husband made the life-style alteration with me and, within three months, no cancer could be found anywhere in me even though it had initially metastasized into my intestines. I felt wonderful, and the bonus was ideal weight for both of us even though that had always been a priority for each of us.

I was asked to speak about my miraculous healing at various functions from small groups, a well-attended women's ministry luncheon/fashion show, to large conferences in a noted hotel. We began to travel again, taking long vacations at various locations within the United States.

However, by the end of 2001, I began feeling a fluid buildup in my stomach. I went from a naturopathic doctor to my oncologist to a gastrointestinal doctor and endured three different cancer tests during the following Spring. All of those confirmed that there was no cancer anywhere within me. Yet, about every four to six weeks, I needed a paracentesis to remove the fluid accumulating in my abdominal area. No one had a concrete answer except for the naturopathic doctor. His tests on me revealed that the fluid was in the form of toxins building up within me from chemo treatments back in 1999, before I elected to drop them listening to and obeying God with biblical nutrition (Genesis 1:29) as He instructed me.

For the first year after my nutrition change, my body reacted positively but, thereafter, the toxins began to dominate. This weakened my body considerably, but my faith remained strong as I followed God's direction with the food that He so graciously bestowed upon His creation. I was reminded of Daniel and his friends refusing the king's rich food and being nourished by God's fruits and vegetables and becoming healthier by those choices.

By August of that year, as I continued on my healthy lifestyle, my fluid decreased and within the next three months was completely gone. I was able to enjoy the holidays with family. I felt strong and healthy. The New Year found my husband and me teaching a nine-week Biblical Health Class at our church and, then, traveling once again as well as enjoying and caring for our five grandchildren when time would permit. This summer, we traveled to a Health Conference in California and learned that toxins do indeed lodge in the liver, and the bile therefrom empties into the stomach causing fluid buildup.

My recent routine oncology checkup showed that I am 100% well, and I continue to praise God for His healing in obedience to His leading me to health.

Life's milestones can be sobering – those times weighted with ponderous realizations and a sharpened sense of one's approaching mortality. Not so, as **Faye E. Chechowich (1974)** describes her upcoming half-century mark. With exuberance and creativity, Faye takes her celebration in hand and shows us how life can become richer as we age.

I am not sure when it was that I began to dread my 50th birthday. After 28 years of professional life working with adolescents and young adults, I suppose it was only natural that much of my perspective about the age of 50 had been shaped and framed by the often less than flattering remarks young people make about aging. For most of my 40 something years, I had relished the compliment, "You're over 40? You sure don't look it!" Much in our culture communicates that younger is better. I was living that viewpoint as I approached my 50th birthday.

Sometime during the weeks before the big day, I began to rebel. I realized I wanted a richer, more holistic perspective about aging – one that focused on the gains that came with aging instead of the losses. I decided that I wanted to arrive at the infamous day being able to say, "I am 50, and isn't that great!" I wanted my 50th birthday to be a rite of passage that inspired celebration, instead of mourning. I wanted to stop feeling a sense of shame about my age. A dear friend reminded me of the biblical concept of the Year of Jubilee, the 50th year when God set apart for his people a time for celebration and restoration. I began to pray that God would allow me to experience my 50th birthday and year as a jubilant occasion.

My prayer was abundantly answered. The gift of friendships nurtured over the five decades of my life moved me from mourning to a jubilee celebration. I planned a party and invited 25 women who were friends and family members. Every decade of my friendships was represented in this group. These were the women who helped to form and shape me. Some were high school friends, some were college friends, some were professional colleagues, some were travel companions, some were Bible-study partners, some were former roommates. All were friends with whom I had a long history, and thinking about this group of women made me feel that my life was rich and beautiful. Just the act of creating the guest list evoked a spirit of joy.

As it turns out, turning 50 was the best birthday of my life. The best part of the day for all of us was when my friend from South Africa surprised us all with her arrival. She and I had lived together during the 1980s when I worked in South Africa, and we have maintained a sisterly friendship in spite of the distance. We all laughed and cried as we shared our memories and expressed the joy and heartaches of our lives. The whole day was a celebration of friendship nurtured over time and cemented over distance.

As I basked in the joy of having so many of my dear friends with me, I realized that the depth and richness of my friendships are only possible because of the years of caring and communication. This wisdom has come with life experience and it has made me a better friend at 50 than I was when I was 30. What is great to me now, I am telling people as my 50th year comes to an end, is that, "I am over 50 and I have significant friendships to prove it!"

During a recent, warm, and memory-filled phone conversation with **Jean Frances Bergwall**, whose husband was president of Taylor University from 1951 to 1959, she told me the following, and gave permission to publish this account. Jean described with charm and poignancy a life that cannot fail to inspire us all.

On Tuesdays and Thursdays, I read to the blind. On Wednesdays and Fridays, I visit the old folks. For Sundays, I search out good devotionals. Oh, and everyday there is the prayer line to record for the church. This spring, I renewed my driver's license. This summer my vision was declared excellent. And all this time, my teeth are my own. I live in my own apartment. I live alone and love it. I have just acquired a computer and am determined to hang in there until it becomes my servant – not the other way around.

And when I chance upon a moment to reflect, sometimes I ask myself why it is that I'm living so long? Then, just as quickly, I ask myself how it is that when I read to my Alzheimer patients, they suddenly call me by name? Or, how is it that I never want for a means to drive to my shut-ins? Or, that I can hear so clearly? Can see with no difficulty? Can make my own decisions? Even muster the determination to wrestle a computer into submission?

I guess I'm just an independent woman. A *now* kind of gal. But then, I just turned 89.

Feeling "Not OK"

Everyone feels a little "not OK" now and again, but for some 17 million American adults annually – and for more women than men – major depression makes normal life impossible. Exactly why women fall victim to the disorder at a higher rate than men remains a mystery, although research is focused on reproductive, hormonal, genetic and other biological factors, as well as abuse and oppression, interpersonal factors, and certain psychological and personality characteristics. The disorder is most common among women who are unhappily married.

Studies indicate that women tend to be more connected to their feelings and the language of feelings than are men. Consider the way they're organized biologically and how they're acculturated; men aren't taught to talk about their feelings. In addition, it has been found that women are more inclined to search out help when needed, therefore, statistics are more readily available.

Before adolescence, the rate of depression among girls and boys runs about even. Between the ages of 11 and 13, however, the rate for girls rises sharply and by the age of 15, girls are twice as likely than boys to have experienced a major depressive episode.

Although depression is a debilitating disorder, it is highly treatable with medications and psychotherapy. Medications work by increasing the levels of neurotransmitters in the brain, such as seratonin and norepinephrine, which allows the brain to communicate with itself.

Of the different groups of antidepressants available today,

the most commonly prescribed are selective seratonin reuptake inhibitors, or SSRIs. These include Celexa, Lexapro, Luvox, Paxil, Prozac, and Zoloft. The SSRIs are shown to have three main benefits: (1) they have few side effects, (2) you can't overdose on them, and (3) they're effective for a wide variety of problems.

If SSRIs don't work, a doctor can try alternatives, such as Effexor, Elavil, or Wellbutrin.

All of the above information is very helpful for those who feel free to step out and make their needs known. For others of us, however, especially those of us conditioned to the notion that as a Christian we are to be victorious over all that life presents to us, or that because of the manner in which we internalize our ideas of God, we should be immune to adversities suffered by others – for those of us once faced with feelings less than positive and joyous – we can be left disoriented, defeated, and isolated.

All too often, faced by feelings of "not all rightness," we are tormented by questions, such as "Why me, God?" "What did I do wrong?" and "What will others think?" The first question arises from the assumption that we should somehow, as loved children of God, be above dark, negative feelings. The second question assumes that when things don't work out to our comfort and benefit that we have somehow broken a divine tenet, that we have not held up our side of a perceived "if – then" relationship with God. Or, as some have told us through their writings, they perceived God as failing to uphold His promises to them.

And the third question arises from a notion that can be especially devastating. When we feel our sense of worth and our identity is tied to the face we put forward to our support community, we set ourselves up for the potential of misery with a capital M.

Being in a social environment toward which we feel we must unfailingly present a countenance of joyful, victorious optimism fails to allow us the level of honesty and integrity so essential to inner stability and emotional health.

And then there arises still another problem, the compulsion to live a personally satisfying and productive, day-to-day life, make important decisions, and conduct successful business, all the while beating down and trying to rise above our unresolved, gnawing inner dilemmas. The expenditure of raw energy is mind-boggling.

Unfortunately for many of us, we've whitewashed ourselves into a corner, and to free ourselves will necessitate slogging our way back across our paint job, leaving our big, black footprints for all to see. And if we felt depressed and low before we found ourselves in such a state, we're sure to feel our world drop out from under us, faced with our felt sense of fraud and guilt.

The following accounts take us into the personal experiences of women who have suffered from a number of types of depression and related conditions, together with helpful and encouraging suggestions for effective treatments.

One in Four Women is Likely to
Experience Severe Depression

One-fifth of women with depression will get
the treatment they need. Women are at
higher risk than men for developing major
depression – about twice as likely – although
some researchers claim that depression is
under-diagnosed in men. (American
Psychological Association, 2002)

Mothers of Young Children are
Vulnerable to Depression

The more children a woman has, the more
likely it is that she will experience depression.

Women with multiple roles such as career,
marriage, and volunteer work may suffer
from less depression because these women
have many different support sources and life-
diversions. (American Psychological Association, 2002)

Symptoms of Depression

Persistent sadness or unhappiness
Lethargy
Loss of interest in previously enjoyable activities
Irritability
Sudden change in appetite
Disruption of normal sleep patterns
Physical discomfort
Difficulty thinking or concentrating
Thoughts of suicide or death

In a 1995 addendum to her book, *To Bend Without Breaking,* **Mary Ella Rose Stuart (1930)** opens wide the window on her severe, clinical depression. She shares with us her symptoms, and the feelings that ravaged her peace-of-mind. And, she courageously discusses the treatments that brought her a level of relief. Her book is meant to be a practical guide for others who suffer similar symptoms. The following excerpts are reprinted by permission from the 1995 Addendum to her book, *To Bend Without Breaking.*

❦   ❦   ❦

My depression was compounded by a mastectomy, in which one breast was removed. The surgeon said the cancerous cells had been discovered very early, and that my risk of the cancer's spreading was about "one-plus on a scale of one to ten." Physically, I recovered quickly from the surgery. However, depression then shadowed me even more deeply. I started being afraid to be alone. I could not sit still. Worst of all, I could not sleep more than an hour or two at a time. I was frantic. I now believe that, as a result of my surgery, there were some chemical changes in my body that contributed appreciably to the tide of depression that engulfed me.

Once again, the old guilt assailed me: "I have every reason to be secure and happy. Yet I am miserably depressed. What is wrong with me?" Others who have faced depression know how debilitating that feeling can be. Already struggling to "stay afloat," our guilt over being emotionally disturbed is like a whirlpool threatening to pull us under the surface entirely. Yes, I practiced what I have written in my book, and that helped. Without those insights I could not have survived. Still – the tide of depression washed over me.

I do not believe that God magically relieves us of all suffering just because we simply pray for a miracle. The loss of two children taught me that lesson. Yet, if we are open to God's grace, it inevitably comes somehow – though quite often not at all as we expect or think we want it. During my time of renewed depression, God sent me two evidences of loving care. First – a book. It was like a life-line thrown to me when I felt I was about to drown. It was *Darkness Visible; a Memoir of Madness,* by William Styron, detailing his struggle with what we now know as a clinical depression, often chemically caused or medicated. Styron has been acclaimed as a major American writer; *Sophie's Choice* is perhaps his best-known work in this country. Though widely praised both in the U.S.A. and in France, with his work being read extensively, he found himself sinking into depression to the point where he thought he was going mad. Styron had every reason to feel very good about himself; yet, he was in despair. His behavior became more and more destructive. At an event in Paris where he was honored with a literary award, for instance, he was insulting to his hostess. He felt as though he was going completely "off the deep end."

I have noted already that God gave me two special gifts.

The first was Styron's book. The second was a highly percep-tive psychiatrist. I was led to go to him after other psychiatric consultations proved unsuccessful. He decided that I had what he described as a clinical depression, probably connected with a permanent or episodic chemical imbalance. He suggested that I try some of the newer antidepressant medications. It took a long time to find the right medication for me, which proved to be Desyrel, with the later addition of Zoloft. In addition to my depression, the need for help in sleeping – a problem that had plagued me most of my life – was acute. With the help of these new medications, I have been able to sleep remarkably well – a wonderful gift in my advancing years.

Apparently, clinical depression often results when the brain of the patient lacks enough of certain chemicals to allow brain messages to be conveyed from one neuron to the next. There are many medications now being used for this problem; the skilled psychiatrist, in careful consultation with the patient, can decide which of these to try. As in my case, several may have to be used before the best one is identified.

I need to make it clear here that I do not believe I have received a "magic pill" that has cured all my problems with depression. I still get depressed – sometimes severely. At times I seem to "fall off the wagon," like a person suffering with alco-holism who had taken a drink that is poison to her system. Then, the old demons assault me again. (I recall again the comment Bill Wilson, founder of Alcoholics Anonymous, made to me years ago when he told me that I was a "dry alcoholic.") However, I usually do not sink down as deeply or remain depressed as long as was the case before the discovery that there was a medication that could help me.

Not everyone who suffers from depression will find its roots in a medical problem or a chemical imbalance. However, this is a possibility that ought to be explored by anyone suffering from depression. I thank God that I have received help because of the discovery of the whole new "families" of medication that can help relieve depression for some people. I know others who are receiving the same sort of help, including a former member of my "Anx Anon" group in Palo Alto. Three of us from that group, in fact, have been helped greatly by various kinds of medical treatment, including medication for a manic-depressive condition in one member that took years to discover and treat.

I have known intellectually for a long time that there is no cause for guilt about depression. Still, appropriating that insight emotionally has been very difficult. I agonized for years because I believed my faith was not strong enough. Why would a person who really believed in God and affirmed Christ's loving care be depressed, after all? I believe my father struggled in agony over that question. I recall hearing him pray in truly anguished words in his study when I was a little child. From what I know now, I believe that he had a clinical depression, but no insight about that medical problem and no treatment for it. He had to hide it away and wrestle with it as an entirely spiritual problem – a particularly serious deficiency in a minister of the Gospel. How I wish he had received the help that has been given to me!

Knowing that I have a clinical depression has been a great relief. Depression is less mysterious and overwhelming than it was before this discovery. Depression is caused by a lot of things, of course. Again – I do not think it can be relieved entirely by a "magic pill," and for some persons who face depression, medication is not appropriate. For many of us, however, the discovery of the physical roots of some depression is a comforting gift. In my 87th year, I share that discovery with you as one more evidence of God's unending love. It seems He never stops picking us up, no matter how often we fall!

Courageously, **Angia Macomber** describes, with insight and deep feeling, her long-time struggle with clinical depression. Angia brings up important issues for reader consideration. What are healthy ways of looking at perfectionism? How can we effectively cope with thwarted expectations? Difficult changes in our life? A sense of hopelessness? Of abject despair? The following article by Angia is reprinted from the Taylor University's student newspaper, *The Echo*, November 2, 2001, with her permission, and offers a frank look into this troublesome condition.

❦   ❦   ❦

I suffer from chronic clinical depression. My first episode occurred when I was a sophomore in high school, brought on by my being driven by perfectionism. My second episode occurred when I was a sophomore in college after the breakup of a relationship and at a time when I was experiencing a crisis of my faith, neither of which was really understood by my parents at the time.

I did not have another major depression until eight years later, when my first husband and I separated. Yet it was not until my fourth episode, triggered by my divorce, that I sought any kind of treatment for depression. I did not admit how desperately I needed help until I became suicidal (not the first instance in my life, but certainly the most serious).

For seven years now, I have taken an antidepressant on a daily basis, and I expect to continue to do so for the rest of my life. Without medication, and without three and a half years of psychotherapy (which have helped me correct destructive thinking patterns and cope more effectively), and without my being open and telling my husband and a close friend or two how I am really doing – especially when I begin to slip into a pit of despair – I literally would not be here today.

On Monday night this past week, I attended the seminar about depression, suicide and grief held in the union. Four faculty members and a former Taylor student shared openly about these topics. This truly was an answer to prayer because I have been so burdened the last two weeks for the students on campus who are suffering depression in silence and have told no one about their struggles!

So I decided to share my story in order to help others in the

Taylor community who are suffering from this debilitating but treatable medical disorder. I want to be a model of openness by telling about the battle I wage daily to resist the urge to appear as though I've got it all together. I don't, and none of us does, and this must be shared boldly!

To those who are struggling, I offer this encouragement: *"For I know the plans I have for you,"* declares the Lord, *plans to prosper you and not to harm you, plans to give you hope and a future.* (Jeremiah 29:11) I have taken so much comfort from this in my darkest times, especially when it seems that it surely could not be true. Still, I have hung on, if for no other reason than as a challenge to God to be faithful to His Word! And He has been

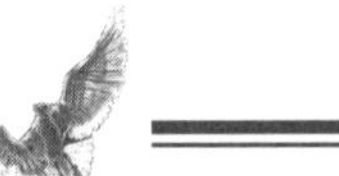

… I have been so burdened the last two weeks for the students on campus who are suffering depression in silence and have told no one about their struggles!

faithful.

Surprised, yet delighted by an unexpected pregnancy, **Roselyn Baugh Kerlin (1955)** reveals a set of symptoms following the birth of her third infant that set her on the path to new levels of self discovery. Roselyn offers valuable information and insight into her diagnosis of postpartum depression.

I stood at the changing table looking at my gorgeous baby girl. To be a new mom was a thrill even though it had been a shock to discover I was pregnant. I was 36 and here I was about to start all over again. I wondered how I could manage a new baby and keep things at home as I always had.

My pregnancy had been uncomplicated and the delivery

relatively easy. I felt I could manage like I always had. I felt I was meeting the needs of my family, nurturing everyone. The older girls were busy seventh and ninth graders. Good students. No problems there.

But what were these other feelings I began to have? Where were they coming from? Why was it that instead of singing happily when I nursed, I would catch myself pleading with God to stop the feelings of turmoil I felt inside? Why was I exhausted all the time, sometimes feeling I could barely put one foot in front of the other? Why did the endless winter days seem to close in on me? A dark cloud hover over me? Why was my milk drying up?

My physician husband had a busy family practice with long days. I always joked that "M.D." stood for "mostly departed." And, in that respect, life really didn't seem to be much different from what it had been before the new baby arrived. Well, that is, with the exception of the construction of a new family room and master bedroom. But then, we had planned carefully for this project and we looked forward to it. Still, what I had overlooked was the impact of these major changes in my life. I hadn't anticipated how inconvenienced and annoyed I would feel with the constant interruption and messes made by the carpenters. I had not considered that I'd be making most of the decisions because I would be the only one at home and available to the builders. And above all, I had thought that because my new baby was cheerful and happy, certainly I could manage things as I had always done before.

But what really happened was that I found myself rushing endlessly from one thing to another, never catching up. I could keep the food ready, cooking ahead when I had some energy. I could keep the house tidy and the laundry done. I was cleaning up, picking up, putting some things here, placing other things there, but still never finishing a job. Then the malaise set in. I'd wonder if I was about to start my period. "Well then," I thought, "If that happens, I'll be feeling better right away." But my period didn't start ... and the feelings of fatigue didn't go away.

My husband arranged for me to see a psychiatrist at the nearby medical school – a physician he trusted greatly. However, the psychiatrist promptly explained his position to me – that he saw people either as "people with problems" or, on the other hand, "people as patients." He was of the opinion that I fit into his category of just a "person with a problem" who was, with time, going to be fine. He went on to explain that it was his view that my obsessions were not deeply rooted and would therefore not be long lasting. He tried to offer an optimistic note by adding

that the compulsive people of the world accomplished the most.

But I felt far from cheered as I left his office. Later, I called the doctor back to ask where the "people with problems" went for help. He finally referred me to a Menninger-trained psychoanalyst whom he said he greatly admired. He went on to explain that in his opinion this physician had great success in the long-term therapy needed to make a difference in the lives of people with Obsessive Compulsive Disorder.

Finally, I had a diagnosis even though it was arrived at indirectly. Armed with this information, I approached the new doctor. A kind, compassionate man, he seemed to sense that I needed to feel more control over my life. He ordered blood work to check estrogen and thyroid levels, explaining the results to me in ways I could understand, and he ordered medication to help me. He gave me reading assignments to further help me understand hormone changes and we discussed what I read. He helped me understand that I was in the midst of a postpartum depression.

An added consolation to me was that I learned the doctor's secretary was a Christian lady whose concern and encouragement gave me a boost. I'd go early for appointments so I could talk with her, giving her opportunity to share from her life what we found we had in common. Having a new friend, who was a person of remarkable insight and compassion, as well as a new doctor who cared, began to make a real difference. I was not in "counseling," rather I was in "therapy," and its benefits were to aid me in opening my feelings – inviting and allowing me to verbalize them. I emerged from postpartum depression realizing that there is indescribable value in having someone in my life who listened, who had compassion, who asked thoughtful questions, and whose caring was not colored by expectations.

Because of my experience with postpartum depression and with the helpful therapy that followed, I look back on the early years of my marriage as though I were almost two different people. I call those years my "Rip Van Winkle Years" because then I was so busy trying to be everything to everyone in my life that I was not at all in touch with myself. During those infrequent times when I'd catch a glimpse of this reality, back then, I'd censure myself by thinking I was being selfish. During early married life, I was willing to make every adjustment possible in order to keep life uncomplicated for my husband as he went through medical school and began his medical practice. Looking back, I think I tried far too hard, rarely attempting to discuss my own feelings, even denying them lest they create discord. What I really thought, deep down, was that if I could just adjust, make myself change, turn myself into something different, then that would be the remedy. I wonder now where this thinking came from.

What I have found is that the positive results of my postpartum depression, in the form of my recognition of obsessive-compulsive tendencies, together with helpful therapy, have been far reaching. Broadened understanding of these conditions together with a fresh, new perception of God's mercy and grace have become mine. And, through it all, I have come to know myself in many valuable, new ways.

Alleged murder, child abuse, incarceration – all are encountered firsthand by **Kayleen Brewer Reusser (1982)** when she takes us with her on assignment. We come face-to-face with what

Kayleen experienced, and that experience will remain with her as long as she has the memory of it – and with us as well.

The clanging of heavy, metal doors and a cacophony of voices surrounded me as I walked through the county jail. Following the guard into a room off the holding area, I immediately looked for an electrical outlet. Spying one, I began to set up my cassette recorder on the table.

"You want Costello, right?" the guard asked. At my nod, he left. The time I had dreaded all week was nearly upon me. Am I finally going to interview an accused murderer!? With that, suddenly my knees went weak and I sat down on a chair, attempting to calm my thoughts.

As editor of the jail's chaplaincy newsletter, I wrote an article for each issue about an inmate who had become a Christian as a result of the chaplaincy program. In the past two years I had talked with inmates whose accused crimes had mostly been the selling of drugs and armed robbery. Murder was by far the most violent crime I had encountered.

But that wasn't all. What set Carla Costello (not her real name) apart was that she had been accused of killing her own baby. I was told it was a boy. Shivers ran down my spine. Who could kill her own baby? With three children of my own whom I loved dearly, I couldn't understand such an action, especially to a defenseless infant. The chaplain assured me, however, that Carla Costello had accepted Christ into her heart, asked for forgiveness, and throughout all of this, she had said she wanted to live for Christ.

Since I depended exclusively on the chaplain's recommendation for interviews and because I wanted to see if I could handle such an assignment, I had agreed to meet her. During the week preceding the interview, I tried to prepare myself mentally. It would be inappropriate to conduct the interview with preconceptions. I reminded myself that, by our system of laws, Carla

Costello was innocent until proven guilty. Nevertheless, each time during the week when I thought about the alleged crime, my emotions assailed me.

I decided to pray for an uncritical spirit, but I barely got my eyes shut when the guard walked back into the tiny room. Behind him followed my subject. The woman, the much publicized, alleged murderer, turned out to be slender, in her twenties, with coal black, shoulder-length hair and dark eyes. She carried a lunch tray. Taking a deep breath, I forced a smile and held out my hand. "Hi, Carla. I'm Kayleen, the editor of the chaplaincy newsletter." She put her lunch tray on the table and we shook hands. "Feel free to eat while the food's warm," I told her. Carla took a couple of bites, then pushed back her tray. Apparently, the meal that appeared to be ground sausage and corn wasn't all that worth eating. Since we had only 30 minutes, I began the interview.

I fully expected her story to include a tattered childhood and a history of abuse, but Carla surprised me by saying she had a good childhood and had done well in school. She never took drugs, she said, and her family went to church on a regular basis, although no one was really acquainted with the Bible per se. Carla told me she attended a large state university where she had earned a degree in marketing in only three years.

A national discount chain had hired her for a management position, and soon after that her daughter was born. Carla wanted to spend more time with her baby, so she transferred to another city for a job in a Receiving department. When her daughter was five years old, Carla moved the two of them across country to live with Carla's father. To all of my questions about her childhood, Carla supplied answers without hesitation, but she hadn't yet broached the subject of her baby's death. I had to be cautious ... if she confided to me some details about it, I might have to testify.

"You had another baby?" I probed. Carla closed her eyes and nodded. Silence filled the small room. Then she spoke up. "A son," she finally whispered, and tears formed in her eyes. She took a tissue, wiped her eyes, then continued with her story. Two years earlier, Carla had married. Several months after this, she became pregnant and delivered the baby boy. A few months after the baby's birth, her husband had come home from work to Carla and their son, but when he looked in on the baby he appeared not to be breathing. Carla's husband called for help, but based on evidence at the scene, Carla was led away in handcuffs.

As for the baby, he died less than an hour later, allegedly having been strangled with a telephone cord. Carla was diagnosed as severely depressed. She was kept on suicide watch for three days. Later, a chaplaincy volunteer invited her to attend a drug class. Carla refused. Since she had never used drugs, she didn't see the need. Her cellmate, however, urged her to go. "It's a spiritual class," she said. "They talk about stuff besides drugs." So Carla went. She was given a Life Recovery Bible. In her cell she read it cover to cover. The more she read, the more fascinated she became with God's love for mankind. The chaplain helped her obtain books by C. S. Lewis and Francis Schaeffer. Carla read them all.

Carla began attending Bible studies and chapel services and eventually accepted Jesus as her Savior. She was then baptized in a jail service. While she talked, I took notes as my recorder hummed along uninterrupted. "I'm waiting for a date to be set for my trial," she continued. "Meanwhile, I spend my time reading my Bible. I've written to my husband, encouraging him to read the Bible, too." The Bible correspondence course she had signed up for was expected in the mail soon.

Carla had given me lots of good material I could use for attention-getting quotes. I knew this could be a powerful story, but I still didn't know many details about the alleged crime. At the end of my jail interviews, I always ask the inmates what they plan to do after being released from jail. When I asked Carla, she replied, "If I ever do get out, I'd like to get involved with postpartum depression support groups to help women with the problem." Her downcast expression and unwillingness to elaborate suggested to me that she believed a chemical imbalance influenced her mind and was responsible for her baby's death. Then, Carla raised her head and her expression startled me. Gone was the bleak look of loneliness and sorrow she had worn since entering the room. She looked suddenly serene. "Even though my future is uncertain," she said, "I rely on my favorite Bible verse to get me through each day." *For I know the plans I have for you, declares the Lord, plans to prosper you and not to harm you, plans to give you hope and a future.* (From Jeremiah 29:11)

Then my time was up. The guard came to get Carla and we concluded our talk with a quick good-bye.

Later, as I wrote the article, I was careful not to present Carla as a sympathetic figure. She had been accused of a dreadful crime and the readers must not be fooled into thinking she was innocent. But somewhere along the way, I realized my initial notions about Carla had long since dissipated. In fact, our talk turned out to be one of the best I'd ever had.

Carla has been separated from her daughter and husband for months. She wonders how her time in prison will affect her relationship with them. She has no control over her future and, worst of all, she has to live with the possibility that she will be found guilty of taking her baby's life. The coming months looked to be stormy and she would need every ounce of her remaining strength to face them. I found myself asking, When was the last time a situation in my life demanded I trust God so completely? The answer was, shamefully, I couldn't think of a time.

I realized then that my life, though ordinary was by contrast, pretty wonderful. Some people might think Carla's behavior with me that day was a ploy for sympathy. Maybe it was. I'm not one to interview accused murderers every day. I'm no expert. But one thing was certain. Carla opened my eyes to the good that can be found in the worst of circumstances. For that I'm thankful.

Note: "Carla" pleaded guilty to a count of voluntary manslaughter. She was sentenced to 15 years in prison. A murder charge was dropped under the plea agreement accepted by the judge.

"Carla" was evaluated by six medical professionals. All agreed she suffered from severe depression when she killed her son. The chaplain affirmed that "Carla" has been a model inmate and is still studying her Bible.

DEATH AND MEMORIALS

Making her own step-by-step preparations for her final journey, **Mary Ellen Gudeman (1964)** transcends these serious matters with realism laced with lightness, and even charm.

"I'd like to discuss some pre-need funeral arrangements at the McCombs Funeral Home on Maplecrest." My words had a professional tone to them that was far from genuine.

"Certainly!" To me, the sweet voice at the other end seemed way too eager. "Our Counselor can meet with you. What is a convenient time?"

Time...? "Well ... there's no hurry ... that is ...," I hedged, feeling the heavy reality of what I was about to do pressing in on me.

"Is Tuesday at 1:00 all right?"

I agreed, my voice sounding hollow in my ears.

I am in my mid-seventies and single; it seemed wise not to burden other family members with these decisions.

On Tuesday, sharp at 1:00, I arrived at the impressive-looking funeral home and parked my car in the empty lot. It looks like no funerals today, I thought as I walked with unsteady steps toward the entrance.

The door swung open before I had time to ring the bell. "Please come in," said a deep-throated voice. "You're Miss Gudeman?" the tall, heavy-set gentleman asked as he extended his hand. "Please come this way to our consultation room," he gestured and gave me his name.

As I followed him, I noted the ornate chandelier in the foyer, the rich carpet in the hall, the plush chapel rooms on either side, and most of all ... the silence.

The Counselor nodded to a chair at the long table and proceeded to pull some documents from his briefcase.

There, in the center of the table, incongruously, sat a bowl of Tootsie-Rolls. How strange. Trivial even, I thought. But then, like a sweet Tootsie-Roll melting in the mouth, life certainly does go quickly, that can't be denied.

"Help yourself." The Counselor nodded toward the bowl as he arranged his papers and began asking in a methodically perfunctory manner: "Let's start with the kind of funeral ... which cemetery ... do you already have a plot ... and what type of grave marker are you thinking about?"

"I would like a Bible verse on my stone," I spoke up. "I'd like, *For to me to live is Christ, and to die is gain (Philippians 1:21 KJV)*, I said."

He paused, frowned a bit, and asked, "What does that mean?"

"For me, it means ... well ... just what it says," I replied, finding it difficult to explain this verse in any other way but in its own words.

"Here, write the words down so we have them exactly correct on the stone," he said and handed me notepaper and pencil.

Next came his detailed explanation of the payment plan.

"Now, would you like to see the casket and vault display?" he asked as he laid down his pen and carefully piled up the papers pertaining to the most final event of my earthly existence.

Following him, we made our way out the door and down the hall.

"Are you ready for this?" he turned and asked as he fit a key into the door lock. All I could do was nod in assent.

He snapped on a switch and dimly lighted lamps exposed a room filled with open caskets. I hesitated a moment and then stepped into a world where the living look beyond themselves to the realm of the dead.

I followed him as he explained, always in business-like tones, the price and quality of each casket.

My thoughts were anything but business-like. How will it feel to have that casket lid closed – no air, no light, no sound – unless it would be earthworms munching or water trickling through the soil? And silence, I thought, ... only silence. I shook myself to attention.

Next he showed me the vaults in an adjoining room and suggested I choose the better quality one – the one guaranteed to be airtight. Airtight? Why? I mused to myself.

We stepped back into the casket display room.

Blue, yes, something blue, I thought as I looked at each one again. The silvery-blue one, there on the left. I looked more closely and saw that quilted on the inside of the lid was a bridge stretching over a chasm into a sunrise with the words "Crossing Over" embroidered below the scene.

"This is the one," I said as I gazed at the scene. Airtight, bug-tested, rust-proof ... how could any of those things matter? I will have crossed over to the other side before that lid is sealed shut. And I remembered my childhood days and felt thankful for a Christian heritage that prepared me for my eternal home. There was a comfort that came from that.

We returned to the consultation room, and I signed the necessary papers.

"Have a Tootsie-Roll," the gentleman repeated as he gathered his papers and put them in his briefcase.

"Thanks," I replied and unwrapped one of the sweet candies and slipped it into my mouth. With the flavor, I was flooded with childhood memories – memories of life and exuberance where there was no hint of coffins with embroidered scenes of bridges or with the words, "Crossing Over."

So, the Tootsie-Rolls served their purpose, I mused. Makes me feel like a child again, I thought, and I pulled the door of the funeral home closed behind me.

—————————————————— ❦ ❦ ❦ ══════════════

Ruth Dixon Truman's (1952) "take" on end-of-life matters turns the usually solemn, dreary approach to death on its head. Her account will put a whole new color to the funeral process, one that is sure to get us thinking.

❦ ❦ ❦

The other day I was attending yet one more funeral. "Memorial Service" is the new name for such events, but no matter what they are called, most everyone looks, acts, and speaks in a funereal way. Sad. Drab. Not at all "rad."

Since I am now 71, and married to a retired pastor, I've been to lots of such events. While I was a student I earned extra money singing at funerals – that is, until the day a mother threw herself across the open casket that held her child while I was in the middle of singing, "Jesus Loves Me, this I know ...." That ended my funeral singing, at least for money.

The first funeral I remember was when my grandfather died. I was about 12. Everyone cried but me. I felt terrible, not so much because he died, but because I wasn't crying. Of course I didn't know how much I would miss him, or how my grandmother's life would change, or how the wonderful summers at their farm would vanish. The people who were crying knew all that and much more. They were already missing him; I hadn't begun.

Now, at 71, tears often come to my eyes in the face of death, but I also cherish what funerals have taught me. Every time I go to one I make a revision in suggestions for my own. You see, I'm a Christian and by the time people get around to my funeral, I expect to be busy at my new life assignment (Christ said, *If you are faithful over a few things, I will make you ruler over many ...*). And I figure that if I live to be really old, most people will be glad to see me move on so they can get on with their own lives, so in that case I might as well get on to planning my own service.

When it came to dying, my Dad set a great example for me. He told his caretaker that he hoped the man would be present when Dad died so "he could see how a Christian dies." Then when the day came, Dad did three things: first, he called his barber to come and give him a haircut because he didn't want to "go into eternity shaggy." Second, he signed all the final papers to sell the house so my mother would have to move to the retirement community near me where they had planned to live together. And lastly, he called my mother into the room, took her hand and said, "Allene, I love you. I love you. I love you." And then he died. What a way to go! He was absolutely sure that "to be absent from the flesh was to be present with the Lord." Dad was looking forward to the next great adventure.

Funerals have made me examine my life. At 30, I had surgery and had to wait three days to find out if the tissue was malignant. I had four young children. How could I die? Facing death made me realize what I wanted out of life: to stay married to my husband, to see my children grown and established, to write a book, and to travel. God permitted all of this, but without looking at my death I would never have launched my life with the same energy and direction. The possible end became the accelerated beginning.

In my filing cabinet is a folder marked My Death. At first, it had the typical directions in it: the hymns I wanted people to sing, the special music, who I wanted to preside, and so on. Later, I wrote some poetry for a final blessing to be read while people released balloons from the church steps as a way of letting go of my spirit. Still later, I added some "wisdom words" for my children and grandchildren. Now I'm thinking about making a tape/CD to be played telling people not to wcep for me, since death is the blessing of release into eternal life.

And at the funeral I last attended I made still another decision. I decided to write out my favorite jokes for people to read at my service. It is my hope that they will call it a "Life Celebration," that it will not be boring or dull, and that they will laugh at my jokes. I hope they will hug each other while speaking words of love, and then depart energized and ready to live each day more joyfully. My hope is that they will be filled with the knowledge that God is present with them in all of life, so that when their turn comes, they can "die like a Christian." That's the way I want to go.

I've learned all this attending funerals. I guess I'll drop these bits of wisdom in my file, too.

QUESTIONS TO PONDER

Alone, or in a group, here are some questions to consider:

1)   From the experiences of the writers whose individual life experiences appear in this chapter, an array of views is encountered. Because numerous challenges make up a life time, what are the constructive, helpful ways you respond to opposing perspectives on life's most serious issues? What is the role of a support group in your life? What characteristics do you look for in the most effective support for you?

2)   Perfectionism is found to characterize many serious-minded, well-meaning, high achieving people. Describe one or more incidents in which you have felt a strong sense of "rightness." How do you think you came to your perception? Consider ways in which a perfectionist attitude toward people and circumstances can work for you, or against you. What is the role of compassion, forgiveness, and patience in the perfectionist's world-view?

3)   Many forms of clinical depression can be hormonally driven: bi-polar disorder, postpartum depression, seasonal affective disorder, and others. Apart from the use of medical intervention, which can be highly effective, list states-of-mind that tend to trigger your downward spiral into sadness.

4)   List methods you have found useful in the intentional interruption of the downward slide into a depressive state of mind. What do you tell your mind? How do you re-direct your thoughts, your inner scenes, and conflicting notions? What role does your environment play in your frame of mind? What role does education and information play? Exercise? Prayer and meditation?

MY COMPANION JOURNAL

1)   Return to your life-events line-graph developed for Chapter One. Do you detect patterns of negative or unproductive responses to people and events in your life? Isolate the common characteristics you find from one significant event to another. List the areas in which you feel stuck.

2)   Review the accounts written by the women in this chapter. Do you see characteristics in common in the manner they chose to cope with their life challenges? What can you take from their experiences that will benefit you and your responses to life?

3)   List all the feelings you experience when you sense you are about to enter a descending spiral into depression. Can you isolate triggering events? List characteristics common to the events. What therapeutic or medical intervention have you considered?

4)   Do you have an effective support group? Do you need to make some changes perhaps by seeking out other persons or groups? Do your friends or support group offer you freedom to express yourself and to experiment with helpful therapies and treatments?

5)   Assess the nature and value of your physical exercise program, your diet, and your environment. Do you find these elements helpful to you and, if not, what is your plan for effective changes?

THROUGH A GLASS DARKLY

**Dusk and Dawning: Insights Gained Through
Time and Events**

*For now we see through a glass, darkly; but then face to face:
now I know in part; but then shall I know even as also I am
known.* I Corinthians 13:12 KJV

Life in this present era is a whirlwind. Everyone lives faster, but perhaps not necessarily fuller lives. There are the demands of domestic life. Demands of our community and nation. And added to the tensions of this period of the early 2000s are the inescapable challenges from lands beyond our once secure borders, and from ideas yet to be fully considered.

The women who contribute their experiences and thoughts to this chapter will inspire and encourage you. Their stories will comfort you; their decisions will reassure you. Their struggles will help you look on life with greater wisdom, equanimity and good humor. You will feel reassured. You will know you are not alone. You are sure to feel a little more at peace within yourself. As you approach the world at large, you will feel a little braver.

We have only one shot at this life. We want to play the game by the rules. We want to win, we say to ourselves. We want to know we have consciously avoided the obviously wrong turns on the road of life. We want to know that when the chips are down, we are not found wanting. We are going for the big prize. We want the acceptance and adulation of the significant others in our life. We want the smile of God.

But, what if it doesn't happen? What if we take what we've internalized to be all the right steps only to find they carry us in strange, unpredictable directions? We lead what we think is a healthy lifestyle, only to turn up with a catastrophic diagnosis. We comport ourselves in ways we understand to be right and appropriate only to find our husband leaves us, or a child turns from us. We do what we do by the rules we've been taught, but what is at work when the results are not the expected? When we are abandoned? When we're uninformed and fearful? When we feel washed in guilt? Or disillusionment? Or betrayal?

The thought of coming up imperfect is, to many of us, almost more than we can accept and integrate into our sense of self and our relationship to God.

Can it be we have disappointed God and have no clear reason why? Is His Divine countenance bearing a frown where we are concerned? The thought of coming up imperfect is, to many of us, almost more than we can accept and integrate into our sense of self and our relationship to God.

Perhaps first, we look outside ourselves. Surely, we may think, we are the unwitting, innocent victim of all that is happening to us. Or just as curiously, why do we seem to look endlessly to someone or something to make our life work for us, offer us a sense of direction and completeness? To make us feel good? To instill within us a sense of OKness? Of worth? Of identity? Only to have all this inner restlessness intensified when we attempt to measure ourselves against others who seem to be contented, balanced, and at peace with themselves. Why do their lives seem to work for them while ours are in shambles?

Perfectionism, for example, may actually serve to undo us. On the surface, it would seem that to live our lives by our concepts of rightness and goodness ought to result in a level of perfection that would offer the highest satisfaction. And yet, all too often, doing what we do, thinking what we think according to our internalized concepts of rightness, instead of accomplishing our deepest and most satisfying objectives, actually may turn upside down and take us spiraling downward with them, only to be consumed by sensations of depression and worthlessness. What is this all about?

Or, what of fear? Fear we may fail. Fear we may succeed – too well. Fear of forces we perceive to be larger, more cunning, more capable than we. Fear is a very real emotion with very real power. Grappling successfully with paralyzing, inhibiting sensations can be important to growth. But what are the best tools? What are the most effective methods?

Some of us may find ourselves back at square one, faced with the most elementary of life's questions: "Who am I, God?" "Why am I here?" and "Why is this happening to me?" Or perhaps we lash out at God, hold Him responsible for our misfortunes, especially if we perceive we have conducted our lives by the life-rules we have accepted to be God's own. Certainly there are as many ways of perceiving a rationale for what we assess as the unjust wrongs we suffer as there are facets to our imagination and our capacity for hurt. But some things hold firm: a life, no matter how well or how ill it is lived, will contain challenge and unpredictability, as well as joy and adversity.

Assuming the above, it is at this point that our question may shift. Our focus can change from deeply-felt helplessness, victimization, or indignation to the healthier and more creative perspective of, "So, what do I do now?" and "How do I accomplish it?"

The women whose experiences are found in these pages are women of remarkable honesty and bravery. Some have opened their hearts and tell us about their "dark nights of the soul" – their times of deepest anguish. Some have wrestled with gnawing sensations of not-all-rightness. They have struggled with their unique adversities. Some have fought the good fight and, at times, lost. And in the losing, they have found far more and have gained far superior experience and insight than they may have otherwise. We thank them for sharing themselves with us and we are inspired by their personal real-life stories.

With focus, determination, perseverance, and great, good humor, **Paige Comstock Cunningham (1977)** works her way through trials to triumph and throughout the process she opens to us wondrous new ways of worshipping God.

I skied a black! Granted, it was a short run and I could see the safety at the bottom from where I hesitated at the top. But for an awkward woman who is athletically challenged, conquering my fear of skiing, more than 9,000 feet high in Steamboat Springs, was a personal triumph.

It was 30 years from my first disaster on skis until I found the freedom to fly. At 17, my brother taught me to ski (or tried to) on a bunny hill in Lake Geneva, Wisconsin. After a few hours, I shivered from wet jeans and ached from a bruised bottom. I'd had enough.

Fast forward to my 10th wedding anniversary, when my husband and two of our best friends surprised me with a trip to Lake Geneva. More warmly dressed this time, but still terrified, I struggled to learn on that same Wisconsin hill. While the three of them conquered the mountain, I retreated to the ski lodge with a book and hot drink.

What was my hang-up? Profound physical fear, coupled with psychological resistance. Simply put, I'm afraid to fall down. I don't like the physical pain. And I don't like trying anything I can't do well the first time. It's perfectionism at its worst. Coupled with fear that speed would make me lose control, I didn't have a chance.

How did I conquer these fears and learn not just to ski, but to anticipate the sport with enthusiasm? As I reflected on how

I overcame deep inhibitions, I realized it was an expression of love. In my case, I happen to love my husband and I love my family and I was determined to be part of this bonding family activity – especially since it was the first outdoor athletic activity they were all passionate about. I didn't want to hold them back, and I didn't want to miss out on all the fun!

The third go-around did it. Six years ago, my husband and I tried skiing one more time. Before a business trip to Aspen, we went to Silver Creek for a crash course. The Colorado powder was a far cry from Wisconsin ice-crusted snow. My husband "got it" immediately. On the other hand, I experienced that first ride up the gondola as a prelude to a trip to the hospital with broken legs and cracked skull. That is how terrified I was. Ski school was the remedy. It eased my worst fears and introduced me to a possibility, the learning of a new skill that my husband loved and that our children would relish.

The next month, we drove the whole family to Ski Brule, a ski resort in the Upper Peninsula of Michigan. By the end of the weekend, even our six-year-old son was flying down the toughest run. With this, they were hooked. As for me, I was still struggling.

Each year, the psychological battle mounted. The first snowfall reminded me that it wouldn't be long before I was pulling ski pants and jackets out of closets. I wavered between: Yes, let's go, Yes, it's going to be fun, and Wait, I'm petrified.

Finally, on our most recent ski trip – the sixth, to be exact – I "bet the farm." Either I learn to ski better than snowplowing down a bunny hill, or I hang up my poles. I decided to take more lessons, at my own pace, until I conquered my fear of the intermediate blue runs. The ski instructor taught a technique that made my body turn the way it was supposed to. It involved holding my arms straight out in front of me, looking where I wanted to turn with my body. It's an intermediate step on the way to learning how to carve broad turns down the mountain. Stiff arms are not pretty, but the technique enabled my muscles to feel a controlled turn. After a few tries, I had enough confidence to "take the brakes off" and gain speed. I yelped with delight as the wind whipped my hair. At the end of that momentous day, my husband convinced me to try Mother Nature, a short, but none-theless official, black ("most difficult") run.

Lessons learned? To have greater control, I had to relax and enjoy speed. My fear of falling down actually made it harder for me to ski, and more likely that I would fall. Instead of trying to inch down the mountain, fighting gravity all the way, I learned to cooperate with this law of nature.

Just as in other areas of my life, I gravitated toward what I focused on. So, to avoid slipping on the icy, rocky patches, I had to look at my goal, the clear path farther down the slope. Even better, catching a tiny bit of air in the trees made me feel like an Olympic skier! And, that old saying is still true: If at first you don't succeed, try, try again. My perfectionism kept telling me to quit, because I couldn't master it on the first, second, or even third attempt. But my determination to bond with my family pushed me out of my comfort zone, and rewarded me with the thrill of improvement.

Because I refused to be defeated by my fears, I gained a prize: the thrill of skimming over sparkling snow. Waiting for me on the victorious side of my trepidation was the ecstasy of enjoy-ing God in a new way, quietly, in the hush of newly fallen snow underneath an aquiline sky, higher than I'd ever been on skis before. There's no worship quite like exulting in the panorama of God's Rocky Mountains on Tomahawk Run. And to think I would have missed it if I had given up too soon!

Jayanne Householder Roggenbaum (1987) compares her personal life to that of the Skin Horse in *The Velveteen Rabbit*, and how it feels to be very "real."

❦ ❦ ❦

It hit me rather early on, I'd say in about 1994. I was 29 years old and the news no one ever wants to hear came as a jarring dissonance to me. I then had to make choices that people usually make much later in life.

We learned that my very closest friend, my mother-in-law, was already in fourth stage cancer. We were told this condition was difficult to treat and that she would most likely have about two years or less to live. My thoughts were in a whirlwind. But as time wore on in the six-and-a-half years that followed, I was to learn more of what it is to become authentic and to love unabashedly.

A passion for serving others, mentoring others, and caring for others had always been my life's mission.

What did it mean to be authentic and to really love? To me, being authentic isn't about the car I drive or the house I live in. It's not about what I do or who I know. It is about going out of my way to show tenderness and ready forgiveness. It's about time spent writing a letter or sending an e-mail. It means sitting with someone and telling the person how much I care about him or her. Or crying with a friend dealing with infertility . . . and then rejoicing and crying again with her when she hears the good news, "You're pregnant!"

Our family made the decision to care for our dying matriarch, my dear mother-in-law, at home, and by ourselves. Since my husband and I lived across the street from his parents, the logistics were not that difficult. But the actual administering of medications and many other "nurse-like" activities were daunting to me at first. The doctor provided the supplies and guidance; we supplied the care. Although I would not trade the experience, there were times when, admittedly, the reality of it all was excruciatingly painful. The emotional toll that caring for the dying took on me required much time and effort to heal afterwards. However, the final weeks and days I spent with her were wonderful times of sharing, just as we had done for so many times before.

There were also times, I confess, that I would think to myself that it might be far easier to lock myself up and hold in my emotions and true feelings. I came to realize that if I lived from my heart and served others in the fashion I believed God had called me to, I would be making myself quite vulnerable.

During this trying time, I happened to be reading a book to my daughter: Margery Williams' thoughtful 1922 children's classic, *The Velveteen Rabbit*. In the story, the young rabbit asks the Skin Horse who has been around the nursery for a while, "What is REAL? And does it hurt?" and "Does it happen all at once, like being wound up, or bit by bit?"

"It doesn't happen all at once . . ." (the Skin Horse replied to the rabbit) and ". . .when you're REAL, you don't mind being hurt," said the Skin Horse, for he was always truthful.

And, what I found through my experience with my dying mother-in-law was that, yes, it does hurt sometimes to be "real." It can hurt to love. People sometimes disappoint us . . . and people can leave us. And make no mistake about it, when I chose to become "real," I had to learn to accept the fact that people don't always know me, nor can they always, and without question, trust my motives. That's when I must search my heart to ensure the purity of my intentions.

Recently, in a group of about 40 high-powered, highly competitive leaders, I was asked to speak about my greatest accomplishment. Would it be some award, some prestigious position? No, it was being with my mother-in-law throughout her terminal illness that spurred me on to new heights as a young person. From that experience I learned early on how to serve and care for others, to be authentic, and to love unabashedly – lessons that I hope will always keep me "real."

With humor and insight, **Ruth Dixon Truman (1952)** describes the conflict that faces many of us as we consider an upwardly mobile move to a new and elegant location, especially in the face of the life-style demands of teenagers plus a home that is already family-friendly. The following excerpt is from Ruth's book, *Spaghetti from the Chandelier*, by permission of the author who currently holds the rights to the book.

❦   ❦   ❦

While I was bent double scraping old paint off the door frame, the telephone rang. Some day I'll learn not to answer it (but that hasn't happened yet!).

"Methodist parsonage. Ruth speaking" – fatal mistake number two; I should have said "Truman residence" and stopped there. The voice on the other end was that of a district superintendent – not from our district though, and, I assumed, not too threatening even though conference time was approaching. How wrong can you be? I handed the phone to Lee and went back to my scraping.

You can get a kink in your back from bending over too long, but from standing up too fast? "Move? They're crazy. They just don't know what's going on here! Look at this place . . . there's a hole in every wall in this house, and most of the plans are in my head, not on the blueprints." Maybe the man on the committee was right – birth-control pills should be in the benefits package.

"I promised him we'd go take a look, Ruth. We don't have to say yes." Lee's reassuring words didn't reach my ears; they were closed while I was using my tear glands. Fortunately, three of the kids were at school and Nate at Nancy's. At least our trauma could be resolved without their eight cents' worth (that's 2¢ x 4). . .

"Didn't you explain, Lee? Didn't you tell him that we are in a grand mess, that moving is just out of the question?"

"He's a friend, Ruth. We've got to at least go look." I took off my paint clothes, washed in turpentine, and put on my face and good clothes. Because of a fifteen-year-old vow to go wherever they sent us . . . (The New Testament instruction not to vow anything came creeping into my thoughts.) Oh, well, we'll just look. Things have changed – at least they're asking, not telling. That's an improvement!

Los Angeles was never my favorite place – at least not the heart of it. No trees, no mountains, no green, nothing to comfort my midwestern hangover. I thought of the birch trees outside our living room window, the kids playing on the lawn, brown shaggy dog at their heels. As we drove, we passed nothing but business-es, office buildings, concrete.

A left turn, and the street began to wind upward until we turned into the parking lot of a beautiful church snuggled into the side of a green hill . . . just blocks away from the ugly concrete. I allowed myself to be delighted, amazed at the sudden change. The steep A-frame building was punctuated with glass – deepest blues, sunlit red, golden orange – inside, the colors flooded the quiet sanctuary. Natural wood and earth-tone carpets set a mood of peace for worship – a haven in the city. While Lee searched out the pastor, I tried on the church to see if it might fit my soul. This was a grand building; maybe a little too grand for us. Our commonness was surely obvious.

After a tour of the educational building and offices, we headed our MG into a circuitous route to find the parsonage. When the number on the curb matched the one on the paper in my hand, we sat speechless.

An immaculate lawn sloped gently upward toward a green-shutttered, two-story white house that might have escaped from Georgia. Plantation colonials stood on the lots at either side. A young man with a tennis racket came run-ning out of the house next door, stepped into an expensive sports car, and sped away. If we had walked clear to the back fence at the house where we now lived, we would just barely have arrived at the front door of this one.

"Are you sure we should go in? We're not dressed very well." I was suddenly aware of the faint odor of turpentine that still clung to me, and nobody sold the particular shade of green nail polish I appeared to be wearing. I really was a painted lady!

The doorbell chimed elegantly. The pastor's wife, fore-warned by her husband, welcomed us . . . I think. I was busy coping with the polished railing of the staircase that curved into the second story. Perfect for a bride to descend – or more appropriately, a perfect railing for a kid to slide down while I was entertaining the women's circle!

Lovely cushioned couches hugged a massive fireplace in the living room, mahogany armchairs were pulled just right for conversation – intimate conversation by firelight with soft music playing. The serenity of the lawn flowed into the room. One football would certainly undo that.

Atop the staircase were three bedrooms and bath, *Better Homes and Gardens* variety. Smaller than the ones we have, I thought. I envisioned them stuffed with toys and children – and all in line with the front door. Mercy!

Walking quickly through an outmoded kitchen (another one to do over!) we entered the "game room, or family room, if you have one. Do you?" Did we! If she only knew! The thought of our four children in this house was interrupted by the breath caught in my throat. I had never seen such a room. A pool table sat at one end, seemingly disconnected from the rest of the room, which looked out on a gardened backyard. Comfortable heavy furniture, overstuffed chairs, low tables, and yet the room expanded beyond them. Obviously, this was where one lived. The rest was just for show.

With a slight apology for the condition of the kitchen paint, our hostess brought us back into the formal dining room opposite the living room. She was about to explain that the furniture in this room was theirs and that we would need to bring our own, when the phone rang. As she disappeared into the kitchen, Lee and I stood close together, drinking in the elegance. My eyes traced the luxurious oak, the etched glass of the breakfront, the floral centerpiece.

Then I looked up. How could I have missed it? Hanging over all was a sparkling chandelier, the colors of its Venetian crystals dancing across the patterned walls, a crown jewel in a house meant to dazzle the beholder.

Transfixed, I began to giggle. Never had I seen anything so hilarious. So much laughter was rolling around inside that I could barely contain it.

"Ruth, what's the matter with you? What's so funny?" Lee whispered.

"The chandelier . . . ." Our hostess returned. We bid a hasty goodbye, with Lee doing all the thank-yous. Talking was beyond me.

Halfway down the long walk, Lee demanded to know. What was I laughing at? What was wrong with the chandelier?

Tears were running down my cheeks. "Didn't you see it? Didn't you see that gorgeous chandelier? We can't take this church, Lee. We can't move here. Not us. Not our family. We have to stay right where we are. . . ."

"But what's moving got to do with the chandelier?"

Poor dear. All this time together, and he still didn't understand how God speaks – especially to me. Move? Us? Not on your life. For when I looked at that elegant sparkling chandelier, I saw . . . .

In a flash of insight, I knew . . . .

In one week . . . there would be spaghetti – hanging – from the chandelier!

(P.S. We didn't move.)

Our culture holds out attractive options for creative initiative and involvement. **Robin Chernenko Chaddock (1981)** brings us into the world of the business in which she thrives. Her success is demonstrated by the many trophies she wins. And then, with a shift in circumstances, she takes a hard look at her professional achievements. What opens to her is an insight that is rich and meaningful.

One by one, I packed them up and shipped them off to purchasers from eBay auctions. My treasures, my trophies, the objects that had defined my success and my priorities for nearly a decade were now being auctioned in order to keep from collecting further dust in cupboards, the attic, and remote corners of the garage. There were my Longaberger baskets and pottery pieces for which I had sacrificed family time, recreation time, and even health-maintenance time over the course of eight years. All gone to the highest bidder and no longer as powerful as they had once been when my worth was assessed by their acquisition.

I had loved my time as a salesperson and sales trainer with a very innovative and heartwarming company. After the birth of my first child, which propelled me to leave the world of outside-the-home-paid-for-services work, I desperately needed an outlet that didn't revolve around being someone's mommy. Although she was (and still is) a remarkable child, I simply was never wired to be a full-time mother with my central focus being nothing but mothering. I needed alternative stimulation.

The structure of my work, together with the prizes I gained, gave me meaning and recognition.

Having always had considerable career energy, I threw myself into rising to the top of the basket heap, snagging prizes, trips, and what I believed to be an impressive "down-line" group of sales personnel recruits whose successes only served to enhance my own achievements. Although the recruiting literature of my company told me I could balance my work and my family time as a consultant, I chose to "unbalance" in favor of my work. The structure of my work, together with the prizes I gained, gave me meaning and recognition. The extra cash didn't hurt either.

I worked like crazy setting up shows, planning recruit manuals, plotting my way to the highest monthly level so that each reward period a nice, big box would arrive with my new prizes. My trophies were displayed all over the house so all who entered would know I was a success, that I had great stuff, and that I was somebody because of my accomplishments and business savvy.

I sometimes mind-boggled even myself when I stopped long enough to consider that all this success took place after my liberal arts Christian education and two subsequent seminary degrees. If anyone should have known where true worth lies, it should have been me. But, somewhere along the path, I was overcome by comparisons and competitions. I came to judge my worth by my externals, rather than my internals. I opted for this bogus identity.

In the meantime, we downsized from a larger, custom-built house to a smaller, patio home, and my biggest trophy was lost. But that only made me more determined to collect more spoils of achievement and regain that most significant symbol of being worthwhile – that house. Longer hours, less focus on the family, more plotting and planning followed on how to build my empire.

And then came the comeuppance. Or, perhaps it was the reverse. Whatever the dynamic, I was forced by a combination 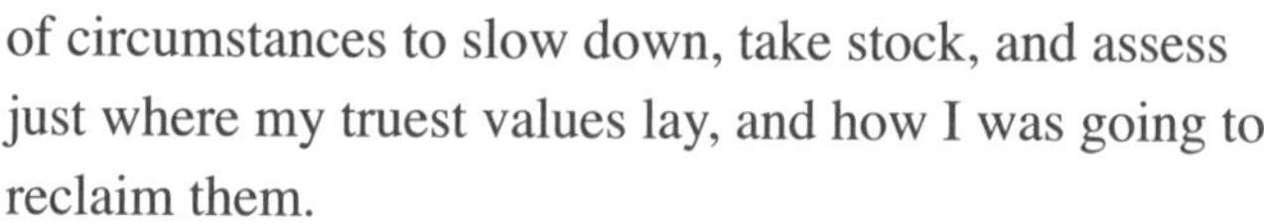 of circumstances to slow down, take stock, and assess just where my truest values lay, and how I was going to reclaim them.

This reordering of priorities was no picnic. What came to me was that what I faced was not about getting everything straightened out. It was not about engineering every day to gain the most recognition and accolades. It was about living day by day, minute by minute in deep, passionate, and eternal Love – God Love, I mean.

What I found was that the process was an ongoing one. There would be times of gentle change – like, for example, the ease with which I resigned my position in the company. But, then, these easier changes could be followed by others that felt like lightning strikes – sometimes electrifying and un-predicted. A truer, purer sense of mission began to emerge. And a newfound passion and pleasure in my family life presented itself – even a sense of the wholeness of a woman's identity that was felt to be comprehensive and comfortably multifaceted.

So, one by one, my trophies were shipped out to the highest bidder. Each, a very realistic witness to my heart becoming re-aligned with where my treasure lay. Oh, I did keep a few, just to remind me to stay on track. Or was it because I still think they're rather pretty?

Through a long and varied teaching career, **Rebecca Lehman Ringenberg** takes the reader into some of the ups and downs of classroom teaching. From her 32 years in the field of education, Rebecca emerges with insights and personal resolves that offer each of us important perspectives and a fresh message about the significance of understanding and incorporating into our lives the values we treasure the most.

There are, of course, unpleasant times in any profession; however, of the 32 years in my chosen profession of teaching, I have observed and experienced not only day-to-day ups-and-downs, but also larger shifts in society as a whole.

During my first 16 years of teaching (1957-1973), my teach-ing positions were largely in rural areas of Indiana and Michigan. Cultural norms were of a conservative nature. There was a basic similarity in the characteristics and qualities of the young people. Most of them showed respect for teachers, for fellow students, and for adults in general. There was a sense of modesty and an attitude of commitment to learning.

But, since the late '70s, student attitudes toward not only educators and fellow students, but toward the importance of the educational process itself has undergone change – significant change. One of the problems seemed to be the number of students who were living with only one parent. We teachers became painfully aware of the shifting family structure that resulted in the one parent, usually the mother, working full-time away from the home. Many children would tell us that they were left to take care of themselves after school. After the parent prepared meals and attended to essential home needs, there was not much time left to help students with their homework or to nurture them.

I certainly have pleasant and positive memories associated with my career, but there are, admittedly, some that are far less so. For example, in one school a number of ninth-grade girls had obtained some valium and, we learned later, made a pact to take it right before school began. It is true that, as the class got underway, I had noticed some of the female students looking at each other with that certain "knowing look," but I went about conducting the class as I usually would. The students were given a writing assignment and the effect of the drug on the students' ability to focus on their subject became obvious. I looked on as the valium influenced their ability to think clearly and to write coherently.

I told the class I was going to the library but, instead, I slipped across the hall to the Principal's office. Together, the Principal and I returned to the classroom only to find one of the "valium girls" lighting up a cigarette right in the classroom, while other students were acting out in other ways.

Perhaps I should not have been surprised at this behavior. Certainly the Principal of this particular urban school had told me when I was hired that I might be in for some culture shock. But what surprised me the most was that the shock did not result from the misbehavior of the minority students – those of other ethnic backgrounds – but rather the white, middle-class students who did not seem to be interested in being in school.

More than once I came home crying and telling my husband that I did not know if I could continue teaching in some of the situations I was experiencing. His encouragement was valuable to me and I learned to cope. Certainly, I grew stronger because of the nearly daily challenges.

I needed strength the day a black girl came to me and announced that if a certain white boy messed with her again, she would take care of him. At the time, the class was working in three groups. Just as I set about working with one of the groups, the girl charged past me from the other side of the room, chasing the boy. As they went by my desk, all my papers went flying. The girl grabbed the boy by the front of his shirt and began pounding him against the wall. Finally, with the help of two other students, we pried them apart and took them to the Principal to sort out the mayhem.

And then there was the time some students actually tipped a piano on its back at the very time I was supervising the halls. In still another school, while I was conducting play practice on the stage, four young men came into the gymnasium and informed me that they were driving by and they saw a tire on my car had been slashed.

And, it is true that I found my tire slit, but upon police inspection, it was concluded that it was impossible for anyone to drive by and see the slashed tire, unless, that is, the reporting student had done the deed himself. The police and Principal took care of that case and the student was suspended.

In the face of this difficulty, I reflected on my own youth, my own early school years, and am sobered by the difference. My own grade-school teachers, Miss Mary, Miss Beulah, and Miss Edna were a high inspiration to me. They were kind, and I never felt afraid of them even if I failed to meet their standards. Their practice was to encourage us to do our best. Since there were only a hundred or so students in my country school in Indiana, and because all grades from one through 12 were in the same school, we knew each other. The majority of the families lived in the area. Many of us attended the same church, and the standards of behavior, derived from religious precepts, made for a relatively conservative and predictable way of life.

What spoke to me was that the life I had known seemed far

less complicated – more simple and straightforward. The use of drugs and overt sexual activity among the young were nearly nonexistent. Movies were not sexually explicit or as ruthlessly violent. In fact, there was no television in my parents' home until about 1959, when I was already out of school and teaching. Much of the vocabulary and many of the visual images that have become a part of our television world today were not a part of television programming when TV first made its appearance in our nation's homes.

As I look back over all the years I have been a part of this country's educational system, from my own small, Midwest beginnings, through to the '80s and '90s, I have experienced firsthand the movement away from innocence and toward the arena of profanity, nudity, sex acts, drugs, and alternative lifestyles.

The value of virtue or of living the virtuous life has undergone a major change. No longer did I have the opportunity to live comfortably within a society with which I shared similar values as I did when I was in my youth. As the years went by, I began to find myself regarded as old-fashioned, outdated, and not

with it, as the young people would say.

And yet there remain, through it all, questions I ask myself. One question has to do with what I want in my personal memory bank. When I close my eyes, or relax into reverie, what memories can I count on surfacing before my mind's eye? Are they positive? Are they life-enhancing? And another question is, what do I want to subject myself to? I realize that I have not only the right but also the ability to make these choices even within the broader culture as it has evolved around me. I am able to construct a way of life that is consistent with what is important to me and to my family. This country allows for that, and it is a blessing that I am free to choose friends and develop associations with others who share those values I came to know in my youth and that I continue to respect.

I know myself well enough to realize what, for me, leads to health, wholeness, and great joy. This, I hold dear.

❦ ❦ ❦

Linda Carlson Bagshaw (1968) takes us into her world that is about to undergo an inner seismic shift. Linda looks boldly at the dynamics of major life change, which happens to all of us at one time or another. Is what I do who I am? The dilemma of identity – just who are we when separated from our occupation, independent of the activities that claim our time and attention? Being uncovered and without the cocoon that surrounds us and acts as our face to the outer world usually gives few problems unless, on the one hand, we have not as yet constructed that persona, or conversely, having come to accept our external persona as our true self, we are suddenly bereft of it.

❦ ❦ ❦

Finally, after a year of visiting and revisiting the idea of quitting my teaching position, I reach the point of firm decision. I had always loved teaching – not only the subject (writing), but also the dynamics of the student/teacher relationship and the energy of a college campus. I was in my element, or so I thought.

After 10 years at this particular college and numerous previous years of part-time teaching, the colors began to fade; the fizz began to flatten. I began to question whether God wanted me to continue spending my time and energy in my current job or to branch out into new territory.

The certainty that this decision was from God's leading strengthened my resolve. Inner feelings of restlessness and dissatisfaction in my job as well as compelling external factors such as aging parents, unfinished home projects, and a possible short-term mission trip all served as catalysts for change.

The day I drove away from campus for the last time, I felt a joyous sense of freedom and excitement about the future: working on my creative writing, spending more time with my granddaughters, becoming more involved with ministries in my church, and taking that month-long mission trip to Ethiopia.

Those were my feelings the day I drove away from campus. A few weeks later, I began to feel tiny whispers of panic. I had always classified myself as a teacher. That was who I was. Now that I was no longer teaching, who or what was I? Somehow the label "retired teacher" failed to convey the exuberance of my new status and direction in life. Slowly I began to bog down into my personal "slough of despond." I had always defined myself as a teacher, a comfortable category in which to fit myself. Now I was suddenly at a loss without the boundaries of definition.

One morning during this time of floundering, two very famous verses caught me by surprise. It was as if God had been watching me in my self-imposed panic and then tapped me on the shoulder to remind me of a simple truth in Matthew 5:13-14: *You are the salt of the earth. You are the light of the world.*

Salt and Light? I had forgotten this in my all-consuming concern about being a "teacher." My true identity, that which defines who I am in Christ, is salt and light to a needy world. I suddenly realized that any particular vocation I pursue or position I hold in the course of my life serves only as a channel for the salt and light God requires me to be. My priorities readjusted themselves as I was reminded of the true "bottom line" of my search for identity.

Ruth Dixon Truman (1952) opens for us not only a view into the life behind the well-ordered appearances of the typical minister's life, but also offers encouragement to all of us who tend to place our concern for others' needs far ahead of our own, with the possible result that we may threaten our own good health and emotional balance. The following is an excerpt from Ruth's book, *Underground Manual for Ministers' Wives and Other Bewildered Women*, by permission of the author who currently holds the rights to this book.

❧   ❧   ❧

The hand at the small of my back was insistent. The voice matched.

"Go ahead, dear. I want you to meet every one of the ladies!"

Before me were over a hundred loyal members of the local WCTU, come to our church for their annual Christmas party. None was younger than my mother, and some older than my grandmother. My feet felt glued to the floor. The hand pushed with more determination. . . .

And so it went, time after time after time. I met them all, and a thousand more like them. . . and some of them became wonderful people in my life. Some weren't so wonderful, but I learned a lot from them about what not to be and how not to act!

You see, I had dragged my feet from the beginning. As a girl growing up in a Methodist parsonage, I had vowed I would never, no never, marry a minister. A favorite boyfriend became an ex-boyfriend when he announced his intention to enter the ministry. So when I met this exciting young

As a girl growing up in a Methodist parsonage, I had vowed I would never, no never, marry a minister.

man who was headed for the mission field I knew I was safe. Little did I dream that a seminary professor would change his direction or that a bishop would discourage him from entering the foreign mission field because he needed pastoral ministers in his conference. It happened though, and there I was – a reluctant minister's wife who distrusted church people, was determined to have privacy for her family, and equally determined to do all the right things so her husband could succeed. After all, I was pledged to be his wife no matter what he chose to do with his life, and his wife I would be even if it killed me – which it almost did. Six years after our first appointment I lay in a hospital bed recovering from surgery and rediscovering life and people.

Emptiness and bitterness had become my companions. There was no sense of self left. I had lived my life at the whim of children and church, and the real me was almost dead – but I got a second chance. I learned a lot about me, about other people, about life and death, joy and sorrow. And I discovered that many of my friends who were ministers' wives were also in trouble because no one had prepared them to live as full persons regardless of their husband's job.

Lori McGuffin Tipple (1989) looked forward to her new high school experience with high anticipation. Her expectations were fueled by the prospect of attending a Christian school, which would surely be far different from the previous school she had attended. But what Lori encountered proved so challenging that she was faced with disillusionment. And yet, through this experience, Lori took valuable lessons for life. She learned more about herself, and more about tolerance and compassion.

I hated high school.

I had been in public school through the sixth grade, then in the seventh grade I began to attend a Christian school. On the first day I walked into my new school full of the expectation that, because we were all attending a Christian school, we were all going to be good friends . . . loving, kind, caring, and compassionate. We would all be close and far more "spiritual" than the kids at public school.

But what happened was that I was completely and utterly devastated when this particular Christian environment contradicted the great expectations I had. I felt a sense of anger toward my fellow students. This new realization was very disorienting to me.

I wish I could have had someone I connected with to discuss my feelings. My class was very small, with only 24 students, and I could not find a niche where I would fit in and connect with the group. I thought I was the only one who was trying to do the right things. By right things I mean: obeying my parents, obeying my understanding of God's Word, resisting peer pressure, trying to develop the character of Christ, and being thankful and honest.

What I didn't realize was that for all the good values I respected, I was really a very rigid thinker, and intolerant of my classmates.

My senior year was my worst year of high school by far. I started that year full of hope and excitement! But a couple of weeks into the Fall term, I knew it was going to be a very long year.

Several of my classmates decided to have a Senior party. There was to be no adult supervision and the word got around there would be alcohol and a variety of other activities that I regarded as inappropriate. I knew it was not a party I wanted to attend. I knew that not only would my parents not approve, but God would not approve either. It was my heart's desire to engage in activities that would bring honor to both my earthly father and my heavenly father.

I found myself at a crossroad. Would I compromise the desire of my heart by seeking the acceptance of my peers, or would I say no to the party and be different as Christ calls His followers to be?

Actually, the decision was easy for me to make at the time, but I was not prepared for the consequences.

The day came when I was asked if I would be attending the party. In my head, I had relentlessly practiced what my response would be. My heart raced as I prepared to speak the words. Even to this day, I can hear myself say, "Thank you for the invitation but I will be unable to attend."

The looks on the faces of my classmates around me were my first clue that my decision was unacceptable to them. So the rest of my Senior year was one challenge after another. Daily I felt the sting of being unaccepted by my peers. Each day I prayed for enough strength to merely get through the day. Each day I cried. But the sun set and the sun rose and I was learning that God's grace was proving sufficient for me.

I survived high school and, in particular, my Senior year. As I reflect on the painful events of those years, I am struck with the awareness that I was not alone. I sensed that no matter how painful the experience, my character was being developed. Although I had no clear understanding then, I have come to understand that God was working through each heartache and each tear to prepare me for future times and even assignments when these qualities would be needed.

Now, I look back at each memory and it is as if I am looking at myself through a window. I'm standing on the outside of the window looking in at myself. I see all my pain but now it is filtered through the glass God has placed before me. Now what I see is God's loving kindness, grace, and mercy. With this new vision I look at my assignment of being a woman, a wife, and a mom. And now I can love other people who find themselves unaccepted by their peers, or who have different values, or are standing at a crossroad in their lives.

I no longer view those painful days with anger, resentment, or bitterness. I cherish them. I cherish them because I now see more clearly the path along which God began many years ago to develop my character into the person He needed me to be for myself and others.

How did I come to the place where I could let go of my negative emotions, forgive those around me, and be thankful for those high school years? For me, it has been a process – one that began about six years ago. I was studying about Abraham. I read in Genesis how God had promised Abraham, many years before Isaac was born, that He would give him a son. It was 40 years before God fulfilled His promise. It took 40 years for God to develop Abraham's character into what it needed to be for him to be the best father for Isaac. Then it was as if I had been sitting in the dark and someone turned the lights on for me. Surely, I thought, that was what God had been doing for me.

I looked back over my life and saw, weaving its way through the events of my life, a path leading to this moment. My senior year was not a waste of my time but, instead, was a part of my journey. Because I felt God's love in my life, it gave me the ability to forgive others and let go of the hurt.

So what did I do? I prayed for the Lord to forgive me for the bitterness and anger I held in my heart. Mentally, I pictured each person I felt had abused me. Then I called them by name, and I told them that I forgive them. I even went further. I adopted a general attitude of forgiveness for everyone and everything that had been a part of those painful years. I even forgave myself.

Suddenly I was free! My heart was full of joy! I truly felt that God had lifted a great weight from my heart.

It's such a cliché, but so true for me, "I really couldn't see the forest for the trees." I love the Bible verse in Ephesians 1:9 – where it says, *He made known to us (me) the mystery of His will, according to His kind intention. . . .* The way I see it is that I didn't give up on my journey and now, through God's kindness, I have a clearer sense of the purpose for the particular road I traveled. And my destination is that I'm finally ready – I'm ready to help those who need what I have learned.

Alicia Helyer Brummeler (1992) takes us on a bold journey into her strongly felt anger at God. Alicia's honesty and her willingness to revisit these feelings offers us insight into the minds and hearts of many who dare to face openly their disappointments and thwarted expectations. This is an important story for all who share similar inclinations within their own thinking, and for those who interface, either at a personal or professional level, with others who may hold these views.

❧   ❧   ❧

I still remember that warm, Fall day during my freshman year of college. I was walking back to my dormitory after class, my head down, and in spite of the bright sunshine, I felt emotionally low. Slowly, I was beginning to realize that the life I anticipated and longed for and the actual reality of my life were at opposite ends of the spectrum.

I had such high hopes when I thought about my future college experience. I was sure I would develop lifelong friendships quickly, be the first choice for a date by any guy, succeed in my classes and in my extra-curricular activities, and in general, have one great experience after another.

But, this was not happening. I was disappointed with my dormitory situation. Many of the women on my floor were very different from me and had interests I did not share. I did not want to sit and watch TV when there was an entire campus waiting to be discovered! I began to think that women on other floors in other dorms had a better situation than I did.

Then there was the matter of dating. I had not been asked out on one, single date for weeks. Not to mention that my photo in the student handbook was absolutely awful. Why hadn't anyone called for a date? There must be something wrong with me.

To add to my conflicted feelings, I was overwhelmed by my classes. Suddenly, I really needed to study. On top of that, I was running cross country and I felt pressure to succeed athletically. I could literally work my stomach into knots just thinking about class deadlines and weekend cross country meets.

I wanted to call a time out and ask for a do-over. This was not what I had expected. Part of my disappointment and frustration stemmed from believing God owed me something. During high school, when friendship or dating relationships were tough, I had consoled myself with the thought that once I entered college, all that would be behind me, and things would go smoothly. I had excitedly listened to other women share about their college experiences – late night talks with roommates, romantic dates, and other life-changing high points. I wanted that, too!

And so, on that warm Fall day, the full impact of all I was feeling hit me hard. I wish I could say I was mature enough to identify my problem as unrealistic expectation, but that was not the case. I don't even remember what I did the rest of that day. I probably went to practice and studied in the evening as I always did. But that particular moment has remained with me despite the years that have passed.

That experience started me on a journey of discovering who I am, and how easily I allow unrealistic expectations to dictate how I live my life. I learned that living by a set of standards, dreams, wishes, and expectations that are not realistic only leads to disappointment, frustration, and anger. It is not that I cannot wish for wonderful experiences, but slowly I am learning that to base my sense of self-worth and security on an ungrounded expectation is foolish. Life is full of ups and downs. In hindsight, I now see how disappointing experiences teach me to trust God with the details of my life. As hard as it has been to let go of firmly held views, I am learning that a different result from what I first expected is not necessarily bad. I am learning that alternative outcomes are often merely different.

On occasion, I still struggle with unrealistic expectations. However, I catch myself sooner when I begin a downward spiral into frustration and self-pity. With each life-experience, I become more confident in my ability to distinguish an unrealistic expectation from a realistic perception and, in turn, work toward a more balanced and integrated view of life.

Judie Assad Keller (1972) dreamed childhood dreams that would release her from family problems of her youth only to find she would need to address similar issues as an adult. Judie perseveres and shows how she successfully replaced unrealistic expectations with a new set of workable life dynamics.

❧   ❧   ❧

Dreams were born one day, a long time ago, as I sat nestled in a secluded hollow of a ring of stately oaks. I drank in the freshness of the crisp autumn air. Leaves floated aimlessly in the breeze, adding to the rust, burnt orange, and golden yellow carpet that extended as far as I could see.

With the yelling voices, the hurtful accusations, the threats of divorce, and the insecurity that comes with living with a mentally ill family member unable to affect me in my secret hideaway, I dared to envision what my life might be like in the years to come. Even as a nine-year-old, I knew I wanted something better.

I dreamed about my grown-up life with a wonderful husband, several children, a yellow house with a white picket fence, and endless happiness. As I stared at the vast array of wild flowers swaying gently a few feet away from me, I felt confident I could make my dreams become a reality.

Childlike faith in Jesus came naturally to me, encouraged by regular church attendance and a Christian school education. To me, Jesus represented security – the something better I dreamed about.

Those simple days of childhood passed, but the dream I imagined on that fall day so long ago remained a vital part of the person I was becoming. Faces changed, but the essence remained.

Years later, I look back at that childlike dream. Although I may chuckle at it, still, I feel a gnawing ache deep inside.

My childlike faith wavered throughout the many storms that came my way. Miscarriage, infertility, divorce, remarriage, and the death of a spouse – all of this was far from the life I had planned for myself that distant autumn day. My house was brown, not yellow. There was no picket fence, and any happiness I experienced was overshadowed by grief.

Slowly, acceptance of the hardships of life allowed the grief I felt for a lost dream to be replaced with a new reality. Jesus seemed to become more real to me in those weary days.

Sometimes I long for that old clump of trees, a moment of peace, and quiet serenity amidst the chaos of life. No longer do I dream my own dreams, but rather strive for God's direction. I am reminded often of Proverbs 19:21, *Many are the plans in a man's heart, but it is the Lord's purpose that prevails.*

As I reflect on the longing of my little girl's heart back there in my hidden sanctuary, I feel that I was never really alone. Nor did my desires go unheeded. Now I have a wonderful Christian husband, and two lovely daughters. I still live in the same house, although it is no longer brown. I couldn't convince my family to paint it yellow, but that's all right. They have given me many happy memories.

In a foreign land, faced with sudden tragedy, the memory of which has become a part of her life, **Marion Brown (1946)** encountered both physical and spiritual challenges that will offer us valuable insight.

It was midnight, and somehow my body and mind would not give in to sleep. Curiously, my mind traveled back in my life, 40 years ago, to an experience that influenced the rest of my life.

During the fall and winter of 1963-1964, my friend of many years and I planned a trip around the world. Our goal was to visit and assess the effects of mission work in the lives of women and children the world over. Each of us had been on the staff of our respective church conferences. This trip would take us to Paris, Algiers, the Holy Land, West Pakistan, Cairo, and India.

We visited dispensaries, family-clothing and equipment outlets, schools, even classes in sewing, cooking, and carpentry work.

About a month into our trip, we had reached Lucknow, India. Then without warning, my friend suddenly fell seriously ill – so serious that she was hospitalized immediately. But just as quickly, her condition became critical and I was told she would have to be moved to a teaching hospital 15 hours away by train.

The magnitude of this situation fell heavily upon me. Here I was in a foreign country for which I did not have the language. I was thrust into a highly complex situation with demands I could scarcely meet. Through the confusion, I was able to obtain the last compartment on the train. But by this time, my friend was drifting in and out of a coma. Concerned by what I was facing, a woman doctor took note of my anxiety, stepped forward, and offered to accompany us on the trip. My relief was palpable.

A station wagon, used as an ambulance, met us at Ludhiana. Four strong men placed my friend on a stretcher, raised her high above their heads, and transported her to the waiting wagon.

For the next 34 days her condition vacillated from having a good night to one where her fever spiked to 103 degrees. And throughout this 34-day period, I stayed with the family of a missionary eye specialist who lived nearby.

It was the morning of the 34th day when I arose early so I could share in the doctor's devotional period. That morning, I felt I was given a promise directly out of John 11. In this passage Jesus was speaking to Mary and Martha concerning Lazarus and he said, *This illness does not lead to death; rather it is for God's glory. . . .* That was it, I felt. That message was a gift directly from God. I felt relieved of anxiety, of not-knowing. I felt certain direction. And I sensed I was propelled into the future with hope.

Then came word that my friend must have a particular medicine, available only at a hospital across town. So I hired a rickshaw and asked the driver to take me to the hospital. But, soon, into the journey, the wheel suddenly worked its way off the rickshaw. I was thrown onto the ground, bruised, but not seriously injured. Determined to continue, once the driver repaired the wheel, we completed the trip and I returned to the hospital where my friend lay, now critically ill.

By this time, Easter was approaching. I was encouraged. My friend responded to the medicine enough that we had dinner together one evening in her room. I had found a used record of Handel's *Hallelujah Chorus* and a small record player. Together, we read the Easter story and listened to the music. I felt hopeful, only to learn how hope can be dashed.

The following Monday, the doctor decided to operate. It was then that he discovered a brain abscess. But all the while I was holding fast to the perspective that we had been granted a gift of certainty. I felt stabilized. I felt strong in that conviction.

Two days later, everything would change. It was 4:10 a.m. when it happened. A caring woman doctor awakened me to say my friend had died. Immediately, I was asked for my decision regarding an autopsy.

At the time, the Scripture to which I clung still seemed real in my mind, but something went wrong.

In retrospect I realize now that I was looking at a portion of scripture literally. I had needed hope and confirmation that my friend was going to live. Later, I revisited the situation from which I have learned numerous things.

In re-reading the entire biblical portion, I realize the promise was only a part of the entire account. Jesus was speaking to Martha in John 11:23 and in verse 25. Jesus said to her, *I am the resurrection and life. Those who believe in me will never die. Do you believe this? She said to him, Yes, Lord I believe that you are the Messiah, the Son of God.*

The biblical commentary indicates that Lazarus represents every believer who loves Jesus Christ. When Jesus said, *Take away the stone and unbind him and let him go*, Jesus was speaking to every believer's condition. Release from the stony heart of sin; let go to the life in God.

Can it be that I took the scripture so literally that I was hung up on physical death only, rather than the spiritual meaning of the words? In further analysis, I realize my friend's illness was evidently rare and the doctors were puzzled regarding the remedy. I had to monitor personally the entire situation every day and inform the doctors when there was a change in my friend's condition. Also, to be factored into this situation were the lack of sufficient medicine, the needed technology, and the level of expertise on the part of the doctors.

In times of stressful situations and when personal responsibility is great, decision making and understanding become difficult. Was the diagnosis questionable? Did something go wrong there? Or perhaps it wasn't God's will that my friend die, or perhaps the Scripture was speaking of physical death, as well as speaking about life beyond death.

A portion of that Scripture is: *This illness does not lead to death; rather it is for God's glory, so that the Son of God may be glorified through it*. Certainly my friend's life had glorified God in her ministry of missions to children.

My prayer is that my personal and professional life in the church has also been to God's glory.

Linda Carlson Bagshaw (1968) describes experiences that make the theoretical real and that attach a face and feelings to conjectures and assumptions. Inherent in Linda's poignant account are important insights that, when she applied them to real-life experiences, became charged with vitality and meaning.

Shortly after my marriage, I was visiting my parents and attended church with them one Sunday. I can still see the minister's large, open hand, palm upward, fingers spread apart as he extended his arm to illustrate the point he was making. "Always hold loosely that which God places into your hand; then He will be able to easily take it away, if He so desires." The thought slid into my mind and heart agreeably and pleasantly – as so many unapplied, untried thoughts do.

Through the years since that Sunday morning in the '70s, I had many occasions to discover how difficult it was to react with that attitude in my life. I experienced God's giving and removing various people and things over the years: jobs, friends, health, church families. . . to name a few. Each time a loss occurred, I gained strength during the crises and readjustments by remembering the need to "hold loosely what God gives me." I learned to release my hold, although not always without a struggle. Sometimes I tightened my grip. For example, when my husband lost his job and it became necessary to sell the home I dearly loved, I balked at calling a realtor. After many of these uncomfortable changes, I began to feel that I was gaining spiritual ground by recognizing God's sovereignty in all events of my life and following through with the acceptance of the direction that, obviously, was before me. It was never easy to have something or someone taken away, but I felt I was growing in this area. The choice before me was always either learning and growing, or pursuing the bitter path of resentment and self-pity.

I never realized how tightly I held onto my father until God removed him from my life. Once more I remembered the sermon illustration. I knew all the appropriate responses that should have emerged: acceptance of God's sovereignty, peace that His timing is always correct, and assurance that I would again see my father. I had often comforted others with these reminders, but I suddenly realized that this time the truths were theoretical and academic in the face of my raw grief.

Then came a loss that far exceeded any before or since and revealed to me in painful clarity that my hand was closed tightly and possessively into a clenched fist. Unexpectedly, and in the span of a few short weeks, my father became ill, had surgery, and entered into God's presence. The laughter-filled phone calls, his warm hugs, his godly advice and prayers for me, his ready responses to my joys and sorrows ... all over in this life. This cut deeply – closer to my heart than loss of friends, or jobs, or church families; I cried out in agonized grief before God.

I began to realize that holding loosely does not mean that I love any the less, but that I love recognizing God's total right to give and take and his wisdom in doing so. I sensed God beginning to slowly pry open the fingers of my clenched fist, one by one; but, of course, what was actually happening was a process within myself of letting go, beginning with that recognition. The next step was allowing my heart to fill with warm gratitude to God as I thanked Him for all my years with Dad – all the special moments of my life that God allowed me to share with him before his 84 years ended.

My natural response to the gifts God placed in my hand is thankfulness; the natural response to the removal of a gift is not usually gratitude. I began to understand the need to keep my focus on the Giver, not the gift. The result is a new freedom born of trust, a release from clutching what is "mine." Now, everything I hold dear falls under a personal scrutiny to ensure that I am holding that gift loosely, with upward palm and open heart.

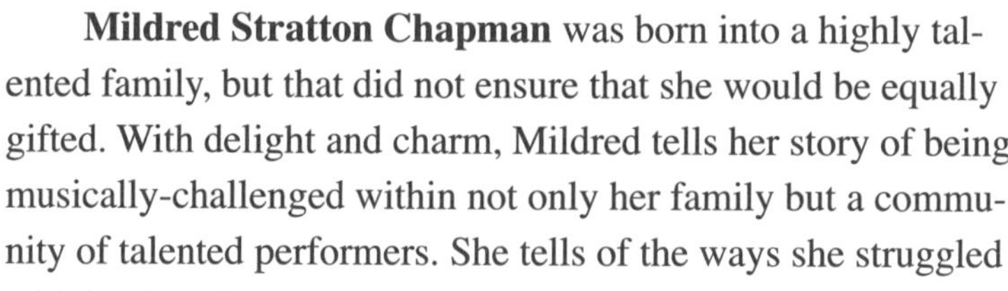

Mildred Stratton Chapman was born into a highly talented family, but that did not ensure that she would be equally gifted. With delight and charm, Mildred tells her story of being musically-challenged within not only her family but a community of talented performers. She tells of the ways she struggled with her handicap to make it work for her.

I grew up in rural Kentucky as Mildred Stratton. Numerous Strattons of varying ages and kinships lived throughout our area. As in all families, there were variations in the Stratton approach to learning and living. There were also, however, obvious commonalities.

The most widely recognized commonality is that the Strattons were faithfully Republican in counties that were Democratic strongholds. The second community-noted family feature is that the Strattons enjoyed singing and merited compliments for their vocal skills. The choirs of area Baptist and Methodist churches featured Strattons as faithful participants and frequent soloists. Our rural, consolidated schools emphasized music. . . especially the high school glee club. . . almost as much as basketball. Everybody who was somebody participated.

When he wasn't too exhausted, my farmer father often ended his workday spending an evening with the hymnbook. As a toddler, I would climb upon his lap and request that he sing Storm Clouds ("An Unclouded Day") and Ring the Bells ("When They Ring Those Golden Bells"). Very early, when he tried to teach me to sing with him, I knew that I didn't quite make the desired sounds. Thankfully, he never evidenced or spoke of the disappointment I knew he must have felt. I didn't know the word monotone, but I knew early that I had missed out on the Stratton musical heritage.

In school and church I soon sensed that, to avoid the stares of classmates, I should do more with lip movement and less with voice expression. I don't remember specific taunting or unkindness, but I tried hard to compensate for what I viewed as a major inadequacy through academic success and friendliness.

Both my home and our local church placed high emphasis on personal salvation and each individual's public response to the altar call of the evangelist or pastor. As an only child, my favorite meditation place was beneath a persimmon tree on a far corner of our farm. Here I often bargained with the Lord, promising multitudinous evangelical participations if He miraculously gifted me with a good singing voice.

Frequently, at both church and school, I was summoned for inclusion in a small vocal group. When I responded honestly that I didn't sing well, the invariable reaction was "You are a Stratton. All Strattons sing well." Obviously, those well-meaning individuals quickly learned about exceptions and never again accosted me with the "All Strattons. . ." remark.

The glee club at our small high school was widely recognized and received invitations to sing at major area events.

In spite of previous embarrassments, I so much wanted to be included that I decided to risk participation. By just working my lips within the relatively large soprano section, I survived a few enjoyable performance trips. One day, however, our director decided to test voices, and I knew my ruse was terminated. Thankfully, both she and the students dealt very kindly with me.

I had planned from early childhood to become an elementary teacher, but neighbors attending the nearby teachers' college told of a required music education course for which all must do a solo. I asked if the same requirement faced those choosing secondary education. Learning that it did not, I immediately chose a career path for secondary teaching, which resulted in a double major in English and Social Studies.

Although my initial motivation was not totally admirable, the choice proved to be a good one and eventually led to college teaching. Along the way I married a Presbyterian choir member and became the mother of two sons with musical skills.

So I have to conclude that my prayers under the persimmon tree have been answered – but in God's own way.

A young mother faces her worst fears when she finds her child not responding normally and as he usually would. **Lois Haycock McKuhen (1968)** invites us to come with her into a living nightmare. Through this experience, Lois becomes informed of a medical condition about which she had known almost nothing. Refusing to be overcome by the circumstances of her child's sudden illness, Lois demonstrates her spirit of commitment and compassion and, in the process, brings valuable insight to us.

"Why are you awake, dear?" I asked as I passed the bedroom of my three-year-old son and saw him sitting up in his bed, staring sleepily at the wall to his left.

I went into his room and stroked his back, "Why are you sitting up?"

I had just finished getting ready for bed. It was 10 p.m. and the spring night was warm. My husband was still somewhere with his real estate clients.

"Dear," I said again. But there was no response.

I had come in for a routine check of my boys before going to bed. That's when I first noticed. Something is wrong, I thought. Then my little boy lay back down, still staring to the left, but he felt cold, and his breathing seemed strange too shallow, I thought. Startled by what I saw, I knew I needed help.

Quickly, I called 9-1-1 and described the situation, then I told the operator that I had to get back to my son and would leave the front door open for the emergency workers.

I ran back to my child's room and found him even colder. He was limp and breathing irregularly. Not wanting to awaken my younger, six-month-old son, I scooped our three-year-old son up in my arms and ran the length of the hall to our bedroom and laid him gently on the bed. I checked his mouth and throat for any obstruction, but I found nothing.

I ran downstairs to unlock the front door, then hurriedly returned. This time, I found vomit in my child's mouth. At this, I began praying out loud in fear and helplessness. Suddenly, a man's voice called from the open door. Then I could hear him bounding up the stairs. In his hand was a medical bag. By a curious coincidence, this man turned out to be our close neighbor that I hardly knew because we had only recently moved to that new location. Later, I learned our neighbor was an experienced paramedic and had heard my call on the police scanner.

Taking one look at our pale, cold, limp child, the man went to work immediately. Soon, the neighbor was joined by other emergency workers, all of whom crowded around the child. By now, my son had become bluish and lifeless. The workers held the child over the bathroom sink in an effort to remove the vomit, wondering, I'm sure, if he had aspirated any of it. With the bathroom crowded with emergency workers, I ran to my room to throw on street clothes and phone my mother to come stay with our baby son. My heart pounded, and my mind, shredded with anguish, began to ask: Could our baby be dying?

Quickly, I phoned our church prayer line and hurriedly explained the situation to our pastor. I felt encouraged that people would soon be praying for our little child.

The next minutes went by in a blur. My Mom came. The Pastor came. Soon our little boy was bundled into the ambulance in the arms of our paramedic neighbor. The Pastor and I climbed aboard. Just as we drove out, my husband came home and was directed to follow the ambulance.

During the 15-minute ride to the hospital, my son showed no signs of life. The flashing ambulance lights colored everything crimson, and the siren screamed almost as loud as my emotions. My little one had urinated, his eyes were mostly closed, and I could see no signs of respiration. Could I be losing my beloved first-born? Surely, God, this isn't why You gave him to us! Save him! I pleaded.

We parted at the emergency room door. Medical personnel took over and vanished behind closed doors. It felt like our baby was being taken into the cloisters of life and death. Alone with the Pastor and my husband in the waiting room, I recounted the story in detail. We tried to recall anything that might have contributed to my son's condition. That evening we'd had an admission conference at the church and the Pastor had given candy suckers to all the children. We hastily relayed this to the nurse as well as that our son had recently taken several falls while he was playing. But ordinarily, he was a healthy, normal, bright little boy. We sat, each of us alone with our prayers. When the doctor finally appeared, he gestured to me, "Come with me, please." In an instant a host of fearful possibilities crowded my exhausted mind.

"We need you to calm him down," said the doctor.

Calm him down? Calm who. . . my limp, lifeless child? I thought incredulously, and then the doctor pulled back the curtain and there on the bed, red-faced and sobbing, sat my very awake and frightened little son.

He reached out for me and we clung to each other, then I searched the doctor's face for answers, but he gave me none.

It took two days of tests in the hospital to find out that our son was a normal, perfectly healthy little boy, but there was one exception. It was discovered that his brain waves were not normal. The most feasible diagnosis we were given was grand mal seizure. He was placed on Phenobarbital at once.

Our son was discharged from the hospital. We were so happy our family was together again, but a growing fear said that it would never be the same. As I learned about seizure disorders, I realized that our son might never be able to stay overnight at a friend's house, or swim without close supervision, or ride a bike, or even get a driver's license.

From my years of Christian training, I had been introduced to the perspective that "rain falls upon the just and the unjust." Because of this, I wasn't consumed by the question, "Why me?" or "God, this isn't fair." Instead, my nearly instinctive response was, "Why not me?" To me, this was the appropriate response to what was happening, even though I felt so very unprepared.

For us, anxiety became a frequent visitor. I crept in to check on our son more than once each night since then. I couldn't wait to see him awake and alert each morning, then I'd keep a close eye on him during the day. Every few months we made the trip back to the hospital for another EEG. Each time, I'd have to repeat the story of the entire incident to the hospital personnel. Why? Didn't they keep records? Each visit confirmed that our son had the same irregularity in his brain waves, yet there was never another seizure. Deep inside, I thanked God, and I pushed forward.

Over time, I began to relax in the hope that the condition was actually a fluke — a single, solitary, developmental occurrence. Living with a child on Phenobarbital had its own challenges, but after five years, two consecutive EEGs confirmed that our now eight-year-old son had normal wave patterns. Slowly, and cautiously, we weaned him from the drug.

Today, our son is a Purdue grad and a "computer geek" who's never had another seizure. As he eases toward 30, he's normal, healthy, married, and the father of our three precious grandchildren. Looking back on this early trauma, and the years

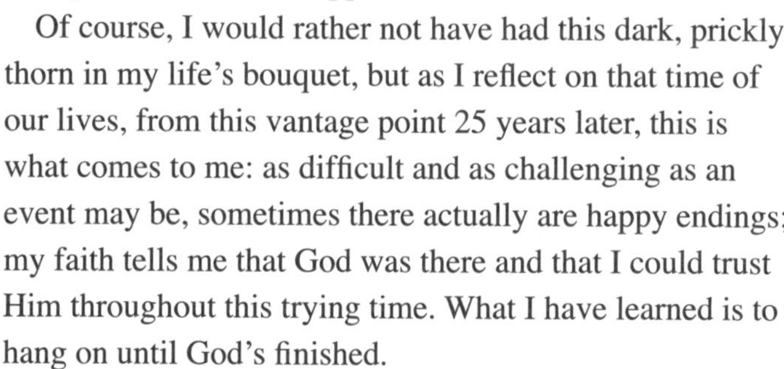

of concern that followed, I can't say I have any idea why God permitted this to happen.

Of course, I would rather not have had this dark, prickly thorn in my life's bouquet, but as I reflect on that time of our lives, from this vantage point 25 years later, this is what comes to me: as difficult and as challenging as an event may be, sometimes there actually are happy endings; my faith tells me that God was there and that I could trust Him throughout this trying time. What I have learned is to hang on until God's finished.

Finding ourselves in a place where we experience more questions than answers can challenge us at every level. Intellectually, we want to know the facts of a situation. We want to understand what we are dealing with. At the emotional level, our peace of mind is set in turmoil and our sense of well-being is threatened. At the spiritual level, our hearts can cry out for relief and resolution, and for the meaning of what we are encountering. **Billie Dusing Manor** unfolds just such a tormenting situation. She tells about all the emotions she experienced as she struggled to understand and then cope with her daughter's medical condition, and in so doing she offers us helpful insights.

I made my decision in all of five minutes. That's the amount of time it took me to walk to the elevator and descend to the ground-floor of the Children's Hospital in the city near my home.

It was a bright, clear day and the brief walk to the car in the sunshine spread both acceptance and encouragement through my soul. The warm sun seemed to invite me to linger awhile in the parking lot. I remember this as if it took place yesterday, yet in reality, it happened back in November of 1972. That day changed my life.

I was now the mother of a child with a "label." Finally, to the questions I had lived with for such a long time, there were answers with explanations attached. For the first time I saw a bright future for my child. Now I understood there were reasons why teachers seemed to point blame at the parents of this child, as though we had employed poor parenting techniques at home.

But let me back up a bit. Let me mention some of the factors that brought about my decision to seek help and how they have influenced my life. My husband and I had a referral for my daughter to see the chief pediatric neurologist in the large, urban hospital for children. Our daughter was a sweet child who, for unknown reasons, presented me with a challenge almost every day of her life.

Already, she had been diagnosed with a medical condition that was commonly termed at that time, a "lazy eye." The day I took our daughter for an appointment with our local ophthalmologist, it was his advice that we make the trip into the city to the specialist that very day. He told me that he thought there was "more going on" with our daughter than merely a lazy eye.

This was the opportunity I had been hoping for. I knew my little girl was a bright child but she was, at the same time, definitely different from other children in her approach to learning. As a baby, she walked at nine months, was curious, liked to climb, but did not talk in full sentences until she reached the age of four. In many ways, she was truly a remarkable child. At the age of two, she could whistle, and she could blow her nose. As time went on, I noticed that she learned in "wholes." For example, she did not draw stick figures as most children do, but at the age of four, she drew a stick man but with eyelashes, fingernails, buttons down his front, and she colored in his face. I quizzed her on why she had done this and she responded, curiously, that the coloring in the face represented the hair on the back of the man's head.

In kindergarten, the teacher noticed that while our daughter merely scribbled on her paper, she could tell her classmates correct answers. I soon learned from the ophthalmologist that because of her lazy eye, she had double vision when she looked at her own paper but could see across the table just fine. We then found that she also had complete mirror imagery.

Armed with better understanding of our daughter's condition, I could be more patient when, at the age of six, she would come home from school, walk to her bedroom, toss her small desk on its side, and repeat over and over, "I can't do it! I can't do it!"

It was discouraging to find the public educational system in the 1970s so incapable of addressing the learning needs of a child with mirror-image problems. We tried diligently to follow the advice of the specialist that "our job was to love" our daughter. This came as a challenge because both my husband and I were educators and I, in particular, was a reading teacher. Nonetheless, I took advantage of as many tutoring and learning opportunities as I could find within driving distance from our home. And there were many, since there are colleges and universities nearby. In my case, it would be easy to say that I could have benefited from good "hindsight," but I followed the doctor's advice and did not tutor our daughter myself.

Now, our daughter is 35 years old. She affirms me when she tells me that I did understand her as a child and that I always let her come home and play, with homework undertaken after supper. She tells me that I knew she needed a break from schoolwork, and that she was a "good girl," and that she would work hard after she had eaten her evening meal.

I must face my inner conflict: I estimate that if I had drilled our daughter on reading components, I would not only have taken away much of her playtime as a child, but at the same time,

I may also have succeeded in increasing her reading ability by a grade level or two.

To this day, I am amazed at her tenacity, her will to "hang in," and not give up. I am encouraged by how much she has accomplished in life. She lives in an apartment by herself, drives a car, and works in the dining area of a local university. I am especially amazed at her abilities because she was 28 years old when she was finally diagnosed as both autistic and dyslexic.

I am content with my decision to accept the specialist's advice and not push our daughter into educational and emotional overload by teaching her myself. With the assistance of others, she has reached her educational potential. I have accepted that sometimes it is better that others, beyond the family, assist in these matters. To paraphrase a well-known expression, I would say, from my experience, that it does sometimes take a village, a Christian community, a town, a city, a state, and even a nation to raise a child. It takes knowledge and information, and most of all, it takes wisdom.

Do any of us who are about to have a baby not dream of a fine, healthy boy or girl? Who does not fantasize, hope, and pray that the new life about to be brought into the world will be special in many ways? But things don't always happen according to what we want to take place. **Kathy Lauber Blume (1960)** tells us her story of shock and sadness and how she coped with what confronted her. Her journey from tragedy to triumph is sure to offer each of us valuable insights and skills for facing similar adversity.

The horrible realization of the doctor's words had begun to sink in. I had suspected it for several months, but didn't want to believe it. My precious infant son was deaf. I was devastated and numb.

My numb disbelief quickly turned to anger. I had come to a crossroads in my journey at which every serious child of God eventually arrives. Why would a benevolent God allow such a cruel burden to be placed on a tiny baby boy? I railed at Him for days.

Eventually, when I was quiet enough that I could hear beyond my own cries, I remembered several years back another crossroads I faced. At that time, I was in college, trying to find my niche. I thought about nursing because of my desire to help others, but I found that profession just wasn't for me. Then

one day a professor observed me in the classroom full of children. She said, "You have a special gift for teaching." So I looked into teaching, was intrigued, switched my major, and never looked back. I loved it.

Reflecting on that memory, I allowed God to show me that by this choice of profession, I would be equipped in advance to help my little son. I was being given the tools I needed to make the most of what would take place. I still don't understand this. It is a marvel to me.

I began to do what I was equipped to do for my son. Tutoring him, encouraging him in the art of lip-reading, speaking and eventually signing, pushing him to discover and develop the unique abilities that were his, and above all, not lamenting over the ones that were not.

Sometimes I would find myself being fearful about whether he would finish high school, go to college, get married, and have a meaningful career. Again, these were areas I could not control, and again, I learned to allow God to remind me to let go of the fear and focus on the important things at hand. Little did I know what I would be looking back on later. We forged ahead, and I know now that our perseverance was honored by God.

Today, at age 35, my sweet son has a list of astounding accomplishments. He did indeed graduate from high school and college, and he went on to teach at both those levels in the field of American sign language. He was the first deaf person to take a bicycle trip across America with the Wandering Wheels program, taking three trips total. He not only married, he is the father of two gorgeous children. . . my grandchildren.

My son is currently pastoring a deaf church and he travels internationally several times a year ministering to the hearing impaired. In his spare time, he is writing devotions and developing videos for deaf teens.

Did God have a plan in all this? Oh, yes. Are God's thoughts infinitely higher than mine? Again, a resounding yes. Has He finished with His plan for my amazing son? What do you think?

QUESTIONS TO PONDER

The expression, ". . . through a glass darkly," suggests a process leading toward increased understanding of life – that we have come through a time without clarity of understanding, and for which we may have only a vague sense that meaning lies someplace beyond us. This is in contrast to the experiences of women that appear in Chapter 1, which focuses on life's firsts and highly charged life events that tend to carry sharp, clear, and often instant meaning. Consider, for example, the abruptness of an unanticipated miscarriage, an instantaneous accident, or words that have intense and immediate impact – all of which may serve to make life-long impressions.

Alone, or in a group, here are some questions to consider:

1)   Once more, scroll through your memory. Reflect on situations that seemed to have an "unfolding quality" to them – circumstances that had a beginning someplace in the past but which have taken time (weeks, months, years, perhaps even decades) to assume shape and definition within your thinking, rather than an indistinct and immediate impression. We do not need to be advanced in age for this process to complete itself, nor will we necessarily experience only one or a few of these apparently related dynamics. Review your experiences with the intention of obtaining fresh understanding not only of the end results, but also of the nature of the process. Were there times when you felt inadequate to the challenges facing you, or perhaps resistant to them? Or consider those times when you tried to be open to new learning and receptive to understanding but they did not come to you. Reflect on your periods of confusion and frustration. In what ways did you deal with your restless mind and emotions at these times? What workable methods did you find that helped you through the process toward understanding and therefore inner peace?

2)   Do all of life's questions come with neat, readily understood answers? Reflect on your unique life story: your parents, your school, church, community. Look for ways these important influences have contributed positively or negatively to your process of maturation. Review your self-story from your high school years, college, marriage, profession, and family life. Can you pinpoint ways in which you have facilitated or sabotaged your own unfolding?

3)   Review the individual experiences told by the women in this chapter. List the dominant qualities and characteristics of their responses to life experience that (a) inhibited their inner growth, or (b) acted to assist them toward maturation.

MY COMPANION JOURNAL

1)   Return to the graph you constructed for Chapter 1. Work backward through your time-line, pinpointing incidents that seemed to relate or contribute to the ultimate insights that came to you. Look for specific revelations and understandings. Draw a line linking each of these points on your graph. Note the amount of time that intervened between each related event. Look for triggering incidents. Look for the process leading to your revelation.

2)   Look again at your graph and take note of the following, asking yourself what meanings these dynamics suggest to you:

    a) Ordinary coincidences: The occurrence of events that appear to be related and that happen, as though by accident, at the same time, but which seem to have no immediate or later connection.

    b) Synchronicities: Highly meaningful coincidences, not easily explained by cause and effect principles, and serving as a connection between something going on outside of you with something happening inside you. Notice ways in which the relationship of an occurrence resonates with your perceived life purposes, or helps you proceed toward your destiny to show love, see wisely, or bring healing to yourself, others, and the world.

c) Asynchronicities: The opposite to synchronicity, these events serve to alert us through a series of negating coincidences that suggest wrong timing, wrong persons, or disharmonious circumstances.

d) Paradoxes: Contradictions so stark as to render us incapable of making a satisfactory decision in any direction. Notice what brings relief to this tension. What reconciling or balancing elements appear to transcend the blockage and offer 1) reconciliation of clearly opposite forces in our lives, or 2) detachment, or 3) otherwise offer us relief from the conflicting elements?

e) Repeated patterns of events: Situations that, while not duplicated in specific outward detail, do appear to repeat themselves in their essence. These may be areas of your life that need conscious attention.

f) Moments of high creativity: Creative moments may happen when a habitual pattern of thought or action is interrupted, or when we intentionally pause to question old habits.

BROAD HORIZONS /
OPEN OPTIONS

I can do everything through Christ who gives me strength.
Philippians 4:13 NIV

Acknowledgment and utilization of the talents and qualities of women throughout history continues to be a matter for ongoing, serious study. Trends suggest an evolving position for women, together with a broadened appreciation for their integration into the affairs of the world.

The perception of the "dual consciousness" of women (the societal notion that the female is to be dependent, nurturing, and secondary while at the same time standing in readiness should she be called upon to utilize her broader talents of independence, resourcefulness, savvy, and strength), ultimately and uniquely equips her to make significant contributions to the world scene.

The women whose life experiences appear in this chapter reveal an inclination toward possibility thinking and effective actualizing of their creative potential, in line with those characteristics traditionally associated with the female.

Our circumstances can shift in ways we may never have expected as we prepare to live out our lives. At such times, we may be called upon to make decisions or assume responsibilities that may change the course of our lives. **Nancy E. Dusckas (1975)** assumed a challenge in the face of family crisis. In so doing, she moved into her life's calling and found herself eminently qualified.

One of the biggest challenges in my life was when I took over my father's business after his death in 1988. I had worked with him for several years and I felt prepared as far as the details of the funeral business were concerned, but when the day came that I had to make all the decisions – both large and small – that was a day of high anxiety. My father was like a modern day Solomon to me. He was wise. He had good insight, and he was greatly loved by our community. He was a large man, so I was facing filling his large shoes both literally and figuratively. I knew I would need his wisdom and I wondered how to develop it because my temperament was to try to please people and make them feel comfortable. While that was a good trait for a funeral director, it was not good where business savvy was needed.

I knew I would need his wisdom and I wondered how to develop it because my temperament was to try to please people and make them feel comfortable.

There had been an unfortunate situation in town wherein a man had set up a program to fund money for funerals – a type of pre-pay program. A younger man who was trying to make his living in sales approached us with his proposal. I knew him to be a good man who would not knowingly have anything to do with scams. While my father was still living, we had set aside time to listen carefully to this young man's presentation. Afterwards, my father had turned to me and said, very thoughtfully, "I'm sorry, but what he proposes sounds too good to be true."

I felt bad about this, not so much for the possible loss of investment potential, but that we had just buried the young man's grandmother, and I thought we should help support him. But, my father's intuition was on target. As it turned out, the program folded, the developer of the program went to prison, and funeral directors who had been lured into the scheme lost a great deal of money.

My father served as a model to me in other ways as well. Never once did I see greed in him. Unfortunately, greed can be found throughout the many ancillary businesses that make up my field. I see families spending more money than they should in response to sharp salespeople. I see people hurt when they should not be.

When my father died, I had an uncle who said to me, "Aren't you afraid of competition?" My response was the same then as it is today, "My only competition is my own father." What I meant by this is that if I could do even half of what he did, I would be successful. I believe he set the bar just that high. And still, it was set at a height I felt confident I could reach.

I was fortunate to have a good teacher in my father, and now it has become my turn to take the baton and run. When I assess all that I have learned, together with the experience I have gained, I feel comfortable that I can do it.

Lisa Huber Toney (1997) takes us to the very cusp of a shift in social consciousness. As professional options opened before her, she listened and heard the directive that, when she responded, took her as through the veil separating one paradigm from the next.

We dated about six months. I liked him and he liked me. It was exciting. It was fun. It felt like the beginning of something beautiful.

Hours went by. Talking. Sharing. Laughing. Trust was taking form.

Sharing dreams seemed comfortable. I opened my heart. "Seminary," I confided to him, "was something I was wrestling with."

Then the wall. My dream slammed head on into a solid place. After the resistance, then uncertainty. Questioning, even condemnation.

"Why couldn't you be a teacher, or a nurse, or something? But a pastor?" he asked.

We plunged into a time of study. We sought counsel. We prayed for direction. We discussed interpretations of scriptures. We contemplated the complexities of culture.

Then the jury came back.

He couldn't do it.

It was either him or the dream.

But I had heard the call.

With a burst of confidence, I confronted him after work in my red, power suit. Did he actually think that if I became a pastor I was about to make a mistake of divinely eternal proportions? Did he really mean to use the word *sin*?

He did.

Six months later, I entered seminary.

I chose the call.

Finding oneself in the position of a "first," without tradition or precedents to refer to, can be a heady, heart-challenging journey. **Roselyn Baugh Kerlin (1955)** shares her experience that opens wide the avenue to new levels of leadership for women.

❦   ❦   ❦

"You have earned the nomination...." Those were the words to me by the Chair of the Nominating Committee for the College Board of Trustees on which I had served as a member for 12 years. Thinking ahead, I realized that if I accepted the nomination and was elected, I would become the first female Board Chair of Taylor University, founded 150 years before as Fort Wayne Female College.

I deferred to the two other women who had "seniority" on the 26-member board, because they had served on the board longer than I; however, these two colleagues were excited about my nomination and it proved to be no problem to them. I knew I would have ample opportunity to prove that I was capable of serving as Board Chair, if it were meant to be.

My first college board meeting was held on Homecoming Weekend at Taylor in 1984. I was so thrilled and honored to be elected. I felt secure in the experiences I brought to the board and thought they would allow me to make a significant contribution. I had firsthand knowledge of the educational opportunities in our state, which came from my years on a local school board and knew I had learned many valuable lessons through opportunities that I had by my involvement in the state school board association. I felt that I understood the subtleties of the responsibilities of an academic board, and that I understood policy issues. What I did not know at that time was how much my love for my *alma mater* would permeate all of those subtleties, challenging lessons learned in other educational arenas.

At the time I assumed the board's leadership in 1996, becoming the first female Chair, there were several problem situations of concern to the board. Enrollments were down in all of our state's small colleges due in part to tuition increases and rapid changes in technology. There was concern about how that might affect the institution. The satellite campus acquired three years before I became chair needed further study. There were many challenges on the horizon for higher education, with some special ones for Christian colleges. Some board members were moving to "Emeritus" status, and new members were being added to the board. Still, I felt secure in this leadership position because I had been blessed with a talented mentor from the state School Board Association who graciously shared with me information and insights on "boardmanship." Confidently, though a bit naively, I began my tenure as Board Chair armed with my faith in God's guidance, my belief in the power of prayer, my passion for academic affairs and curriculum, as well as my love for the institution.

Because communication and peace-making have long been integral to my personal leadership style, I have an innate respect for being well-informed and assisting others to be the same. I felt gratified as the board atmosphere became more animated and board members began to be more involved.

Significant goals for the institution were achieved during my tenure. A $75 million capital campaign was begun at the time of my installation as chair, concluding successfully and on time. Academic programs were strengthened with more attention being given to faculty concerns, such as heavy teaching-loads and salary issues. The position of Chancellor was established, thereby retaining the previous, much-loved President's continued institutional involvement. Important building expansion was accomplished and enrollment increased, creating a waiting pool of students for the Office of Admissions.

The experience helped me develop a greater understanding of the subtle forces at work within a unique, small college culture. I learned that some traditions must continue to be honored, but that others may need to be set aside in favor of new ones developed from new insights. From a still broader perspective, I recognized that my position was one involving transition. I count it my privilege to have been that person who provided a bridge into the new perceptions for my alma mater and her Board of Trustees.

Yes, I wholeheartedly agree with the words expressed by the Chair of the Nominating Committee before I was elected

Chair of the University Board of Trustees … I did indeed *earn* the nomination. What I also earned was a position of enormous challenge – challenge far beyond the simple, straightforward principles and guidelines set forth in my Governing Handbook. Throughout my three years as Chair, I received acceptance from fellow board members and friends, and I recognized that my leadership earned their respect. I have a new sense of the ongoing presence of God who promotes harmony and good will. As I accepted the position and its challenges, the support of others and God's guidance were important to me as I faced significant board leadership opportunities. I am grateful for these three years that stretched me and allowed me to exercise new levels of wisdom and love.

Having heard and heeded a call that, for her time, was about to set her apart from the norm, **Lisa Huber Toney (1997)** describes her journey using a movingly poetic stream-of-consciousness method of expression.

Consecrated to God: That is what my name means.* Little did I know that my profession would one day match the name my parents chose for me as an infant girl. They raised me to live for my Creator and declared my life no longer my own, but His. I was consecrated at birth, I learned.

Called: The unmistakable voice of one greater than myself gently prodded my heart and mind to follow. After years of refusal and personal ambition, I yielded. Completely unsure of what this would mean, I stepped into the unknown. I was compelled beyond myself.

Chaos: Uprooted from everything familiar, I left them all. Good-byes were dispensed with tears to family, friends, and home. I left all I knew to pursue something few understood. Out of the chaos came a new day with a clear purpose.

Commencement: It began. I began. Life became clearer, sharper, and fuller. The doors of seminary opened wide to enrich my heart and mind. Validation flooded my being after years of questioning. Life commenced accordingly.

Conditioning: They were few in number but faithful. Embracing my leadership, they invited me in. I joined them with fear and enthusiasm. Midst their warmth, I tried out my new pastoral skin. It was thin and tender, but was growing stronger with time. A new layer was expanding and conditioning my life with expectation.

Confused: Some stood with shaking heads and questioning tongues. Could females lead? Could women be divinely called? Was she stable, her mental and emotional faculties intact? A few threw out catcalls. Others cheered. Some clapped and encouraged me on my way.

Courage: I stood firm behind my call. Doubt, I found, is best dealt with through time, relationship, and grace. My thin skin grew thicker, yet it could bleed. Thorns can do that. And the courage to be authentic midst condemnation is, I learned, beyond myself.

Clarity: Still, the sun rises and sets. The routine persists, even takes on new life. I marvel at changed lives. With hope, I fight my own cynical nature. I embrace the power of healing and life within brokenness. Dawn brings clarity to the day and obedience brings clarity to my life. I celebrate the call.

Commissioned: It was a moment that stood still in time. As is the tradition of the faithful, they laid their hands gently upon me. They spoke a circle of blessing around me. Validating and fortifying the mandate with divine power, protection, and provision. Ordained by the church and compelled by my Creator, I was commissioned with Holy orders.

Consecrated to God: Consecrated, and committed, all the days of my life.

Elizabeth means consecrated to God, or God's oath and is the

English derivative of the Hebrew name Elshaba. In Greek, the name is Elisabet with derivatives of Lisabette, Lisbeth, Lisel, Lisa.

Coming into young adulthood in the '70s and early '80s, and being a woman of strength, vision, and ability brought **Rebecca Kerlin Haak (1978)** times of solitary introspection and lonely pursuit. Being true to her deep sense of calling, Rebecca persevered to become highly respected in her chosen profession.

I am 47 years old and have been a practicing OB-Gyn doctor for 20 years. When I look back over my life and am prompted to ask myself if I had to do it all over again, would I? I would have to say, yes. I would indeed. I feel comfortable, integrated, and positive about the direction my life has taken, even though my chosen profession may seem to some people a side venture from the mainstream of women's career choices.

As I look back to my high school days, I have to admit that my strengths lay in math, science, and music. I was naturally inclined in these directions, and in those areas I earned my highest grades. I would have liked to have been proficient in other areas, but in my case I just wasn't. Therefore, it seemed both natural and prudent to follow my innate abilities rather than to contort myself to fit into a program different from the one I chose.

I remember how much I enjoyed music – actually I progressed considerably in this area and for a time entertained the thought of going still further, but then I felt dissuaded. There was an inner sense of hesitation. This was not because of a lack of talent for music, but rather because there was something about music as a profession that, while appealing, seemed to offer me very little sense of deep, inner peace, a condition I came to understand more fully later.

It was during my senior year in high school that I felt particularly compelled to think seriously about the program I would follow. At about that time, it occurred to me that really, bottom line for me, music would – and of necessity had to – focus on me. During this same time, I considered the field of medicine, which would be a natural mix of my twin interests in both math and science. Of course, it is important I mention that my father is a physician. My memories of accompanying him to the little hospital on the American Indian Reservation where we lived while he served out his Public Health requirements, are vivid in my mind. As are the times later when he would take me with him to the hospital emergency room when he was in private practice and when mother would be busy elsewhere.

But I did see my relationship to my doctor father as a kind of apprenticeship. To me, his being a doctor was just what he did. Accommodating and integrating his profession into our lives was merely our way of life not unlike other families who adjusted to their parents' lines of work.

What became clear to me, in time, was that the practice of medicine, more than the pursuit of a career in music, would concentrate my attention on others and their needs. Suddenly, I experienced the inner peace that served to signal the right choice for me.

But I was a woman. Back in the '70s and early '80s the social climate would have women subjugating their natural gifts for the culturally accepted "female professions" of teaching, nursing, and secretarial work. What I decided to do in the face of these circumstances was to go on to undergraduate studies, to take the courses I gravitated to and loved, give them a try, and assess my situation as I went along.

As it turned out, there were only two chemistry majors in my college science department in the mid '70s. Any encouragement I may have failed to receive from the larger student body was more than fully compensated for by the supportive college faculty. They took delight in their students' interest and hard work. They offered themselves to us as sources of encouragement and inspiration.

All of this is not to say that my undergraduate years were in any way a microcosm of paradise. What I can say is that, within the confines of the Science Department, it was rather heavenly. But beyond those borders, out where the general student body partied and participated in what gave their lives meaning and sense of belonging, I just didn't seem to fit in all that well.

For one thing, perhaps the most significant event of my young life was an experience I had when I was 13 years old. I had been a timid, first-born daughter in my family. In fact, I was so introverted that I was reluctant to move out into the life of many of those around me. But, one day we, as a family, attended a Christian Retreat. I happened to be standing within hearing range – but beyond the sight – of some young people deep in conversation. First, I caught snatches of what they were talking about, and then I found myself wanting to hear more. What they were discussing among themselves was something I found intriguing, even tantalizing. What they were talking about in their youthful, energetic ways was how they wanted to know more about God and to learn how to live lives that brought joy and goodness into the world. This, I thought, is what I want.

Silently, and very alone, I took the path up into the mountains that bordered the camp retreat. I didn't really know what to do or say there in my aloneness, so I just opened myself and asked God to come into my life in His fullest – to make me strong, and to make me loving.

From that moment forward, the process seemed to be underway. The very timid child I had been, uncertain of who I was or where I fitted into the scheme of things, began to give way to greater confidence in who I was. I sensed, like the locust that sloughs his shell, that I was growing less concerned about self, and more open to others. And perhaps most significantly for me, I came into a nearly palpable sensation of being loved, of being in this life for a purpose, and that there was a valuable role for me in life.

By the time I was in college, what had begun in my adolescence showed itself in my being more comfortable in my own skin. I felt genuine. I felt in balance, and I felt authentic. Trends in fashion held little interest for me. To sweep my hair into a Farrah Fawcett flip, so popular in the '70s, held little interest for me. To wear clothing that emphasized my gender attributes seemed unnecessary. To make myself into anything other than what I regarded as purely and genuinely me, if that was a requisite for attracting male attention, well, then perhaps there existed guys elsewhere who were not so attached to these characteristics as hallmarks of what they regarded as the ultimate female.

And so it was that I continued my focus on pre-med courses with the intention of gaining admission into medical school.

Women, I came to understand within my particular collegiate culture were meant to *dress up* their men. They were to *show well*. To be a kind of appendage used to enhance the social standing of the male counterpart. Women were to limit themselves to the "female professions," and they were to learn how to play out their predestined role within those limitations, and do so quietly and gracefully.

It was not until later when I was in medical practice that I experienced firsthand the debilitating fall-out from these arbitrary, but nonetheless powerful, social injunctions placed upon women. Much of my practice evolved into what I call "Mothering Mothers." By this, I mean the consuming need demonstrated by my women patients to have someone to talk to, to listen to them, to honor their experiences, to respect their feelings, to enter into dialog with them about viable life options – options that would offer them their own unique *sense of self* that is denied to a person within the confines of conformity to group attitudes.

So, I look back over the span of my life and all that it encompasses. There were the indignities shown a young woman who sought to pursue her deeply felt dreams. But there are also the satisfactions of a young woman opening herself to others whose needs were not unlike her own. There were the stresses of family and profession. But there were always creative ways to bring the two into sufficient compatibility. There were the criticisms. There were the praises. And through it all, when I ask myself, if I had the opportunity, would I live my life differently, I would respond from the deepest part of me that there was a calling on my life and to that calling I was true. My life, both personal and professional, has been ordered and conditioned by my desire to reach out and to offer help to others through the practice of medicine. This is what my professional choice has been and continues to be all about.

Stephanie Golden Earhart (1991) chose to pursue a demanding career that, by the time she came into adulthood in the late 1980s was, as she says, "not a particularly big deal." Almost seamlessly, she moved from her undergraduate studies into graduate school and on into her chosen profession, which she balances together with family and married life.

By the time I was an undergrad in the late '80s, my choice of medicine as my profession was not particularly a big deal. From Junior High on, I knew I loved both science and people so it seemed almost natural that I would gravitate toward a career in the medical field.

When I was taking pre-med courses, there were only a few more guys than gals in the college program and we women students had no problem holding our own. The curriculum was demanding, that can't be denied. But most of us hung in and were rewarded for our commitment. Not

My life, both personal and professional, has been ordered and conditioned by my desire to reach out and to offer help to others through the practice of medicine.

only did we have the support of our professors, but our fellow students accepted our career choice and urged us on.

This was a time when young people were of the mind that life was to be explored. For me to pursue the demanding field of medicine did not put me on a pedestal, nor did it suggest that I was, in any way, unusual.

I knew what it was to work independently and to work hard. I was the oldest of two daughters of an Army Chaplain. With my family, I had moved frequently and lived in many parts of the world. When I completed high school and set out for college, I was leaving the place that had become home to me – Germany.

A broad world view was a part of me when I settled down at a college in the Midwest. It would not be honest of me to say that I had no adjustment issues ... mainly I found myself longing for friends who, like me, had exposure to a larger picture of life. But, in time, I found many areas that my classmates and I held in common and when my peers became upper classmen, we were quite compatible. By that time, students had been on study-abroad trips and they had opened themselves to other cultures and ways of life.

The option of continuing my medical training through a military scholarship was another "natural" for me. When I was accepted into the Army Health Profession Scholarship Program, it meant that I would owe a total of eight years of time in service after medical school. I was still single at the time, having not yet even met my husband, though I hoped to marry someday. I knew it was possible that being an Army physician might intimidate potentially interested suitors. After much prayer, I was at peace with this possibility, and with the real potential in the Army for danger and even death, depending on the world situation. Interestingly, I was engaged less than a year after being sworn in as an Army reserve officer!

Life in the military was merely a way of life to me. I had observed firsthand the opportunities for ministry to military personnel and their families. I was aware of what it was for young men and women to be moved out of their comfort zone and into foreign settings. I saw how many would turn from their original church affiliations, move into a kind of spiritual void, then become confused in the face of even deeper spiritual hunger. I experienced, along with others, the very real presence of death because of its being integral to military life.

Juggling all these elements, while sometimes difficult, in the overall I see them as a grand adventure. From my place now as a young doctor in Family Practice, a wife and a mother, the ingredients that combined to make my life work were a sense of creativity, an openness to new options, a freedom from restrictive tradition, and underlining it all, the commitment my husband and I have to each other and to making our family a success. I do not deny that it is a significant challenge to coordinate our crazy, demanding schedules, but what I found is that it can be accomplished to the benefit of all concerned. Admittedly, any move – especially to move frequently – takes its toll on youngsters and parents as well. For this reason, we now hope to remain settled so that all of us may assume a more predictable life.

Years ago, when I was in junior high, I was touched deeply by the book, *Christy*, by Catherine Marshall. The character who impressed me most was the doctor. I saw, through him, the many opportunities for ministering to those in need. That has stayed with me all these years. And throughout all of this time, I have found that the urge to minister extends not only to patients, but to marriage and family as well.

Each segment of life opens into the next. This is an exciting reality to me.

A daughter born to a mother's high ideals, instead of rebelling against or sloughing them off, may well rise to, even exceed, the heights that she was first encouraged to achieve. Her mother's slogan, *Blessings Demand Responsibility,* settled deeply within **Carole Hoel Godfrey (1981)** and propelled her beyond the usual women's professions at that time of secretary, teacher, or nurse to a calling in which she works in a legal setting to influence and elevate the lives of the less fortunate.

As a child, I had always believed that my mother was a superwoman. Blessed with an exceptional intellect, she excelled at everything she pursued. A natural teacher with gifts of diplomacy and humility, she was born before her time – a female pioneer in a man's world. And at that time, there were limited opportunities. Today, she would have undoubtedly discovered a cure for cancer.

From as early as I can remember, the words she indelibly imprinted on me were, *to whom much has been given, much is required*. What they meant, she said, was that *blessing always demands responsibility*. Whether it be knowledge, talent, a home devoid of violence and insecurity, or simply the blessings of a good temperament – whatever it may be – all that comes our way must carry a fair accounting.

My young mind somehow translated all these lofty words into a deep desire to become a lawyer. Many of the specific ideals that often spur one to the study of law meant less to me than the simple conviction that I wanted to be a lawyer.

And so, I began my training. I attended a university and completed bachelor degrees in psychology and philosophy followed by graduate work in theology. It is said the best preparation for a law degree is an education of diversity. So I pursued the arts, sciences, the classics, travel, and the conscious acquisition of valuable life experience. As it turned out, this advice was not only sound, it was life changing. My liberal arts education proved to be the most valuable training I received.

With careful preparation, I applied and was admitted to law school in 1983. But what I found replacing my heady studies of the nature of man and questions of meaning and existence was the study of real estate law, corporate debentures, and minority shareholder interests. I felt I was stepping from meaning into non-meaning. This was not what I wanted to do in my chosen profession.

Finally, I graduated with my law degree and began practicing immediately, and almost exclusively, family law. This choice was due in part to society's volatile nature, which translated into plenty of available work. But it was also due to my academic background in the humanities. All around me on a day-to-day basis I watched as the agonies and ecstasies of the human drama played themselves out in the family courtroom. All of this touched on much of what I had studied earlier, and it seemed to be a closer fit than the corporate boardroom. I settled into my practice in a large city with a population of 800,000. I began to have success and soon became an established law partner.

Admittedly, my law practice is challenging and meaningful but, as with all professions, there are times when it can be a difficult taskmaster. The hours can be long, the work demanding, and the pressure relentless. My ideal of leaving work at 5:00 in the afternoon and having my life returned to me on weekends was shattered before I could figure out where the erroneous perception had come from. Awakening two or three times a night to anguish over files and deliberate over the next step to be taken in a case, or despair over the next step that should have been taken, was likewise not what I had anticipated. The pressure inherent in a law practice was never adequately described in any of my textbooks, nor had it ever come up for classroom consideration.

But I have survived, even thrived. Throughout the years I have practiced law, I have been involved in adoption cases, simple divorce situations to complex and protracted custody battles, and matrimonial property disputes ranging in value from a few forks and spoons to millions of dollars. I have seen clients returning for second and third divorces and those wanting to divorce after 40 years of marriage. I have seen the thrill of parents with their newly-adopted babies, as well as the relief of those surviving the highly emotional divorce process. I have seen greed, poverty, deceit, hatred, and sorrow.

But, despite its difficulties, the issues inherent in family law are compelling. The fabric of the community hinges upon the structure and dynamics of the family. How are children to be cared for upon the breakdown of the marriage? What is fair and reasonable in assessing the amounts of maintenance to be paid for children, or for a former spouse who because of illness or disability cannot return to the workforce? What property should be divided in matrimonial disputes, and in what manner? The answers to these questions can affect virtually everyone within a family unit.

Over the 14 years I have practiced family law, there have been positive changes. Fathers are finally beginning to be treated more fairly in custody disputes and visitation regimes. Maintenance awards for children, which have been grossly inadequate, are being raised to reasonable and long-awaited levels. Laws are being enacted demanding the responsibility of both parents for the long-term care of their children. Counseling to educate parents on how to minimize the effects of divorce upon their children is now mandatory in some jurisdictions.

Women, over the years, have made considerable strides in the profession, and I look with awe and gratitude at my predecessors who have battled hardships that I, very possibly, would have been unable to endure. There are many benefits to being a female lawyer, yet even in our time, it is not without a price. Many female practitioners forsake the opportunity to have a family because it is viewed as a disruption to the upward climb in their career. Some, like myself, have delayed having children until later in life.

Integrating family with career is not without its complications. Much to the disbelief of my partners, I chose to take a temporary leave of absence after the birth of our second child and after 13 years of full-time practice. Even though my husband and I knew this decision was best for our children and for the smooth functioning of our home – and, in the long run for me as well – still, it was a difficult decision to make. To be considered were financial security, the thrill of the battle, and the sense of accomplishment – all important to one's sense of professional success.

I have subsequently returned to my practice; however, I now work only part time, which allows time for my children. Unfortunately, options this gracious are not available to all women.

It is an understatement to say that I am thankful and humbled by the opportunities that have enabled me to pursue and continue the practice of law.

The greatest lesson I have learned from my career, although handed down in a courtroom of sorts, was not the understanding of a new legal principle or the application of a new statute. Rather, it was an understanding of myself and my most basic strengths and weaknesses as a human being. And through it all has been my mother's admonition: *to whom much is given, much is required* …. Certainly I will never stop.

A combination of intelligence, curiosity, a healthy self-knowledge, spiritual acuity, and high energy coalesce and propel **Beverly Jacobus Brightly (1964)** into life choices by which many within her sphere of influence stand to benefit. Not willing for her abilities to be either undeveloped or unused, Beverly's life reflects authenticity and integrity.

Whatever I have accomplished in life has come from just putting one foot in front of the other. I just did what I felt I had to do in the time and place I had to do it. I walked through doors that I perceived God graciously opened for me, and I walked away from doors that slammed shut in my face.

I can't talk about my life without being somewhat analytical, and also idealistic, because that is who I am. I have come to believe that being intelligent and actually enjoying hard work, are what it takes for a woman to balance all the demands, challenges, and opportunities presented to her in life.

I know God endowed me with extra drive, a penchant for
doing things well, making things right, and giving my best to
anything worth doing. To my way of thinking, He gifted me with
an abundance of empathy to sense what others need, as well as
the ability to organize, and a generous amount of tenacity. Even
as a young child, I remember feeling the needs of others and the
urge to respond and help where I could.

Perhaps I am naïve, but I do believe that a woman can rise
to the top of any field, even those in which she must defy gender
biases. But she will pay a greater price than any man to do so.
She will be called to sacrifice and balance to keep far more "balls
in the air." She may be required to work harder and be better
at what she does. If women have not "broken through the glass
ceiling," or are not making as much or more money than men,
it is not because of their being less capable and conscientious.
Rather, it is because they have not traditionally had the same
goals, the same purposes, or need for the drive, or the consistent
commitment of time necessary to achieve the same goals.

Some women do not wish to further their education or
pursue a professional career. That is fine for them. My concern
is about who we all are inside, that we are working hard and
well at whatever we choose to do. I also believe that whatever
else we women may care to do, our greatest calling, our greatest reason for being, our greatest responsibility is the mothering,
nurturing role. I do not perceive life as a competition between
men and women. There is no inequality in my eyes – only different choices or a combination of choices. To serve has been my
Christian calling.

Work, I believe, is my "love made visible" – hence, my
purpose, my justification. That is not to say that work never feels
dutiful, or is even drudgery at times. But for me it has always
been my positive attitude, my compulsion to organize, to set
priorities and accomplish closure that I utilized in seeking to
meet others needs and dreams. All of this became the expression
of my inner song. *Making a bouquet out of all the flowers within
my reach* became my reason for being, my style of living – and it

never mattered whether anyone noticed or not. I noticed. I think God notices.

The wonderful adventure for me has been that higher education has led me to an ongoing life of learning. My undergraduate education opened up for me a wide new world of knowledge and cultural pursuits, which propelled me to new intellectual heights, but I still had no idea where I was going professionally. Because I loved to "listen with the third ear" and to study society, a double major in psychology and sociology was exciting to me. And when I began to look at graduate schools, I found I could not refuse a full scholarship to New York University, the only requirement being that I specialize my training in the area of disabilities.

Just prior to the birth of my first child, my son, I completed a Master's program in psychology; but I never stopped taking postgraduate courses, and privately I read the course texts on the subjects I felt I had missed whenever I felt the need to know. Ultimately, I completed the Doctorate (in administration/supervision) at Boston College, commuting from the Washington, D.C., area to Massachusetts several times each month for several years, all the while working full time and fully devoting myself to the responsibilities of family, home, and church.

That is not to say that work never feels dutiful, or is even drudgery at times.

The Juris Doctor degree, which I have presently completed, came much later, following the support of my two children through their own postgraduate programs. For me, attending law school came as a result, I think, of spending so much time working with so many State and Federal laws in my government jobs. With the encouragement of my children and other friends, I took advantage of this "window of time" in my life to pursue a legal education. Was it easy? NO! The time, intensity, and expense involved in filling this wee little brain with so much knowledge (while working full time) have provided me with a great challenge and sense of fulfillment.

My "career" path is a much longer story (and there are so many ways to tell it). So much of what I did was based upon where I lived, what my husband was doing at that time, and the practical demands of life and family. The luxury of planning and the advantage of geographic stability were never available to me, since I was married to a man who required a change in his professional commitments about every four years. Thus, lots of moves and changes, with the lessons and growth that come from all that, were constant factors in my professional development.

I entered the world of work when my son was a preschooler. I had never expected to go to work at that time; and, I confess, it was a painful decision for me to leave my child, particularly since it was not entirely voluntary. I went to bed one night in New Jersey, expecting to wake up to a move to upper New York state and the role of a minister's wife, married as I was to a man who had recently completed a Master of Divinity degree and accepted a ministerial position. But, alas, I was instead informed by him that he "would never serve the local church" and had made plans, rather, to attend another graduate program, this time in Boston, with an internship at an educational TV station. Being the accepting and compliant wife that I was, that seemed okay. But, in fact, my life changed overnight and the responsibility for supporting our new little family fell suddenly upon me.

As I had done with my son, I returned to work full time about the time my daughter began preschool. The move to this new job was truly a providential door-opener for me. I rose to the top of the list of candidates for this challenging position and became the first director of special education for a very large and affluent Massachusetts school district. The school superintendent and board had decided to take a chance on me.

I could not be more thankful for what I have, for who I am, from whence I have come, and for where I am going. Above any educational and professional accomplishment, I am most joyful and grateful to have experienced firsthand the challenges of parenthood and the blessing of future generations. In the end, I recognize that it is faith and family that give all else in my life meaning. Finally, I know that seeking God's will is not some great mysterious game of search; but, rather, living before Him, wherever we are "planted," with constancy and love, and passing with duty and fidelity through the doors He opens before us.

Exploring the mix of a demanding profession and her role as wife and mom, **Ruth Dixon Truman (1952)** takes us with her on her journey during the 1970s and forward as she shows us – with gravity and light humor – her life of noteworthy achievement.

Triumphantly I finished my Ph.D. in 1976. I was a UCLA commencement speaker, topping off a four-year journey of both the mind and the freeway. From the town where my husband was pastoring a new church, I had commuted hundreds of miles through Los Angeles traffic, always juggling my schedule around three teenagers and church activities.

A summer internship at the Department of Education in Washington, D.C., came next. I exulted in the responsibilities at the department, and negotiating the maze of city streets on my own. My life was at an apex. I was 45 years old and hitting my stride.

When I returned home, my family was all there to greet me with hugs and kisses and the inevitable query, "What's for dinner, Mom?" There I was, just off the airplane, exhausted from the trip, out of my time zone, and I was expected immediately to put dinner on the table. Inside, I felt crushed.

But, no matter. I would get a job, then everything would normalize. But Proposition 13 had just passed in California, shutting off money to colleges and universities and there were, quite simply, no jobs. Every position I applied for had 100 to 500 applicants, all well qualified, and I had been employed only four years. Why would an employer want to take a risk on a 45-year-old woman with so little experience? Even so, every time I either tied with, or was second to a man, the man was always hired. Less than one percent of college administrators were women then, and most of those were nuns.

The next three years, I did pick up consulting jobs, wrote a book, put in applications, and got older. At the same time, I was going through extreme surgical menopause, so severe that at times I wasn't sure I would ever be able to trust my body again. If that were not enough, my husband was assigned to a new church after a nine-year pastorate, so that ended deep friendships, and at the same time the last of our children left for college.

I fell into desperate depression. My prayers hit the ceiling. I considered taking my life since I didn't seem very valuable anyway. My husband tried to be of help, but I was too immobilized by depression.

Convinced I had misread the Spirit's leading in getting the Ph.D., I decided to enroll in a high school program for women reentering the job market, learn medical transcription, work as a temp, and do freelance writing.

One day the teacher came to my computer station and said there was a secretary's position open at the USC Cancer Center. "Secretary?" I protested. "I've never been a secretary in my life. What would I say?" Her reply was, "You'll think of something, but you really should go for an interview."

Humbled yet again, that night I asked God to take over because I no longer knew what to do, and what seemed like an *audible* voice spoke: "I can't help you if you don't go through the doors I open for you." I was stunned into obedience. The next morning I made an appointment for an interview.

The meeting went well until there came the inevitable question: "So tell me about yourself, your experience … you have a bachelor's degree … that is fine. Anything else?"

Cringing inside, I responded, "Well, I also have a master's in counseling."

"Wonderful!" came the response. "You can help me with my research." Then, "anything else?"

I had stuffed my resume into my purse so I pulled out the wrinkled paper and hesitantly handed it across the desk.

To make a very long story very short, here is the result: My rumpled resume went to the assistant director of the hospital. The following week, I was hired as a part-time hospital administrator at level 7 on a pay scale of 12. About two months later, a job came open at level 9, and my part-time job was folded into this fulltime position. Seven months later, my superior resigned and I was hired to take his place at level 11. When I went in to file the personnel papers, the director said, "You know, this never happens."

But it did. And, there's more.

My husband was appointed to a church farther from my work leaving me with a long commute. About a year later, a rain storm caused me to be on the freeway two-and-a-half hours trying to get to work. When I finally arrived, I phoned my husband and asked him to go to the small, private university close to our home and get applications for two job openings. With that, I was hired as an administrator in the Extension Division – at a raise from my current salary. Two years later, I was promoted to director of all university extension programs. Another two years and I was appointed acting associate vice president in charge of extension, cooperative education, faculty research, and television and media divisions. I had a glorious year of doing everything I knew how to do – all in one job. And though I stepped aside as interim and returned to my prior position for my last year of work, my pension – along with the golden handshake – was based on that one highest paid year.

I shall never forget that voice – loud and clear: "I can't help you if you don't go through the doors I open for you."

❦   ❦   ❦

Open to potentials, receptive to opportunities, and free of restrictive conditionings, **Jewell Reinhart Coburn (1955)** views life as a great and wonderful gift. She has succeeded in climbing professional mountains and gaining meaningful life experiences, and found herself a transitional figure between the norms of the 1950s through the 1990s and those unfolding to women facing the new millennium, with its broader horizons and open options.

❦   ❦   ❦

Life is, to me, a great gift. A gift to be opened, to be explored, to be used, and to learn from … to be respected, held dear, appreciated, and enjoyed.

I can't remember when this thought crystallized in my thinking. I suppose I was rather young. But then, perhaps I grew into the perspective through the natural course of my life, being born to what I call wonderful, "can-do" parents. An engineer father with an excitingly inventive mind and an awesome respect and appreciation for – as he would say repeatedly and with which I resonated deeply – *God first, then others and nature, and myself last.* It was Dad who brought the gift of scientific exploration right into our home, his ideas drawn meticulously on paper and processed into endless rolls of blueprints stacked behind his drafting table, and his experiments stationed in the basement and garage.

Or, for that matter, the influence of an energetic, "learn-by-doing," project-oriented teacher-mom who routinely took over both kitchen and dining room to practice her classroom presentations. Like the heavy cord drawn taut from the chandelier to dining table top and with various weights attached. That day, they were the principles of the block and tackle, the pulley, and the study of balance and fulcrum points. Or, open the oven door expecting to slide in the apple dumplings for supper only to find in it Mom's experiments with papier-mâché or plaster of paris already drying slowly in the oven's low, dry heat.

How could anyone, I have often thought, not benefit from so creative, yet disciplined, an environment … even to the cultivating of our rolling farm land and the care of the livestock? With Dad, as the Sunday School Superintendent, and Mom, as Church School Teacher, I was the beneficiary of their loving biblical instruction in our little village church as well as at home tucked away in the wooded hills of the Ohio Cuyahoga River Valley. Even my education had a multifaceted quality to it. There was the small and provincial, the larger and more urbane, and a third, stronger academic, college prep program.

And, living in that Ohio community that lay just about equidistant from the burgeoning rubber industry of Akron and the thriving steel production in Cleveland back in the '50s made for an atmosphere tingling with creativity and possibility. Open, expansive perspectives grew quite naturally from these environments. Inquiry was invited. Questions were encouraged. Acquisition of knowledge was applauded, and the heady search for new understandings, encouraged. Consideration of biblical precepts was integral to our family discussions … as was putting them into practice via a staunch work ethic and nurtured empathy.

"If it won't work this way, then try it another," was my Mom's stock response to my childish frustrations, routinely followed with her added admonitions, "and don't fail to consider the consequences of your decision," then always the zinger – "and, please, Dear, do be frugal about it."

Life became, to me, a living laboratory – and it still is to this day. I learned early the importance of independent thought, deep devotion, the value of humor, and that taking one's self too seriously could result in needless roadblocks.

As a child of the Great Depression of the 1930s, I learned resourcefulness and the ability to find joy through want … even deprivation. Through the great World War II of the 1940s, there were lessons in man's inhumanity to man juxtaposed with the largeness of the human potential for goodness. There were lessons in walking through insecurities, through fears … lessons in working with life, of utilizing opportunities at hand, of accepting challenge, of turning negativity and limitation into a positive, yet-to-be-realized potential.

That I have been able to add to my vita extensive world travel, including missionary work, and resulting in the study of many of the world's cultures became a natural progression unfolding from early curiosities about other peoples and others' ways. To probe deeply the workings of the human mind and spirit has contributed to my passion to know more about the nature and blessedness of God. That I have been able to add to my resumé considerable research and writing, experience in business, non-profits, and then first, the Vice Presidency, followed by the Presidency of a university follows from the accumulated education and life-experience gained to that point.

I learned methods for balancing family and profession into a cohesive, "work together" unit. And now, as a senior, life for me continues to be a great gift … one that fascinates, and endlessly inspires. It shows itself to me as having qualities capable of replenishing themselves and offering their newness as gifts to be opened with gratitude and joy. In the face of this wonder, I am humbled … and, as always, with child-like awe, I am enthralled.

Events of our youth have the power to color our entire life, but when childhood memories are of a distant and exotic land, one can expect those colorings to be vibrant and deeply felt. **Lisa Curless Ford (1992)** gives us a peek into a culture vastly different from those in which most of her peers were brought up, and which provided experiences that enriched her greatly.

I sat amidst the clutter, rummaging in boxes, leafing through files, day dreaming about the figures in the old photos … girls in white dresses, with black curls and sullen faces. There was the picture of a young (now late) King Hussein of Jordan at 18, barely old enough to drive, carrying the weight of Jordan's monarchy. As I shifted, dust rose from a pile of mattresses where I sat. Against the slope of the ceiling rested the white, iron bed frames that once held these mattresses when those girls in white dresses slept here … back then, this was a boarding school rather than the day school it was now. Sunlight filtered through the dusty window pane and I moved to prop open the window and look outside.

It was June in Ramallah, the Palestinian town where our family had moved when I was seven. We lived on the compound of the Friends Girls School, a 100-year-old school founded by Quaker missionaries who had arrived in dark dresses, on boats, and carried with them the rugged sea trunks that now cluttered the web-woven attic where I spent hours reading and at play.

I looked out the window, down the old, crackled tennis court, past the green iron gate and out over the streets of "Ramallah Down," which was literally the low part of town, at the bottom of the hill and the bottom of the economic ladder. Boys ran in the street, barefoot, rolling a tire with a stick. Chickens cackled, a donkey brayed. Bells rang from the domed Orthodox Church on the corner. "Booza Rukab" sang the ice-cream man, trying to sell the treats in his cart. A few blocks away, "Allah Hu Akbar" echoed from the minaret as faithful Muslims were called to pray.

Memories of our arrival there sifted through my mind … the first night, sitting in the old dining room, laying the starched napkin on my lap, eating honey on flat bread, playing "Survivors" in the fig tree, laying the tile in the garden shed, now our playhouse. Bargaining for bananas under the tents of the food stands. Singing Bob Dylan songs as Becky, the American teacher with the straight, long, brown hair, sat on the floor and played the guitar … our backs to the pot-bellied stove where Jalilah cooked lamb and rice for dinner. Far too many hours had been spent bent over my little "loom" weaving nylon potholders, or under the table-tent reading my "Little House on the Prairie" books and dreaming of the States, now so far away. And hearing the bomb blast as our mayor's car exploded, leaving him handicapped, I learned later.

Again I peeked out the window, smelled the sweet jasmine, its scent carried up from the garden below. We would soon be leaving. Moving back to America, and to home. But this, too, was home and I wasn't sure that I was ready to say "Maa-Sala-ma" … or, "With Peace" … as we boarded that ship in Haifa and set sail toward Athens, and eventually back to Indiana.

From my Arabic reader, I had read many times: "Who am I? I am an Arab. My tongue … that of an Arab. My love … that of an Arab."

According to my passport, I am an American. But in my heart, I think, I hold the heart too, perhaps, of an Arab. Like many of those black-dressed missionaries who came bearing sea chests full of books, clothes, reminders of "home," we too had come. Now we were to leave with those sea chests and all of those treasured memories. The memories of the fig tree, of armored tanks, of Mrs. Hawit, who wrapped my knuckles with her ruler if ever I spoke out of turn in class. Of my little navy blue uniform, of watching our breath trail to the ceiling in winter when we stood beside our desks to say, "Good morning, Miss!" as our teacher entered the room. Of springtime in the Jordan Valley amidst poppies and cyclamen. Of snow sledding on Mt. Hermon. Of camping in the Sinai. Of Easter sunrise service on the back of the Mount of Olives. But mostly … of the attic.

Being subjected to not one, but several, richly diverse cultures as a young person makes for an unusual and wonderful background. In addition, it can serve to expand one's sense of place. **Heidi Halterman Chupp (1986)** reveals her cross-cultural nature with charm, humor, and poignancy.

❦   ❦   ❦

Last night I went to my local Wal-Mart dressed in my two-piece Indian punjabi dress and I spoke to the lady behind the deli counter in Spanish.

I was standing there, waiting for my turkey to be sliced, when two Hispanic ladies came up behind me. They heard me speaking Spanish so joined right in on the conversation.

I had two distinct feelings.

One was a sense of belonging. I felt welcome. I felt included. Talking in Spanish felt familiar, like being at home with an old friend. And at the store I went to before Wal-Mart, the lady who checked me out was from India and she noticed my dress. There was that warm, fuzzy feeling there too.

Moments like these bring fresh realization of how being a missionary kid has influenced my life. My exposure to a variety of cultures has given me a great appreciation for each new one I encounter. For example, I shop at a grocery store that sells lots of Mexican products but caters to all kinds of Asians as well. I often visit a Vietnamese market where I can actually find items I need to make my favorite dishes from Thailand. The little Indian store near my house provides ingredients to make some of my favorite Mediterranean cuisine.

Yet, there is another side to this. Another feeling. It's a sensation of not truly belonging to any one place. Yes, there's a part of me that's familiar and comfortable with various Hispanic cultures – but it only goes so far. And I wasn't raised to be Indian. I've only had a cultural implant.

Standing at the meat counter, a deep sense of joy washed over me, followed by an equally profound loneliness. I felt a part of many cultures without belonging to any, including the culture into which I was born.

Such is the life of many a child of foreign missionaries. What I really grew up in was a culture uniquely different from all others – one that will never truly be duplicated.

So I'm destined to complete my journey with this continual

sense of cultural imbalance – the sensation of not belonging anywhere, yet – in a fragmented sort of way – belonging everywhere. It's a tension I've lived with every day. It's pain – sometimes very deep. And it's joy. What kind of parents would raise their child to be consigned to such a life? Mine . . . and I can't fully describe how glad I am they did.

Despite whatever discomforts I may experience, the benefits far outweigh them. Actually, the discomforts *are* the benefits.

I remember reading the first part of I Peter where Peter writes about living as strangers and aliens. I understood immediately. Jesus never intended for me to get too comfortable in any one place or to feel as if this life was really *home*.

This sense of continual displacement is actually a blessing in my life, I've found. It prods me and pokes me when I might be tempted to settle in and put down my spiritual roots in the wrong place.

When I cry out to God and tell Him, "I don't feel like I belong anywhere," He speaks to my heart and says, "You're right. You don't. Except heaven."

So I will keep traveling on this odd journey of mine. I will wear my Indian punjabi dress and shop at Mexican grocery stores. And I will embrace my non-belonging status and keep on looking and longing for heaven … knowing it's the only place where I fully belong.

Large events, such as nationwide trauma, have the power to shift the thinking of an entire culture. September 11, 2001, will be forever referred to as 9-11. Terrorist attacks on our World Trade Towers in New York City and the Pentagon in Washington, D.C., are etched in our collective memory. **Mary Ellen Gudeman (1964)** tells us of a similar event that gripped us both as individuals and as a nation: Sunday, December 7, 1941. This is the date of the Japanese surprise attack on Pearl Harbor, marking the beginning of World War II.

Is it folly to ask where forgiveness exists in such mayhem? Mary Ellen challenges our thinking on this issue when she takes us into an unforgettable meeting with a man behind the horror.

I knew from various sources that Major Mitsuo Fuchida, the pilot who had led the 1941 Japanese attack on Pearl Harbor on the island of Oahu in Hawaii, was still alive. The word was that his home was not too far from the Osaka-Kobe area where I was serving as a missionary.

By that time, the year was 1971, but still, after 30 years my memories of Pearl Harbor ran deep.

"We're at war!" President Franklin Delano Roosevelt's controlled voice with its New England inflection had spoken out over our radio.

"Mom … Pop …! Listen!" I called, and turned up the volume. In grave tones, the President reported Japan's surprise attack on Pearl Harbor.

An overcast sky and cold wind made us shiver that Sunday, December 7, 1941. President Roosevelt's startling message set an uneasy tone for that day and many to follow.

My brothers and sisters came in and joined us. Tense silence filled the room, and we listened closely.

"Oh, no … Milton …!" Mom said in agonized tones as she listened.

Milton, my older brother, was only 17, a prime choice for the military.

I danced a little jig around the living room and aimed an imaginary gun in the air. "Let's get those Japs," I snarled with vengeance. If only I were a boy. No one seemed to pay any attention to my antics, but in a few days Germany declared war on us, and with our forces involved in both the Far East and European zones, loss of lives quickly mounted. Few families were left unaffected.

Following my high school graduation ceremony in 1943, my mother invited some friends over for cake and ice cream. Among them was Maurice, my brother Milton's buddy. Maurice was soon shipped overseas, and in a short time he lost his life in a flying mission over Germany. We all grieved.

Some of the fellows in my class had enlisted immediately; some waited to be drafted. Although Milton was exempt at first because of farm production necessary to the U.S., eventually he enlisted and was shipped to Hawaii to await further assignment.

The war waged on and my mother was heartsick with worry.

How I longed to help in the cause! While working on a nearby university campus, I often begged my mother to let me enlist in the WAVES, but she flatly refused. So, I contented myself by serving at the local USO Center. There I dated Steve, a sailor whose father, captain of a ship at Pearl Harbor, had lost his life in the December '41 attack.

Later, we learned that one Major Mitsuo Fuchida had been the officer selected to command the first group attacking Pearl Harbor. He was, so it was reported in a magazine we had all read, an ace among aces within the aircraft fleet. As I read this, I felt renewed anger.

Two of my classmates lost their lives. Other close friends never returned. The war waged on. My brother Milton received orders to leave for the Far East.

Eventually the allied forces were victorious in Europe and the war finally came to a close in Japan following the atomic bombs America dropped on Hiroshima and Nagasaki.

But now it was 1971, and I was already too busy with my missionary responsibilities. Reluctantly, I agreed to chair the first Kobe Christian Women's Luncheon. I had come to know that Major Fuchida lived in Nara. I had also read about his conversion to Christianity. With the consensus of the luncheon committee, I wrote, asking if he would be our speaker.

More than 500 ladies attended our first luncheon in the Kobe Oriental Hotel. Major Fuchida was the featured speaker and he told about his war experiences and his marvelous conver-sion later. As he had led 360 planes toward Hawaii, he told the audience, his only concern was in achieving a military success for his country. At 7:49 a.m., he uttered those fatal words, tora, tora, tora (tiger, tiger, tiger – the code for "we have succeeded in surprise attack"), bombers had shelled their targets below.

He was jubilant, he said, when he learned of the widespread destruction and hundreds of sudden deaths: eight battleships hit in the harbor, 3,077 U.S. Navy personnel killed or missing and 876 wounded, 226 American soldiers killed and 396 wounded.

I sat listening to Major Fuchida, recalling that day so many years before and my outburst of childish hatred as I danced a jig in our living room.

He went on to tell us about the discouragement that came later when the tide turned and eventually the war ended with the atomic bomb attack on Hiroshima and subsequent surrender of his country.

He shared how he had eventually met an American pilot, Jake DeShazer, who had flown in the Jimmy Doolittle Squadron in a surprise raid on Tokyo and who became a prisoner of war. DeShazer, later released, had returned to Japan as a missionary. His hatred had turned to love.

Major Fuchida told us that after reading DeShazer's pam-phlet, "I was a Prisoner of Japan," he felt motivated to read the Bible. As he read, he came to Luke 23:34, the prayer of Jesus Christ at His death: "Father, forgive them; for they know not what they do." At that moment, he realized this prayer had been for him. He met the Lord Jesus for the first time, and his life was changed.

Later, after Major Fuchida finished his talk, and we were about to enjoy our luncheon, he took his place at the main table. I looked over at him sitting there next to me and I couldn't help but think to myself: *Those are the hands that held the mike and those are the lips that ordered, "All squadrons, plunge in to at-tack!" followed by those fatal words, "tora, tora, tora!"*

I could never have known that someday, far into the future, I would come to know this man, not as an anonymous, terrorizing enemy, but as my brother in Christ. Sitting next to me was one of those "Japs" for whom I had felt such hatred as a teenager!

Father, thank You for forgiving us both.

*Ed. – The above firsthand experience is reprinted by permission of Mary Ellen Gudeman and appears in her book of personal life experiences, *Survival of the Unfit* (Xlibris Corporation, U.S., 2001, pp. 213-217).

The horizons of **Barbara Rioux Novak's (1952)** world stretch far outward, and the life options she has chosen have taken her on a journey compatible with her independence, resourcefulness, and pioneering spirit. Through Barb, we are transported into a way-of-life filled with challenge and majesty.

The lake was magical this past week. The full moon brought back the old camp song so much a part of me, "…across the silver lake, the moonlit ripples break, their path a magic highway seems."

It is this mental picture, and many others, that I try to impress on my mind and make a part of my memories so they'll be easily recalled when I might no longer be here. For example, when I close my eyes, I see myself crunching my way across the ice last winter when the temperature hovered around 10 degrees. Or the music the ice makes as it freezes and expands – the thunderous booms, the fragile tinkling. Or the north wind that can be so strong that even wearing snowshoes, all of us living here on the Presque Isle have to walk with our backs to the wind.

So I think back over my life and how I arrived on this

beautiful island in north central Wisconsin that lies about 70 miles from Lake Superior. My island lies in a three-lake chain, is spring fed, and excellent for fishing.

One Victor Streator homesteaded this island sometime back around 1907, so our local history tells us. The island slopes somewhat to the west and is covered with great old trees. Getting to the mainland requires a boat and navigable waters. During the frozen-in months, which we call our "marooning time," I tend to hunker down and stay put, secure in my island home.

But, I'm straying from my story about the chain of events that brought me to this remote place of unending beauty. What I recall vividly is a trip to the Ford Hospital in Detroit. I was about five. The problem was that my parents noticed I tended to turn my head to the left to see to the left. After the medical examination, we were told that I had scar tissue on the retina of my eyes. It

So I think back over my life and how I arrived on this beautiful island in north central Wisconsin that lies about 70 miles from Lake Superior.

covered the central vision in my left eye and narrowly missed the central vision in my right eye. Either then, or later, we learned the scarring was caused by a parasite called toxoplasmosis. My family had a cat and my mother must have had an active case while she was pregnant with me. We were told I would probably be unable to go to college or drive a car.

As it turned out, I had only a few problems in elementary school. Admittedly, I didn't like having to sit within the first three rows of all my classrooms, and I certainly didn't enjoy being called "Four Eyes" because I wore glasses.

When I was in the 5th grade, I joined Campfire Girls and the next year joined Girl Scouts. These experiences changed my life. From Girl Scouting, I learned outdoor and survival skills and developed my great love and respect for nature. Later, I worked as a camp counselor and even at a camp in Bavaria, Germany.

Back when I was in high school, my mother taught me to drive when I was 14 years old and I have been driving ever since. That took care of that early medical prognosis. And, as far as being told I would be unable to attend college, I determined to overcome that one as well. As it turned out, I not only completed college, I obtained my teaching credential. For many years I worked both as a camp counselor and as a school teacher. It was during high school that I learned more about my visual limitations. But I also learned to compensate. I tried to play outfield on the softball team. What I found was that I could bat fine, but when the balls were hit into the left field, I couldn't catch any. I was devastated. Later, when I studied college psychology, I learned that I had no depth of field. Therefore, I could not see where the ball was. But at around the same time, what I found I could do well was swimming and water sports, as well as basketball, and even though I was not a first-string player, I felt comfortable with what I came to know I could do well.

Someplace along the course of my young adult years, I had still another life-changing experience. A devastating relationship propelled me to reevaluate my spiritual thinking. What helped me greatly was a lay minister's correspondence course together with a woman pastor for whom I had great respect. While working on this course, I sensed the divine message that the measure of my inner difficulties was the degree to which I was my own harshest self critic. Namely, I was not laying hold of the available forgiveness to be found in God, but rather, I was punishing myself as though I were my own judge and even executioner. I had, unfortunately, usurped a role that was clearly not mine and as such, I was meting out to myself, my own self-judgment and therefore my own misery.

Following this time of enlightened understanding, I was able to move forward with my life. Soon after this, I met the man who would become my husband and together we set out on a life that was in harmony with the love we both held for nature.

My husband taught me how to hunt quail and he showed me how to shoot water moccasins and rattlesnakes in Florida. We hunted grouse and woodcock in Wisconsin. We water skied. We took canoe trips. We snowmobiled. When our twins came along, we taught them our skills. We added paddle boating, sailing, and kayaking to our lives.

Two English pointer dogs are very much a part of our family. They took to pulling a plastic sled across the ice when I didn't use the snowmobile so I took the cue and bought a kick sled used in dog sledding. Now here was a dog sled they really loved to pull. When I get out the harnesses, they couldn't be more excited.

But I'd be the first to say that island living is not for everyone. Take last year, for example. The temperatures plummeted to –20 degrees and my furnace went out. For two nights there was no central heat to keep the water pipes from freezing. I had to use the kitchen stove and my ceramic heaters to coax the chill away. With minimum snow cover and extremely low temperatures, most everyone on the island lost either the function of their septic tank or their water line. For me, my loss was my water line on the one and only night I didn't run water through the system in the middle of the night. What I'd like to do is retrench for my water line, dig deeper, then heap more dirt on it and maybe some straw for still more insulation. One thing I know I mustn't do is to use hay instead of straw because the deer will turn it into a meal.

I returned home one afternoon to find both dogs with their faces full of porcupine quills. So, considering the 70-mile trip to the vet, a neighbor and I set about the task of removing the quills. And then there are extra dry cells, gasoline, 12-volt light bulbs and first aid supplies. In fact, I have so many supplies that a neighbor called me the other evening hoping I had a pair of crutches which, unfortunately, my first aid equipment did not include. But her question got me to thinking ….

In this glacial moraine area, it is said one could find diamonds. I have never found any, but I have found ink wells, and bottles from the island's resort days back in the '20s, and the occasional red agate. And there are deer and bears. They will

occasionally swim across to the island, but the dogs have their
ways for letting them know the island is not for them.

It has been 10 years now since my husband first went to the
care facility, followed then by his passing. Sure, I could move
to the mainland but I don't mind being here. I actually enjoy the
days from November through April when the ice is freezing or
breaking up and I am marooned on the island. After all, I have
a phone, and a computer, and a stock of food. I have someone
to collect my mail. I have help winterizing the motors, turning
over the utility boats, putting up the jet ski and the ski boat, and
hauling in the raft. The pontoon boat is pulled up on shore and its
battery taken inside. I have chainsaws, a garden tractor, a wood
splitter, extra paddles, and flashlights, tarps and tie-downs.

And when the weather turns, I sit in the lee of my favorite
tree and listen to the sounds of approaching spring. One definite sign are the rings of bare ground around the base of large
trees. I marvel at the thought that a tree produces that much
heat. And the hemlock grove where the boughs are so thick that
nothing else can grow under their canopy until a tree dies. And

the birches. And the basswood. And the huge tree trunks
scarred from lightning strikes. And the eagles and loons.
And I am amazed at how I can hear and identify with all
that is around me. Everything has its own language, its
own message for a receptive ear and an open heart. The
limitations of my vision since my youth have only served
to open me to more than I could ever have dreamed back
then when my parents first took me to that Detroit hospital.
Or later when I was rejected for a job teaching overseas, or
when I was not accepted as a missionary – all because of
my vision, I was told. And there's the whisper through the trees
when the wind blows and the mournful song of the loon. How
can I not be moved, or not take courage, or not find solace from
all that surrounds me? And I can't help but think with serenity
and gratitude that indeed, while not in every place across this old
globe, but certainly in this one sacred spot, surely "God's in His
Heaven; and all's right with the world."

————————————— ❦ ❦ ❦ —————————————

STRAINS IN THE NIGHT

Like the weird celestial music of the wind
Around the corner of the house.
Strains in the night
Fanciful, lyrical, melancholy strains from nowhere –
Strains from everywhere –
I caught them with my pen;
They taught me life.

Esther Lewis
The Taylor *Echo,* January 21,1943

QUESTIONS TO PONDER

Alone or in a group, here are some questions to consider:

1)   How does your present way of life utilize your greatest talents?

2)   What interests, curiosities, and abilities are yet to be realized?

3)   Explain ways in which your present way of life contains a high quotient of satisfaction and/or stimulation.

4)   In what ways do you balance the Christian calling to self-sacrifice and generosity toward others with the inclination to express freely your unique talents?

5)   List the qualities you are called upon to utilize when interacting with and contributing to the broader world.

MY COMPANION JOURNAL

1)   Return to your life graph constructed for Chapter 1. Look for life influences that contributed to your ultimate choice of lifestyle and/or profession.

2)   Was this influence largely from within your family, from outside your family, or a mix?

3)   What obstacles, barriers, or other hurdles have you encountered that caused you to rethink your dominant life choices? Do you perceive that any of these road blocks or detours have had a positive component? Do you perceive that any tended to thwart the development of your authentic self or that you still feel defeated?

4)   What ways may effectively assist you to enjoy further progress in your life?

5)   Have you unutilized gifts or talents for which the world is waiting?

VENERABLE VOICES/ MODERN MESSAGES

They will still bear fruit in old age, they will stay fresh and green, proclaiming, "The Lord is upright; he is my Rock, and there is no wickedness in him." Psalm 92:14-15 NIV

The year 1846 marks the founding of Fort Wayne Female College that was to become Taylor University in 1890. Throughout those years and forward, the voices of women speak to the universality of shared life concerns, which persist across time and circumstance. Messages from the heart and mind transcend historical and cultural shifts.

Editor's Note: Due to the abundance of valuable writings by women from the past and available in the Archives of Taylor University, more than could be included in this already comprehensive study, the Editors have prepared a supplement titled: *Authentic Voices: Addendum 2004: Women of Insight Speak from the Past.* This enlarged compendium is designed to delight the reader interested in learning more about these outstanding women and to assist future researchers as they undertake the otherwise arduous journey backward in time in search of women's voices.

*W*hen one thinks of institutional archives, of library stacks and special tucked-away coves housing historical books and papers, the smell of dust – even the hint of mustiness – may come slyly to the nostrils. Even the mouth may go unexpectedly dry. *Life-past* seems a dead thing to many. In the absence of a pulsating life-force, of what value is it? Flaccid. Empty. Decaying. Value-less.

If this is how you tend to view the past, the present chapter is sure to change and delight you. Perhaps we could extrapolate from the theory expressed in physics that matter is neither created nor destroyed. Perhaps we might boldly apply the essence of this concept to thought and feeling – in this case, thoughts and feelings communicated through the

Life-past seems a dead thing to many. In the absence of a pulsating life-force, of what value is it?

written word that can have the capacity to outlive the writer and remain accessible down through time.

Rather than confine the contents of this book to the experiences of women speaking exclusively to shared, contemporary life challenges, we have chosen to honor the nearly 160-year history of women affiliated with Taylor University and its predecessor, Fort Wayne Female College dating from 1846. *Authentic Voices*, therefore, offers a first-of-its-kind forum for Taylor women no matter when they appeared in the timeline of history. Just as the voices of the many generous women still living, including our earliest contemporary writer, **1938** graduate **Hazel Butz Carruth Anderson**, are given a vehicle for expression within chapters one to five, so also have we invited, through research into the university archives and many other sources, the voices of women past.

As you turn each page, read each word and message, you will surely begin to enter into many of the life challenges faced by those who preceded you. You will become fascinated, as were the editors, with the ease in which one might develop a sense of kinship with Taylor women past. As the personalities of these dear women emerge from the words they left behind, there can be the unconscious inclination to begin referring to them by their first names. Even to wonder if they were living in our present era would they be our wonderful friends, caring mentors, or colleagues with whom we might interface, share, bond, stimulate and challenge one another to the betterment of all?

You will be delighted by their humor, moved by their concerns, and inspired by the life challenges they confronted. You will soon be referring to the **1910** Taylor University graduate and long-time Taylor faculty member, **Sadie Louise Miller**, as Sadie, the young woman with the charming and moving way with words. From as far back as the early 1900s, her voice, through her poetry, invites the reader to come with her – as in the following poem – to that place she has found that quiets and nurtures the heart:

> I strolled along a common walk one day –
> A roadside where the people hurry by;
> And there I saw the weeds along the way,
> Begrimed with dust, but growing rank and high.
> Men walked with cautious mien and haughty air,
> And women held their skirts in sheer recoil;
> Afraid to come too near while passing there,
> For fear the smirching dust might stain or soil.
>
> I turned and plucked a work of Nature's art,
> Shook off the dust and marveled at the grace,
> While clusters grouped around a tiny heart
> Of purple velvet – dainty Queen Anne's lace.
> Such wondrous things by daily roadpaths hide
> To thrill the heart of him who turns aside.[1]

***The Uncommon Common*, Sadie Louise Miller 1910**

Or move forward in history to the voice of **Grace Olson 1927**. Her heartfelt words are as elevating and ennobling as when they were first written from the depths of her own personal yearning:

How I have longed to find for Him
Who's done so much for me
A worthy gift of His great love,
Who brought salvation free.

O, for a jewel to mirror back,
Within its living rays,
Thanksgiving for the love with which
He guides me through the days.

Though jewels are cold, they do their best
To show their love for Him;
Proclaiming to the world about
The Lamb which saves from sin.

My life with errors seems so dark,
O, God, how can'st Thou shine
To show the world Thy wondrous gift
Through this poor life of mine?

O, Master, take my life and make
A jewel to shine like fire;
That Thou through me can'st show to all
The Christ Who lifts from mire.

I care not, Lord, how great the cost
To polish or to grind,
If I to others then may point
The Lord they seek to find.

> As jewels shine, though in the dark
> And show their rays so bright;
> Let me, I pray, somewhere for Thee
> Turn darkness into light![2]
> ***A Prayer,* Grace Olson 1925**

We are indeed fortunate to have access to the actual words of these women because prior to the current decade of the 1990s and early years of the new millennium, the voices of women were less accessible. Social customs discouraged the expression of the female mind and heart, and custom muffled any outpourings of a highly personal nature. But, times have changed. National and world events – perhaps most notably the catastrophic felling of the World Trade Center towers in New York and the attack on the Pentagon in Washington, D.C., that emblazon the date 9-11-2001 in our collective consciousness – have served to unblock our previously reserved natures. The high sense of rugged individualism so respected among our forebears is weakening. In its place, an inclination toward brotherhood – and sisterhood – is taking a new form. To hold our pain tightly to our chests and suffer in solitary silence will soon seem quaint, an emotionally outdated and no longer appropriate inclination. Increasing recognition and acceptance of our common humanity is drawing us ever closer together.

As we step backward into history, knowing what we do of the reserve of those who came before us, we can be that much more appreciative of our opportunity to peek over the shoulder into those very private lives lived years ago.

Editor's Note: For additional biographical information on many of the women whose actual words appear in this Chapter, we refer you to Winquist, Dr. Jessica L. and Dr. Alan H., *God's Ordinary People: No Ordinary Heritage*, Upland, Indiana: Taylor University Press, 1996.[3]

A DISTANT, SOLITARY VOICE: 1848

Rare is the privilege to make our way back to within only two years of the founding of Fort Wayne Female College in 1846, and there to read the actual words of student **Susan Davis Marsters Smith (1848)**. Six personal letters, written by Susan to her husband while she was a student attending Fort Wayne Female College are available in the Taylor University Archives. Due to the space constraints of the present publication, the Editors have selected two of the six letters for inclusion.

We are indebted to both Taylor University Professor, Dr. Robert Lay, who obtained the following personal letters and generously made them available to *Authentic Voices,* and we thank the Lilly Library, Indiana University, Bloomington, Indiana, for their courtesy in granting permission to reprint the transcripts of the letters together with their introductory material.

❧   ❧   ❧

Letter #1. October 28th, 1848: Susan D. Smith to her husband Hezekiah Smith

Susan D. Marsters Smith's (1819-1905) first letter written home to her husband, Hezekiah Smith (1805-1879), in Greencastle, Indiana, is sent after arriving by a canal boat in Fort Wayne. Susan begins her studies at the Fort Wayne Female College (later known as Fort Wayne College, 1855, and finally as Taylor University, 1890). It was unusual for a woman to attend college in the middle 19th century in Indiana (opportunities were limited), especially if the woman was 29 years old and married. Susan's decision to attend college seems understandable in light of the fact that her husband's ministry as a Methodist circuit rider kept him away from home at least three weeks out of every month. These letters were, of course, never intended for publication; unconventional spelling and grammar is left uncorrected in these

manuscripts. Clarifications are enclosed in parentheses. This first
letter sketches out many details relating to the college's schedule,
staff, curriculum, and costs, and also hints at a Protestant view of
Catholicism (see also Letter #4).

Fort Wayne, Allen County, Oc(t) the 28th 1848

Very Dear Husband

I have just received your letter which I have anxiously
looked for, for the last three weeks. Lois and I have been very
uneasy to hear from you and Mr. Bacon's family. Lois has written four letters to her father and has not received a line from
home. We were left as you know at the hotel. We remained there
until after breakfast then we came here and handed Mr. Johnson
your note. He read it and told us that he would do the very best
for us that he could and so he has. He went and hired a dramen
to fetch our trunks. Our bills at the hotel was 50 cents each.
Lois and I went to a store and got a luster dress patron (pattern?)
apeace for which we paid $5.25 for each patron. I got shoes and
aprons and paper and ink and flannel and soap for washing my
things and we got candles together. We have to pay 12½ (cents?)
per pound. Lois got what she wanted then we went to work sewing our things and we also washed up all the close we had durty.
We was very busily engaged until College commenced then paid
our tuition and incidental expenses. I had to get a new Latin
grammar and a Latin reader and Blair Rhetoric and a slate. This
quarter of college is eleven weeks long. The year is now divided
into quarters (,) four quarters in a year. This quarter will close
on the tenth of December. There will not be any vacation until
the year closes, that will (be) about the last of July. There will
be a holiday between Christmas and New Years. I have paid my
board for this quarter which was 15 dollars, my tuition 5.37*, my

books, slates, and paper was some over 3 dolars. I have but very
little left over after paying for my things. I got a cheap bonnet, it
cost something near 6 dolars. I only got wat I could no do without. I am well pleased with the College and all that is connected
with it but being to much crowded, the new building is not yet
done nor won't be this winter. It will be when done about twice
as large as Greencastle College**. It commands a beautiful view
of the St. Mary's River near to Mr. Edsel's.*** It will when finished accommodate all together one hundred students. We number about one hundred and five students. There are twenty six
that board in the college. Professor Hustess and baby(?)and child
boards with us in the Stuards Hall.**** We have good boarding
here. I think that brother and sister Johnson are first rate people.
I have become acquainted (with) brother Wilson and family. I
think that he is an excellent minister and the best historian I ever
heard. Our president is a minister. I think him a very good man.
His name is Round. He and Pr(ofessor) Hustess do all the teaching except a few classes that Mrs. Hustess hears that is in the
preparatory and college departments. There is a lady teaching the
primary department and one that teaches music. There are forty
four music scholars. We have two societies in college. One is
called the Philamathean and the other the Philosophian. Lois and
I belong to the Philamathean. We have to write and read every
two weeks(,) one society one week and the other the next week.
Our society read(s) Thurs. Last Wednesday for the first time in
my life I read my composition in public. You can guess whether
I was embarrassed or not. It was the eighth anniversary of our
wedding day that I stood before the President of Fort Wayne
Female College***** and read or tried to read my composition.
No one is excused from writing or reading their compositions.
The faculty is very strict with all. They draw us rite to the mark
in every particular. This is what I like. I think that I am improv-
ing sloly in my studies. I have three (classes) Latin, algebra and
rhetoric. I parse in the class that parses in Polisky (?) Course of
Time (booktitle?). I wish that you would send Polisky (?) Course
of Time to me by S.C. Chooper (?) if you can it is among our

books. I have seen a man from Marshall County. He is by the name of Thomson. He came here to visit some of his relations and to bring his daughter to college. He told me that Charles B. Marsters was married. He said that my _________? were all well and uncle Martin (?) and his family has moved from Ohio and settled in Marshall County. Lois and I went the firs(t) Sabbath after we came here to the Catholic Church. We nearly strained our eyes a looking at things that we never seen have before. Two of brother Johnson's hired girls are Catholic so we eat Catholic cooking. Lois has gone out shop(p)ing this evening and I cannot wait for her to come and write. If I do my letter will not go out tonight. I would have written sooner but you did not tell me to write first therefore I thought that you would (have) writ(t)en sooner. I have been very uneasy for the last two weeks until received your letter. That was about 1 or 2 hours before I commenced this. I wish that you would write every two weeks at least. The girls here have letters every week here from home. Lois has taken a hard cry since your letter came to hand because she could not get one from home. She has had one Eli since she has been here. I believe that I have in some kind of way told you all I know that you will criticize this letter I know that you will find a plenty of room for criticism. I hope that as this is the first letter I every wrote to you that you will excuse as far as possible the errors. No more at this time. I remain your affection wife until death.

To H(ezekiah) Smith

Susan D. Smith

Letter #2. February 23rd, 1849: Susan D. Smith to Hezekiah Smith
This letter sheds light on travel to and from the college and matters of curriculum and testing. It also hints about religious life at

the college as well as the challenge of life and study away from
home in the 19th century, including both physical illness (chick-
en pox) and homesickness.

Feb(ruary) 23rd, 1849
Fort Wayne Female College

Very Dear Husband

I have received your letter which I read with pleasure but
was sorry to hear that you were uneasy about the small pox. I
informed you about that in my last (letter), my health is as good
as new with the exception of _______and Lois is well and has at
last received a letter from her father and one from Nancy and her
mother. Our examination is to commence next Tuesday and on
Wednesday evening we are to have an exhibition and that will
close this quarter. I informed you in my last letter what my intentions were concerning my going home to see you. I informed
you that the calculation was for Lois and I to go home with Mary
Rus(s)ell as soon as the boats commenced running. If we should
change our notions in reference to this agreement I will let you
know in my next (letter). Mary Rus(s)ell is very anxious for me
to go to her fathers with her and have you come there for Lois

and myself. I am anxious to be with you and think that
nothing but death will ever separate us as long again. I am
anxious to find myself ready to step on the boat, but sor(r)y
to leave this institution and its advantages. I have become
warmly attached to many that I have become acquainted
with since I came here a stranger. Brother Willson and
family is well and brother "W" is just as good a preacher
as ever. His quarterly meeting commenced last night so we
have meeting, examination and exhibition all most of the
time. Brother Cooper from Green Castle came here this
evening and will remain, and I sup(p)ose till af(ter) the exhibi-

tion. I have be(e)n trying for some time to write but have made poor progress for there has been several girls in my room talking. They have just left the room as it is bedtime and retired to their own beds and Lois is in bed and I am writing and want to finish this so that it will go tomorrow in the mail. I expect a letter next mail in answer to my last (letter) to you. I suppose you are aware that I kneed money but I do not h(ope) you will send it unless by mail. Do not send much at a time by mail if you should send it in that way. I think if the wether should continue as it is for two week(s) the boats will commence running. Then you may expect to see your Yanke(e) wife and be troubled with many questions from her as you know she is very inquisitive. She thinks of teaching a school and commencing the 2nd or 3rd week of April. You will oblige her ver(y) much if you can secure a good situa-tion for her in the country. Brother Johnson appears to be ver(y) for Lois and I to leave. Lois has become very anxious for the time to come when we will start home. Her father did not write anything of much importance, only that if she wanted more funds she must let him know or he would send a check on the bank as that would be the only safe way. He hinted at some things in his letter that you told us about, Ha. Lois has wrote the conclud-ing letter to Eli. I bring my scattered remarks to a close as it is late. Write as soon as you get this. Excuse this unconnected letter. I have never studies as hard in my life as I have the last two weeks. I have to be examined in the five books of Roman history that I have read in Latin and I dre(a)d it more than my algebra but tomorrow and Monday will wind up my studying for this quarter. Then if I could I would see you in three days. But enough of this. I remain your affectionate wife until death. Susan D. Smith to Hezekiah Smith.

This has been writ(t)en in a hur(r)y and by the light of a poor dim candle.[4]

Voices of Humor and Whimsy ...

Humor lightens and disarms. Healthy humor, free of ridicule or sarcasm, has a power to render a curse illusory, to dismantle the forces of the negative, and to catalyze the power of the positive. Humor defuses. Humor elevates. Humor shifts the train of thought abruptly and delightedly to the unexpected. The women from Taylor University's past whose writings were found in archives and other obscure locations show us that humor was a part of their lives, just as surely as it is meaningful to us now.

For starters, the demanding activity of writing – putting one's thoughts and experiences into a written form interesting and readily understood by the reader – is a shared challenge across the ripples of time. Just as many of the contemporary writers whose pieces appear in the first five chapters of this book admittedly wrote and rewrote their works to achieve the highest level of clarity of thought and written expression, so the same feat posed similar demands on women-past. Notice, for example, how **Sadie Louise Miller (1910)**, who became a seasoned poet, reveals her own struggles with words and ideas.

Sadie arrived at Taylor University as a student in 1908 with an already impressive career as a teacher of piano and voice. Upon completing two degrees in music at Taylor, she became a faculty member in 1910 and continued her teaching career with the university for 40 years. In addition to her position in the Department of Music, Sadie developed a solid reputation as a poet, with several published collections listed for reader interest in the *NOTES* at the end of the chapter. Although the greatest number of her poetic works are of a serious, inspirational nature, selected poems included here demonstrate her charming sense of humor and her delicate dance of words.

In the following poem, Sadie delights us with her cheeky, charming, poetic considerations of the tough stuff of writing. Fresh and relevant to us now, such poems could have been written by her this very morning.

IT CAN BE DID

I have just laid me down, pillows under my head,
For I can write better while lying in bed.
For weeks I've been trying to grapple a thought;
It will not be begged, hired, rented or bought.
So I said, "Though ideas have flown clear away,
I must write, though I've nothing whatever to say."
Then I closed tight my eyelids and racked my poor
brain
To see if good Muse would not come once again.
If someone would only a subject suggest –
That's always the hard part – I'd do all the rest.
But titles and themes followed Muse in her flight –
I wonder whose pen she is pushing tonight.
I'll guess she is visiting Barton Rees Pogue,*
And he is just hanging right to her – the rogue!
And out he will come with the spiffiest poem -
Well, let him go to it, I'm just going to show 'em
That I can write too, and without Mistress Muse,
Or rhyme book, or synonyms – What is the use?
With a half hour, a tablet, eraser, and lead,
I've a sheet filled plumb full, and who cares what
was said![5]

Editor's Note: Barton Rees Pogue, an Indiana poet of considerable reputation, was graduated from Taylor University in 1918 and later returned as a professor in the Department of English.

Jessica L. Lohnge entertains us through the following excerpt of a longer article appearing in the Taylor *Echo*, May 1, 1916, with her outrageous and charming consideration of the role played by idiomatic expressions in communication down through history.

Slang

Slang, according to my dictionary, is low, vulgar, unauthorized language; popular cant; or jargon of some particular class in society.

Slang has existed through all ages. Back through the centuries to Shakespeare's time; Shakespeare himself uses slang that was popular in his day, and there are many others to be found. Back to Caesar and Cicero; that it is found again and no doubt Adam and Eve "chewed the rag" at the beginning of creation; and when Abel tried to put one over on his brother, Cain slugged him once in the belfry with a beam.

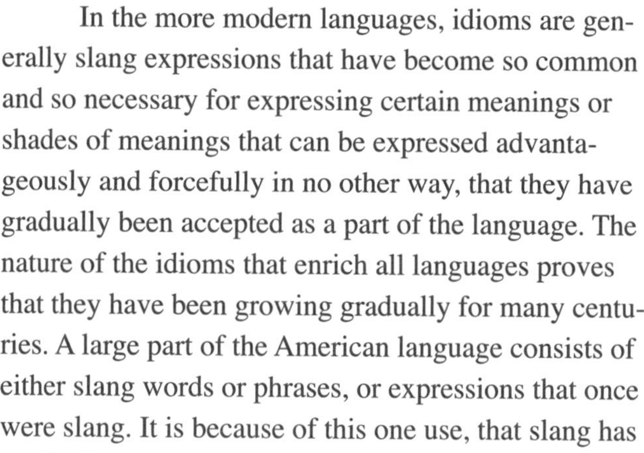

In the more modern languages, idioms are generally slang expressions that have become so common and so necessary for expressing certain meanings or shades of meanings that can be expressed advantageously and forcefully in no other way, that they have gradually been accepted as a part of the language. The nature of the idioms that enrich all languages proves that they have been growing gradually for many centuries. A large part of the American language consists of either slang words or phrases, or expressions that once were slang. It is because of this one use, that slang has its greatest value.[6]

Fernmae Goyings (1916, according to 1915 Taylor *Gem*) collapses time and circumstance into a breath of whimsy as real to us today as the experience was to her, all of nine decades ago. Who of us has passed through life untouched by the pressures associated with our nation's emphasis on universal education? And who has escaped the jitters associated with meeting deadlines and acing tests?

The Test

One evening I sat in my study
When the cares of day should be o'er
With a book lying open before me,
Page after page to devour.

The clock that sat on the mantel
Was ticking the hours away
And shadows thro' the window were creeping
Which warned of the on coming day.

I fumed, I worried and fretted,
The books were piled o'er the floor,
The leaves were stained and crumpled
As though they had been thro' the war.

I tried but in vain to find solace
I tried but in vain to find rest
For everywhere thro' the silence
Came the icy whisper "Test."

It came from the remotest corner
It came from the one easy chair
It fanned my cheek with hisses
It filled the fresh balmy air.

The time flew faster and faster
The hour for the test grew near,
I buckled and rebuckled my armor,
And did penance with many a tear.

I marched bravely out to the battle
That terrible Waterloo!

Faced the cannons and muskets bravely
E'en tho' the air was blue.

The shells came faster and faster
The smoke grew black and thick
My brain seemed whirling and dizzy
I grew faint, weary and sick.

'Tis over, the battle is finished.
Am wrinkled and bow'd as with cares,
But the test in algebra is finished
Under our professor – Dean Ayres.[7]

Inez Miles (1921) spirals back in time, holding fast to the thread of wonder and asks those still further into history even more remote than Inez is to us, to enlighten her as to how it is that they could produce writings of such mastery? What she tells us she learns from those in ancient time is as fresh and applicable to Inez in her day as it is to us today.

Inez served as President of the Student Senate during the academic year of 1921, and returned to teach in the Taylor University Department of History beginning in 1922.

INSPIRATION OR WORK?

Was Virgil, when he wrote his tale of old,
Inspired by glows of morning's purple light
Sent by Aurora, chasing shades of night?
Did Jupiter in clouds of glory hold
That soul, and words of gods to him unfold?
Were meter, words and style disclosed aright
Without the poet's care and oversight?

And were they naught but what the muses told?
"Ah, no, not so:" an echo answers through
The avenues of time. But as a bird
Doth build her downy nest, he wrought it line
By line. It was a labor long and true
Which he carved each thought, which set each jeweled word
And bore at last that child of master mind.[8]

Dorothy Freese (1928) offers an example of humor at its most charming when she dabbles with the unexpected. Dorothy reveals that not only young folks, but authority figures as well – in this case, a professor of English – can have a witty turn of mind.

The Most Embarrassing Moment in My Life

It happened in my first year at a school in town. The characters involved were myself, awkward and newly arrived from the country, and a certain English and History teacher. I had spent the week-end at my home in the country and had returned on Monday morning. I had failed to write the required English theme for that day and had nearly decided not to go to school at all.

But, at last, I decided in favor of going and I hurried up the steps as the last bell was ringing. I started up with a run, hop, skip and jump, and was almost successful at taking three steps at a time when the wrong thing happened. I caught my toe; then fell on the stairs and went rolling and bumping down until I struck something which stopped my descent. Looking up, to my chagrin I discovered that the object that had stopped me was none other than my English teacher.

When we arose from the floor, I meant to say "Excuse me."

However, I was so confused that I said, "Thank you!" instead.
Gratitude for the accidental halt was not uppermost in my mind
just then!

The teacher did not seem very friendly and conversational
so we proceeded to the class in silence. When the themes were
being taken up I was seized with sudden inspiration. The day being the first day of April, I printed in large letters across a theme
sheet, "APRIL FOOL," folded two or three sheets with it and
handed it in.

A week later the teacher read some of the worst papers and
gave her corrections. At the last, to my embarrassment, she read
my paper and remarked that it was excellently done except that
I needed a severe hint on etiquette. She then told me that name
cards should be smaller and **engraved**, not **printed!**[9]

… And Then, the Ubiquitous Gender Issues

Gender issues are as old as the world itself, it would seem.
The following poems and essays voice opinions held by early
women writers. The selections are fascinating not only in the

force that comes through their words, but by the number of
pieces whose writers seek anonymity, as well as entries for
which no author is given. **R.M.**, for example, takes a strong
initial position in her poem, "Our Aim," Taylor *Echo*, **1918**.
Her first three stanzas are a clarion appeal for women to be
seen as having a just and important place in the scheme of
human creation. R.M.'s sixth stanza becomes charged when
she states, "Then men will awaken to the error they made
when they thought that to rule was our aim." R.M. then
expands her consideration of what she sees to be a twisted
relational psychology, "It is not their place we are striving
to grace, but to love and serve on their plane."

❧   ❧   ❧

"Let the women keep silent,"
Was said; they obeyed.
But the world has made progress since then.
We have shown long ago
We can do and can know,
And we've proved as efficient as men.

Some say we are missing
Our purpose and sphere;
That we're leaving our God-given throne:
We were made in this life
But to be some man's wife
And know nothing outside of the home.

In this they're mistaken,
As soon they shall see;
We're not leaving our place to God's plan.
But we wish to become,
In the world, in the home,
What God meant us for: equals with man.

For a helpmate He made us
And so shall we be,
When the world recognizes our place;
Equality's charm
Will do us no harm,
But will add a more beautiful grace.

When the world is attracted
By beauty of heart,
And a face has less value than soul,
When natures are kind
And mind copes with mind
We'll be nearing our long-desired goal.

Then men will awaken
To the error they made
When they thought that to rule was our aim.
It is not their place
We are striving to grace
But to love and to serve on their plane.

And when we have risen
To ideals that will make
Better women and mothers and wives,
We will use every gift
The world's burdens to lift;
We will serve man with talents and lives.[10]

Editor's Note: A useful description of the prevailing ethos regarding gender issues, including the argument against the value of educating women – the theory that excessive education leads to the unsexing of the female, that women were insufficiently intelligent to assume the demands of the larger society – are available in *God's Ordinary People: No Ordinary Heritage* by Drs. Jessica L. Rousselow Winquist and Alan H. Winquist, Taylor University Press, 1996.

Sadie Louise Miller (1910) reaches beyond her usually serious poetic approach to life and offers us a touch of realism wrapped in whimsy in her "In the Rough." The theme, the proverbial appeal to look beneath the surface to find life's greatest worth, is Sadie's vehicle to portray a young woman blinded to the gem before her.

She was offered a diamond gem in the rough;
She looked at it there –
Neither brilliant nor fair.
"I want a polished one," she said,
And turned away a haughty head;
But she knew not the hidden value, that lay
In the stone she pushed from her hand that day –
That diamond gem in the rough.

She was offered a pure, young heart in the rough;
She gazed on the face –
It was just commonplace.
"I want a handsome one," she said,
And turned away a proud, young head;
But she missed through all her life on earth
A precious gem of priceless worth –
That pure, young heart in the rough.[11]

"My Ideal Husband" appeared in the Taylor *Echo* (March 1, 1916), and sets forth an impressive, if not timeless, list of characteristics that the anonymous writer suggests the potential suitor should be wise enough to cultivate, in order eventually to "make a better and much more desirable mate for the woman of his choice (no matter who that might ultimately be.)"

If every man would ask himself what kind of a husband would I want if I were a woman, he might be enabled to live his life and form his habits in such a way that he would eventually make a better and much more desirable mate for the woman of his choice.

If it should be my duty or privilege to select a husband I would first demand that he should be a manly man. All real men and the majority of women detest "a sissy." Thus my husband would have to have red blood in his veins and ambition in his make up. He would be interested in virile sports; contests which called for trained, hardened muscles, a quick thinking mind, and perhaps even courage and grit. When my husband walked he would place one foot at a considerable distance ahead of the other and when I heard him approach the house his footsteps would be firm, strong and steady in place of light, quick and pattering.

Again, I would wish my husband to be a leader. He should be aggressive and perhaps somewhat domineering although by no means excessively so. I would want him to really rule over me but not in such a way that it would be unpleasant to me.

The characteristic which I would demand above all other traits in the man whom I would prefer to have as my life mate is purity and scrupulous righteousness of character. In order to realize in him my ideal I would have to know that he was as respectful and courteous to other ladies as he was to me. He would reverence womenkind. My ideal husband would have no vicious habits; after he had bidden me good night at the door of my home he would not indulge in some practice which would injure, degrade and undermine his body, mind and morals.

Once more my ideal husband must be a good provider. He must be willing to work hard and earnestly in order to obtain comforts of life for his family but he could not be a man who was able to work only under the supervision of others. Besides being an aggressive leader he must possess brain power enough to discern and seize his opportunities and thus he would accomplish something of value for himself and the world.

Lastly and most important of all the man who would be an ideal husband for me would have to be a Christian. He would have to possess a simple but deep love for and trust and faith in his Maker. This characteristic covers a multitude of desirable traits. If he was a real Christian he would be kind, true and gentle. He would bear the annoying daily experiences of life with a steady patience and an even temper. He would love and respect above all other women the woman whom he had asked to be his wife and in turn he would merit her admiration on account of his own integrity, kindness and worth. He would be accustomed to place the wishes of other people above his own desires and thus he would endeavor to please his wife and children before he did himself.

Personally I have many enormous doubts whether a man lives who possesses all these traits which I have named but if he did, providing I was a marriageable woman, I would long, wait and wish for him until he had asked for the heart and hand which were already his.[12]

Julliette Corson's essay, "How to Cook a Husband," assumed a prominent place in the Taylor *Echo* (February 14, 1922) and offers the reader a humorous take on gender issues during the 1920s.

A good many husbands are utterly spoiled by mismanagement. Some women go about it as if their husbands were bladders, and proceed to blow them up. Others keep them constantly in hot water. Others let them freeze by carelessness and indifference. Some keep them in a stew by irritating ways and words. Others roast them. Some keep them in a pickle all their lives. It cannot be supposed that any husband will be tender and good, managed in this way; but they are really delicious when properly treated. In selecting your husband, you should not be guided by the silvery appearance, as in buying mackerel, nor by the golden tint, as if you want salmon. Be sure and select himself, as tastes differ. Do not go to market for him, as the best are always brought to your door. It is far better to have none, unless you

will patiently learn to cook him. A preserving kettle of the finest
porcelain is best, but if you have nothing but an earthenware jar,
it will do, with care. See that the linen in which you wrap him is
nicely washed and mended, with the required number of buttons
and strings nicely sewed on. Tie him in the kettle by a strong silk
cord, called "comfort" as the one called "duty" is apt to be weak.
They are apt to fly out of the kettle and be burned and crusty on
the edges, since, like crabs and lobster you have to cook them
while alive. Make a clear steady fire of love heatness and cheer-
fulness. Set him as near this as seems to agree with him. If he
sputters and fizzes do not be anxious; some husbands do this till
they are quite done. Add a little sugar, in the form of what con-
fectioners call kisses, but no vinegar and pepper, on any account.
A little spice improves them, but it must be used with judgment.
Do not stick any sharp instrument into him, to see if he is becoming tender. Stir him gently, watch the while lest he lie too flat
and close to the kettle, and so become useless. You cannot fail
to know when he is done. If thus treated you will find him very
delicious, agreeing nicely with you and the children, and he will
keep as long as you want, unless you become careless and set
him in too cold a place.[13]

The following essay by **Mary G. Wray**, Taylor University
Professor of History from **1909 to 1915**, appeared in the Taylor
Echo and gives insight into the subject of male-female relationships in the early 1900s. Professor Wray writes a thoughtful, but
impersonal essay on "Marriage as a Career."

The present age is full of opportunities for woman – the
Woman's Day, it has been called. It appears that woman has
been emancipated in the last few years. In all religious activities
she has long had part, and in the last half century she has led in

social reforms, but now she has accomplished her great desire to exercise political rights. Women are now discovered in Congress, legislature and law courts.

It is surprising that factory work and its noise and grind appeals to educated women, but they often prefer it to well paid sedentary occupations. A young woman of this type who had taught school successfully but now holds a position of great responsibility in a gun factory said, "I feel that I have more liberty here, more chance for growth and initiative than when teaching school. This work is more real."

The successful competition with men in the industrial world has given women a taste of financial independence which may be cause for careful study on the part of thoughtful people. We may well ask: Will their economic independence complicate the problems of marriage and of motherhood?

There has always been a tendency on the part of the self-supporting women to defer, if not to avoid marriage, possibly because it curtails their liberty as well as their income. If this tendency increases in proportion to the increased success of independent young women in the last four years, what will be the result to the American home and the American nation?

Granting that she has gained some independence, some recognition, some mental poise, what has she lost? There is a rare zest in measuring wits with the opposite sex. The associations of the business world awaken keenness of intellect and observation. But whether in the world of business, of politics or of reform there is another side to the question of woman's development in public affairs. She may have a clarified vision respecting the superiority of the opposite sex, but does she not pay for this change of sentiment the heavy price of disillusionment and lost romantic dreams?

Miss Josephine Strickler, the able secretary of the late Colonel Roosevelt, a young woman herself, makes the following admissions: "For the woman who has been handling thousands of dollars of business a day, or holding great audiences by her genius, wiping the baby's nose and counting the linen for laundry are, to put it without exaggeration, not enthralling." But she adds: "Business does harden us. Business does take from us our old dreams of the mental superiority of the male sex. Business does show us men in the average as predatory and selfish, and if we compete with them, we women become predatory and selfish with ourselves."

Thoughtful men have doubts about the desirability of business women for wives. A doctor was asked, "How about the business woman versus wifehood?" He replied: "Pretty good if you catch them before they're too successful. Too much success means the wrong psychology for an amenable wife and also nerves that don't stand motherhood any too well. But they are good scouts, these business women, even if they have nerves. I prefer them to your gabby society girl any time." When asked, "What do you mean by an amenable wife, doctor?" "I mean a good deal," he replied, after several moments of thought. "Amenable means tractable – responsive to discipline. Now don't get excited. The discipline I mean is the general discipline of marriage, the learning to give up personal desires, to yield to the opinion and decision of another at least half, usually more than half the time. A woman who has conducted a business, or who has had authority and responsibility in some one else's business, finds it quite as hard to be amenable in marriage as does a man. Now the man has got to keep on in his profession. The women must give up, must be the unselfish, the self-sacrificing member. That's merely good biology. It makes for the unity of the home consequently for the protection of the children. Now when a woman has been in business so long that she has become as masterful and as opinionated as the average business man, there is the very dickens to pay! Also when she has worked so hard with her brain that her nerves are gone, she's a poor wife and a poor mother. On the average, the women with the fine, hard-working mind is a much poorer physical specimen than the average woman with the simple, untrained brain."

Shall we be frank enough to discuss marriage as a career?

Will a public career pay if it prevents or compromises a woman's chances of marriage? A girl chooses her career by determining certain personal questions; Is she adapted to it? Is the necessary preparation available? Will it yield satisfaction? If she is devout, she asks: "Will it please God? Let her ask these questions respecting marriage as a career. Is she adapted to it physically and mentally? She cannot make a success of marriage if she is not in good physical condition. She needs health, vigor, nervous energy, a good physique, and attractive personality. She must be responsive, unselfish, self-sacrificing, and self-controlled. Lacking any of these characteristics the would-be wife faces failure.

Will the needed preparation be available? This question may be answered affirmatively, given the fundamental requirements of sound health and a willing mind, for all the foregoing characteristics are within the reach of every girl. She has only to train for them.

Will it yield satisfaction? In other words, will it pay? This is often the paramount question respecting any course of action, and may well claim attention on the part of earnest youth regarding marriage. What greater satisfaction can be anticipated than the establishment of a home – the foundation of society, the hope of the church, and the bulwark of the nation? In it a woman has opportunity for self-development such as she could never have in the business world. Here she may bring to pass her youthful dreams. Here her grace and charm may have their fullest sway. Here she may establish her kingdom in one true heart. She may select the friends who can be admitted in the inner circle of her influence. Her home may be a beacon of light and fidelity and virtue in its community. A happy home solves many a social problem. Divorce, the nation's curse, would be unknown if women loved their homes and recognized marriage as an institution primarily for home building. When the woman accepts marriage with the right psychology, and is willing to center her interests and activities there, and there practice her arts and allurements, she will not need to worry about the vampires of society since she will hold the husband in the hollow of her hand.

In choosing marriage, the right-minded woman also chooses motherhood – the fulfillment of her destiny. This is a career in itself, which yields joys that are sacred, satisfaction that is endless. It demands untold sacrifice and unbounded courage; all of a woman's mind and heart, love and life; but I think we need not discuss the question of its payments, since they are unquestionable, immeasurable and eternal.

And now let us ask: Will God be pleased if I select marriage as a career? Since God Himself decreed it, and Jesus, our Lord, honored it, there can be no argument against it. It is, however, a sin for young people who cannot bring to this state sound minds, sound bodies, and sound psychology. To accept marriage impulsively is weakness. To accept it "reverently, discreetly, and in the fear of God" is well-pleasing to Him and affords woman her consummate opportunity.[14]

Voices of Taylor Women Abroad ...

The history of Taylor University women abroad is unique and compelling. The influence of Bishop William Taylor's missionary zeal was felt in a profound manner on the campus during the early 1900s. Drs. Jessica L. Rousselow Winquist and Alan H. Winquist contribute important researched information about Taylor women in ministry both at home and abroad during this period. Their book, *God's Ordinary People: No Ordinary Heritage*, Taylor University Press, 1996, provides a valuable consideration of those particular inspirational elements that resulted in many women rising above or stepping aside from those societal norms that would have them remain within culturally limited and prescribed roles. Women became active participants in the rigorous activities demanded of missionaries within underdeveloped countries. The actual words written or spoken by as many of these women that could be located by the date of publication comprise the content of the present chapter (*Venerable Voices/Modern Messages*), *Authentic Voices: Women of Insight Talk about Real-Life Challenges.*

Between 1884 and 1896, Bishop William Taylor (after whom Taylor University was renamed) made seven trips to Africa with an initial focus on Liberia, West Africa, where numerous problems had developed with regard to the establishment of early missionary work. **Agnes McAllister** is noted as one of the outstanding William Taylor Missionaries who worked alone throughout many of her years there. Her work is compellingly detailed in her book, *A Lone Woman in Africa*, 1896, a copy of which is located in the Taylor University Archives. (High tribute is made to her and her heroic work by Bishop William Taylor and appears in his handwriting at the front of the book, dated by him as August 14, 1895).

During her 19 years in Liberia, Agnes McAllister was stationed in the Kroo (Kru) coastal area. It was specifically around the Garraway Mission Station there that Samuel Morris (1873-1893) emerges. As a son of an African chieftain, Morris was caught in a treacherous web of tribal violence. The Sammy Morris story, first written by Taylor University president, Thaddeus Reade (his presidency extending from 1891-1902), is movingly retold by Jorge O. Masa and titled, *Angel in Ebony or the Life and Message of Sammy Morris*. Indisputably the most legendary student in the history of Taylor University, the life and death of Sammy Morris has provided inspiration to many across the years.

Agnes McAllister's accounts of life among the Kru during this period are important to the understanding of those people who, to that time, were without significant encounters with outside civilizations with the exception of the occasional traders seeking economic opportunities. No specific record is found of personal contact between Agnes McAllister and Sammy Morris as was reported of Morris' acquaintance with Miss Kroll, a former student at Fort Wayne College, or Miss Lizzie MacNeil, another of Bishop Taylor's missionaries to Liberia. McAllister's vivid descriptions of the conditions out of which Morris is said to have come are effectively communicated through her book, *A Lone Woman in Africa*. McAllister described the tribal practices of harsh social justice that required individuals accused of any one of numerous misdeeds to prove their innocence by ingesting the liquefied bark of the sasswood tree. If the accused lived through the ordeal, he or she was considered innocent. If death resulted, this, of course, proved guilt. Sasswood comes from a West African tree of the pea family whose bark yields a highly toxic poison yet whose timber is useable for construction.

The following is a condensed account of a gripping incident demonstrating the heroism and creativity of Agnes McAllister who, moved by conviction, and armed with boldness, together with disarming good humor, insinuates herself into a "Sasswood Palaver" and reveals to the tribe's people the folly of their justice system.

It all began in the tribe with the unexpected deaths of two brothers, strong young men. One had been unwittingly shot in the leg and the other had suddenly taken ill. But their conditions worsened rapidly. These two events were sufficient to arouse the suspicions of the tribal people and initiate an ensuing frenzy. The common belief was that some witch had most certainly caused the deaths, while at the same time giving heed to the larger belief that when a person dies, "God took him."

The body of the second brother to die was being prepared for burial. The corpse was washed and his face streaked with paint. A large, new cloth was put over him, beads strung around his neck, a pipe placed on his chest with the stem toward his mouth and a comb by his head.

As I approached the site, I heard the call of the "Quee." I had come to know that when I'd hear this particular call by the tribesmen that it meant they had decided they would not bury the dead without what they called a "palaver." The Quee was a secret society of men who referred to themselves as the "Devil Society." When they made their appearance, it most likely meant that someone would be accused of witchcraft and would be compelled to drink the poisonous pulverized bark of the sasswood tree to prove innocence or guilt.

Several men approached me in an effort to persuade me to return to my compound and leave them alone to their palaver. But I stood my ground and said to them, "Don't anyone dare put his hands on me." I knew from my experience with these people that if they once took hold of me they would soon shut me away because it was against their custom for a woman to see or be seen while the Quee were performing. By this time, I was the only woman in the village not closed away in her house. If a woman sees the Quee, the belief is that she has truly set eyes on the devil and is therefore to be severely punished and compelled to pay a heavy fine.

I came upon the chiefs engaged in a secretive conversation. When they saw me, they began to speak up indicating they had decided not to resort to the palaver.

"Teacher, do you hear what we say?" they turned to me.

"Yes," I answered, "and if you do as you say and not give any sasswood, I shall be very glad."

With that, the men made the decision to approach the body and ask it who had killed him, but I could see they had other motives in mind so I remained with them and even said, "Come on, I am going too."

"Oh no," they insisted. "Woman no fit to go there today. Don't you see all women go inside? You must go inside, too."

"No," I said, "I do not go into any house today. I'm going to see what you men are doing."

With that, I led the way even though some said to me, "No, don't go there." But at that, I laughed, and finally they were all laughing too.

We came to a small, enclosed yard where the Quee were at work. As soon as they saw me, some called out, "Oh, there is teacher!"

"Yes," I replied, "and who is this?" At that, I pulled the curtain aside and shoved my way through the warriors who were seated in a circle inside the curtain. Suddenly, they hushed the man who was playing the role of the devil and got him away, scolding me at the same time for being where I was not supposed to be. Some proposed to carry me into the house, and some just continued laughing. I marched around the circle of men and said that I had come for the purpose of a burial and that it was

time now to carry the body to the grave. Some of the men attempted to take me by the arm, saying that I must sit down, that surely it was too hot for me out in the burning heat. But, I assured them that I had not come to sit down and besides, I always carried my umbrella for protection from the sun. I told them how foolish it was to have such a performance over a dead man, and that eventually all must die anyway, and then preached Jesus to them.

In the meantime, the Quee were going ahead with their plans. They told me that it was the devil making the queer noises.

"No," I replied. "I can tell you who is making those noises and it is Zanier," I said, pointing at the man's house.

The chiefs were surprised and said, "Teacher knows everything! Who has told you this?"

"It's not hard to tell," said I. "It certainly is no secret. I have seen this done many times before."

At this, the kings and chiefs in the group all laughed and thought it a fine joke, but said that I must not tell the women what I knew. Of course, I did not make any promises.

But the events were not over yet. Soon a young man appeared with the news that a woman had been singled out from the village to be given the sasswood. At this, I left to find someone who had the authority to put a stop to this. But I had been in town only briefly when they brought in the woman. I learned that she had already been made to drink three basinfuls of sasswood and she even carried the wooden basin in her hand. They all pointed at her and called out, "A witch! A witch! A witch!"

That afternoon, the corpse of the young man was finally buried and I learned the accused woman vomited the sasswood. But instead of the situation drawing to a close, the people refused to accept her innocence and they planned to make her drink still more sasswood the next morning.

With the intervention of some of the Christian tribal men, the woman was finally released, only to have the tribeswomen join together to show the men the truth of the situation as they saw it. At this, the men became afraid because, as they said was their belief, women were stronger witches than men.

For a time, things seemed quiet then suddenly one evening, a local woman, lying asleep on her mat with her infant by her side, was awakened and taken off ostensibly to be given sasswood. I got up, hurriedly dressed, and went out to find someone who could tell me what was happening. What I learned was that it was evident that the people were determined to kill some person in exchange for the death of the young man.

At this, I gathered together all our Christian natives and we set out to face the palaver. There ensued much confusion but because I knew the language, no one could say much of anything that I could not understand and I was careful to let them know what I heard them say.

By this time, a group of victims had been rounded up. There they sat, fearful and surrounded by their accusers. Relatives of the victims were in one cluster. Kings and chiefs in another. We Christians gathered in the shade of some nearby trees. We knelt down, and asked God to help us in this time of great need because we were at a complete loss to know what to do.

We looked on while the sasswood was being beaten and turned into a deadly broth. Finally, one of the victims was singled out and called to come forward. Village women approached the victim, two by two. They rang a bell in her ear and ordered her to drink the sasswood.

One of our men approached me saying he would offer to interpret what was going on. But waiting to have everything interpreted was far too slow for me, so I spoke up in the native language and suddenly, the ridiculousness of it all broke through to me and I began to laugh.

With that, I went to the young men who were beating the sasswood and said: "Here, let me help you. We will give everybody sasswood today. You have not half enough sasswood in the mortar. Let me put in some more. Why, is this all you brought? That won't be half enough. Send men into the bush for more. Don't you see all these people?"

I went to the victim, and, after tasting her sasswood, I said to her: "This is not nice. Don't drink it. It will kill you." Then, going to the women who were ringing the bells, I said: "I am sure you must be tired. Let me ring the bell awhile." All the while, we sang and preached Jesus and told the people of the better way.

I asked the accusers if they themselves had drunk sasswood. "No," they said. I told them I knew they did not like it for the same reason the victims did not want it. While they were amused at the mistakes I made in their language, still, though vexed at me, they could not help laughing.

When the tribespeople continued to push the sasswood on the victim in spite of my efforts, I suggested they go get their cooking pots, bring them back, and we'd all prepare sasswood together.

Finally, I took the victims by the hand, raised them up, and we all set off away from that place. We took them to their homes, and later the chief told us how grateful he was for the intervention, and encouraged us to help put a stop to these evil rituals.

The next day, there came many expressions of gratitude and I don't think that since I went to Africa I shook so many hands at one time. Later, I took the mission children and went home to have a quiet day. I learned later that the accusers had given the king a sign of peace between them and pledged their word that they would never again force anyone to drink the bark of the sasswood.[15]

Susan Moberly Talbott Wengatz (1910) is said, in the 1909 issue of the Taylor *Gem* to have "made glad her mother's home" in Coatsville, Indiana. She was born on January 29, 1885, and was the daughter of a criminal lawyer, who was also a state legislator. She moved to Orleans, Indiana, when quite young and was later graduated from Orleans High School in 1904. The summer of 1903, she spent in the Shorthand Training School in Indianapolis. Later, in the fall of 1905, she entered Taylor University with majors in Music and Education. While a university student, Susan traveled with the university Ladies' Quartette in 1908, was president of the Volunteer Band* during the year of 1908-1909, and was planning to become a foreign missionary. She met John Wengatz (1909) at Taylor University and they were married in June of 1909. Upon Susan's graduation in 1910, they were assigned to foreign mission work in Angola, West Africa, under the auspices of the Methodist Church. While in Africa, Susan is credited with translating over 60 hymns into the dialect of the tribe she and her husband were serving. She also helped found the Taylor Bible School.*

The following two entries (a letter from Susan and a personal account by Cilicia L. Cross describing the circumstances of Susan's death) take us into Susan's world abroad – places far less civilized than those in which she grew up in Indiana. Her adjustment to the less than comfortable circumstances is impressive. Her highly productive life on the remote mission field inspires and challenges.

The following letter, written by Susan from Angola, describes some of the perplexing conditions she encountered in her attempt to minister to the Africans around her. "Joanna," writes Susan, "from childhood was a dirt eater."** Little was known at that time about the practice of ingesting dirt and other unnatural foods. According to Susan, the unusual habit became the ultimate cause of Joanna's death and contributed to the obvious frustration of those who cared about her.

Editor's Note: Useful discussions of many campus organizations throughout the history of Taylor University such as the Volunteer Band (part of a national Volunteer Movement sponsored by such organizations as the YMCA and YWCA, with comprehensive, well-stated, and noble objectives), and the Taylor Bible School, established by missionaries from Taylor University in Africa for the education of the African residents, are available in the Taylor University history, *God's Ordinary People: No Ordinary Heritage*, 1996, by Drs. Jessica L. Rousselow Winquist and Alan H. Winquist.

**Editor's Note*: Dirt eating is known medically by the term *Pica*. This condition is characterized by an abnormal craving for certain unnatural foods such as clay, chalk, paint, or the chewing of ice, and it may occur during pregnancy, hysteria (a condition characterized by emotional excitability, excessive anxiety, sensory and motor disturbances, and the simulation of organic disorders such as blindness, deafness, etc.), chlorosis (a type of anemia that may result in a pale appearance to the skin, weakness, palpitation, or in dyspepsia, which is impaired digestion; the patient is observed closely for the symptoms of anemia.) *Merck Manual of Diagnosis & Therapy,* West Point, Pennsylvania, Merck & Company, 2004.

The following letter is from Susan Moberly Talbott Wengatz
stationed in Angola, West Africa and appears in the Taylor *Echo*,
April 11, 1918.

Joanna Kimbangu was the name of one of those black village women who somehow just work their way into your heart
and before you know it cause you to be interested in every detail
of their lives. She became a Christian in 1911 during the general
awakening about Quiongua and her turning from her "mahamba"
to serve the true God was sincere and lasting.

Joanna early formed the habit of asking us to pray with her
whenever she came to the mission either on Sunday or a week
day. If she came to sell something she always came early enough
to have time to pray, and many times she walked the four miles
solely for the words of prayer we had together. Many times she
would come at the most inopportune times for us. We were oh
so busy and confess we
almost begrudged the time
we gave her; but when the
prayer was over and the
old face shining with trust
in her Lord, we chided
ourselves for having had a
thought of wishing she had
not come.

*If, for any reason, Joanna was absent from a
Sunday service she either advised us beforehand of just what would hinder her from
coming, or she sent word to the service why
she was not there.*

One day we were
much amused when she
came just at noon and found us at the table. She came to the
door and said, "Senhora, I am going away for a few days and I
have come to say good-bye to you, and the Lord." The poor soul
meant it well, so we refrained from giving vent to the laughter
that possessed us, lest we offend her.

If, for any reason, Joanna was absent from a Sunday service she either advised us beforehand of just what would hinder her from coming, or she sent word to the service why she was not there. She said: "I do not want you to think I am staying away from service just because I do not want to come."

Within a year or two after her conversion, she led her blind husband to Jesus, and he is still happy in the faith.

Joanna, from childhood, was a dirt eater. After she became a Christian she struggled against the temptation like one who has a habit of drink or opium tries to reform. Sometimes she would yield, and then would come with repentance and new resolution. This awful habit, so common to many natives, worked havoc with her body and left her a wreck before she reached the age of fifty. Medicine did not help her, though we did all we could. A disease, in its appearance akin to leprosy, finally claimed her.

A short time ago she sent for me to come to her and hear something she had to say. I went immediately and found her very weak indeed, but still able to talk. She said, "Senhora, I have sent for you to come to me that I might leave you my testimony. I am very weak and shall not live, and I do not want you to be surprised some day soon with the news that Joanna has died, and have any doubts about my future." Then with all earnestness and sincerity she told me of her faith in Christ as her Savior and her trust of going soon to be with Him. I questioned her closely if she had any doubts, but she said the Lord was with her and had cleared away what doubts she had. We talked a bit to the people gathered about, praying with her again, and after she led in prayer asked her to choose a hymn to sing. She began "All my members belong to Jesus who could die for such a one as I," a translation of "My body, soul and spirit." We took her hand at parting and promised to meet her in heaven, and four days later Joanna went to be with Jesus.

These are the lives and testimonies that amid all the discouragements make us feel that the work is worthwhile.[16]
Yours sincerely,
Susan Wengatz

━━━━━━━━━━━━━ ❦ ❦ ❦ ━━━━━━━━━━━━━

Susan Moberly Talbott Wengatz (1910) was attacked by a rabid dog on October 25, 1929, while working in the rose garden of her home in West Africa far from urban areas. By this time, Susan had been on the mission field in Angola for 19 years. No anti-rabies* serum could be located locally nor could the required antidote be sent from a distant city to their station with the immediacy necessary to counteract the poison in her bloodstream. Susan died on January 16, 1930, nearly three months after being infected. Six days after her death, the needed serum arrived at their compound. The account of Susan's remarkable courage in the face of severe suffering is recounted in the following pages, excerpts from personal letters written by Cilicia L. Cross, who was in Angola with Susan, and titled "The Last Enemy to be Conquered is Death."

Editor's Note: Rabies (Latin for madness) is an infectious virus, a disease of the central nervous system in dogs and other flesh-eating animals. It can be transmitted to man by the bite of an infected animal and is characterized by choking, convulsions, and inability to swallow. It is fatal if not treated immediately with anti-viral serum. Prior to actual death, medical resources indicate the patient is likely to suffer acute hydrophobia, an aversion to, and inability to swallow water or other liquids resulting in potentially fatal dehydration. *The Merck Manual of Diagnosis & Therapy, 2004.*

❦ ❦ ❦

"THE LAST ENEMY TO BE CONQUERED IS DEATH"

*Extracts from letters written to homeland friends
by Cilicia L. Cross, Angola.*

"The last enemy to be conquered is death." Dear Susan repeated these words many times the last two days she was with us, and she conquered death triumphantly, gloriously. She was more than conqueror in the name of Jesus. Such an abundant entrance as was hers! If only I could be with you for a few hours to tell you of the victories of her last two days, it would, I am sure, take away some of the pain of your great loss. My own loss is over-whelming, for no one ever loved me as she did, and I cannot yet contemplate what life is going to be without her to share every burden and every victory of mine. But dear friends, my own life will always be richer and fuller because of the proof she gave us of the reality of our SALVATION in Christ Jesus during the terrible agonies and horrors of this unspeakable disease.

Both natives and missionaries felt that our hope was in God, and I wonder if any one person anywhere ever had so much prayer going up for weeks as she did for her. She was so beloved by our native Christians that the Churches just gave themselves to that one task while she was in danger. Our Christians know how to pray the believing prayer that brings the answer, and so

we must believe that her work was finished and that the Lord had need of her elsewhere, although we cannot yet see how Angola is going to get along without her. Her own mind was kept in such peace all through. On the day she was bitten when we discussed her trying to get to Europe for help, she insisted that she stay and await developments, for she said she was sure that nothing could come into her life that God did not permit and that accidents do not happen to those who are wholly the Lord's. In her praying, she always reminded the Lord that He was able to keep her from any evil results if it was His will, but if not, then she chose only His will. We all felt so sure that she would be spared to us, and she often begged us not to be so certain for fear that our faith would receive a shock if this proved to be God's time for her. She was so completely in His hands always, that her last days were a blessing to everyone. Even after she realized that she had the disease, she was still victorious. I was with her from the first and shall never be the same again, after having shared those precious upper room scenes. The Everlasting arms that she had trusted so long supported her marvelously during the five days of awful agony such as I hope never to witness again in a human being. How many times she said, "the last enemy to be conquered is death." Could any death be more terrible than one by hydrophobia, and yet she conquered it gloriously and triumphed till an abundant entrance was granted her. Almost every breath during the last two days, was prayer. Hundreds of times she repeated, "In Jesus' Name I will conquer. In Jesus' Name I will keep my right mind until the last, and I will die, not raving mad, but as a Christian." And in Jesus' name she did keep her right mind until the last, and she did die as a Christian. The last few hours were wonderful.

She often spoke of how little she had suffered in the way of sickness during her life, and said that if she had to suffer now, it was no more than her share. The rest of us truly believed that she was to be spared to us. It could not be that her work in Angola was done. Native Christians everywhere were praying and believing for her recovery. People in Capetown and other parts of Africa were praying and all who knew about it in America were praying.

The unmistakable symptoms of the dreaded disease appeared first on Monday evening, January thirteenth. The next afternoon she seemed to be slipping and we got hold of the Lord for her and from that hour on, His power in upholding her went beyond anything I had ever dreamed possible. Sometimes His presence seemed almost visible, and she talked to Him just as intimately as she did to one of us. Every little while she would ask us each in turn, "Is the promise true? Does your faith hold?" When we assured her it did, she seemed to lean a little harder on the Everlasting arms. From that time on, she was so entirely in His hands that she began to conquer the physical fears of the disease. She had not been able to have anyone else in the room, but now she told us to call everyone who was in the house, and she shouted, and praised the Lord to all of them. I will not distress you with all the horrors that are part of the disease, but she conquered them one by one until she came to the most terrible one, the name of which she could not even speak – water. But she finally got the name out and said, "In Jesus' name I will drink it." Oh, the power of God as we saw it manifested in her overcoming this fear of water! Has it ever been known in the history of the world that a rabies patient could even see water to say nothing of washing in it and drinking it as she did? I doubt it. It was so precious I must give you the details of that particular victory. She just talked to Jesus, "Can I do it Lord? In your name can I? He says, 'Bring the water'." We brought it, but kept it out of sight. "Now Lord, in your name, strength to look at it." In His name, she looked and conquered. Then in the same way, just talking to Him as she did to us, she finally got it into her hand and later poured some on her hand. "Oh," she said, "if I could only drink some of that pure cold water!" We prayed that she might, and Jesus answered. It was a miracle. Such things are a physical impossibility. But oh, the presence of the Lord in those hours! About eleven o'clock on Wednesday morning, she did drink that glass of pure cold water for which her body was famishing. Victory, what a victory! Then she said, "Now I can rest in Jesus' Name." After an hour of quiet rest, she asked Mr. Wengatz what time it was. He replied that it was just noon. With a look of rapture, not of this earth, she almost leaped from her bed, "It's High Noon for me, and I see the Sun and Moon and the Stars. Kiss me, John. I'll see you in the morning. We knew then that the healing was for the conquering of the disease and not for her to stay with us as we had supposed. But she lingered. Her work was not quite finished yet. She had often talked to one of the missionaries, of whom she was very fond, about the second work of grace in her heart. She felt that the Lord wanted her to press the matter once more, and there, on the brink of the River, too weak to do much of the talking herself, she opened the subject and had us explain the way, and got the missionary's promise to make her consecration, and not to stop until she knew that the work was done. (This missionary has, since Mrs. Wengatz' death, received the fullness of the Holy Spirit. S.L.M.)

At seven o'clock that evening, she told us that the Lord had kept His promise and she was to die like a Christian, and not mad; and that "He has kept me so that I have never looked at my precious husband with mad eyes." From that time until nine o'clock she was more in Heaven than on earth. "I hear the music of Heaven, I see Jesus; my anchor holds. Does yours? Your faith is going to be tested. Will it hold when the test comes? And you will not fail me? I'll see you in the morning. Now I'm going to sleep in Jesus' Name." Once she seemed to be drifting off, and then she opened her eyes and whispered the chorus of "We have an anchor that keeps the soul." During the night she was semi-conscious at times and talked always about Jesus. The end came peacefully as she had said it would at 6:25 Thursday morning – a natural death, in her right mind, and as she so often prayed, as a Christian. Just about three minutes before the end, she opened her eyes and as we repeated "In Jesus' Name," from her, we caught the whisper, "Yes Lord, in Jesus' Name," and she went to be with Jesus.

Loving hands made the casket, and it was beautiful. Loving hands dug the grave, and none but loving hands touched her precious body. A service was held for the natives at Malange, and another service at Quessua where no less than twelve hundred people were in attendance. In the latter service, three languages were used, Kimbundu, Portuguese, and English. She awaits the coming of the Lord beside the Bible School at Quessua. She loved it so much, we felt that is where she would like to be. It was a beautiful funeral. Mr. Wengatz said it was more like an Easter service than a funeral.

We will need you in America to keep up the interest in all her beloved work. Not one bit of it shall ever be allowed to go down. Her place cannot be filled, but we are all giving ourselves to the work anew to carry on in Jesus' name as never before; and some day we shall understand why Heaven needs her more than Angola does.[17]

❦   ❦   ❦

The three women in this section, *Voices of Taylor Women Abroad*, speak to us from distant times and distant places. Agnes McAllister, from the 1890s, takes us into the social life of Liberia, West Africa, and reveals her firsthand experience with the customs so treacherous that for one to prove their innocence, when accused of some misdeed by tribal neighbors, he or she may be called upon to drink the poison of the feared sasswood tree. **Susan Moberly Talbott Wengatz (1910)** shows us how she encounters medical and psychological challenges which far exceeded then-known medical causes and effective treatments, both on the parts of the native population she served and also the personal health dilemma she faced.

Although foreign mission fields offered severe challenges, there were also times of heady, good pleasure for those serving in far off places. A charming love affair sparked by delightful coincidences captures the fancy and, like a sprightly gazelle on an African plain, leaps into our imagination from the pages of *Kansas Prairies to African Forests* by **Edith Roseberry** (mother of **Ruth Roseberry Herber 1942**). Whereas Edith incorporates family and domestic information in her book, the overriding theme is her experience in British Sierra Leone, and later in French West Africa. She relates many incidents that formed the background for the opening of that large area of Africa to missionary endeavor.

❦   ❦   ❦

The plea was going out continually for new missionaries to meet the challenge. Little did we realize that the Lord was calling and preparing one of these new recruits right in our own home.

Our daughter Ruth grew to young womanhood while we were stationed at headquarters in Kankan. Most of her grade school work was done at the school for missionaries' children, which was located in the foothills of Foula country. She completed her high school work by correspondence, and then left us to return to the States to enter Taylor University.

While Ruth was in Taylor University she met Ralph Herber, a young premedical student, who was expecting to become a doctor. As the friendship developed, I was troubled for many days by the question: "Would my daughter settle down in the homeland and not take up the torch in Africa, or some other land across the sea?" We did not try to persuade her to become a missionary, but prayed that the Lord would lead her. It is difficult for young people to follow the Light when matters of the heart fight for control. The whole matter was to be settled in a wonderful way that caused us to rejoice greatly in the Lord for His goodness and care.

In the summer of 1941 Ruth went to a summer camp in Michigan to work. She had a wonderful time there, enjoying the outdoor activities as well as the spiritual fellowship. One day while Mrs. Ruth Stull was speaking, the Lord suddenly spoke to Ruth and told her that He was calling her to train for missionary service. The struggle that had been going on for two years came to an end as she heard the Master's voice and responded to the call in full surrender. In a few days summer camp would be over. Ruth had planned to meet Ralph in Detroit and spend a few days at his home before going back to school. Ralph had never had a call to foreign service, and during the summer had grown away from the Lord. Ruth knew she must tell Ralph of her new decision to go to Nyack instead of into the teaching profession, even though it would, no doubt, mean an end to their two years of close friendship. Before leaving the camp she wrote a letter telling him, without equivocation, that the Lord's call was to be first in her life. That is the secret of victory. The letter was posted Air Mail Special Delivery and should have reached him by Saturday. However, it was missent to a distant city and did not arrive at its destination until Monday.

In another city about 100 miles away, Ralph Herber, all unconscious of Ruth's call to definite service by the Lord, sat in Sunday service in his godly father's church. A strange feeling came over him as his father proclaimed the truth. He had a deep conviction of the Spirit that he should go to the altar and settle once and forever his relationship to God. Hardly had his father finished preaching when Ralph rushed to the altar. There, after a struggle, he found peace with the Lord, and received a definite call to foreign service. How beautiful it is when two lives are called together in full consecration to go out as messengers of the Cross.

On Monday morning Ralph received Ruth's letter telling of her definite call to foreign service. There was joy and happiness in his heart and praise to God for the wonderful way in which He had worked out everything in their lives for His glory. In a day or two Ruth arrived on her way back to school, and her heart was filled to overflowing when she learned of Ralph's call. They knew now that this was God's seal upon their lives.

They had one more year together at the University and then more definite plans were made for the future. Both had been accepted at the Missionary Training Institute at Nyack when the Army put in a call for Ralph for military service. Again they wondered how God would untangle the maze that seemed to envelop their future. Ralph was rejected by the Army for physical reasons, and the way was then open to go to Nyack. After one year in the wonderful school where they learned much about the indwelling Christ, Ralph and Ruth were united in marriage June 12, 1943.

Their training completed, Ralph became assistant pastor in the Central Church in Detroit. Later he served as pastor to the University Church in Louisville, Kentucky. These were wonderful years in which they experienced heart searching as they came in contact with Bible truths; of new commitments as they realized the need for the infilling of the Holy Spirit; of joy as they saw God leading them along the pathway that He had planned. He opened door after door as they learned to trust and wait upon Him.

The time came for them to leave for French West Africa, and we had the joy of seeing these new recruits – our own daughter and son-in-law – come into the needy field waiting for them in Senoufoland. There they labor, carrying the torch everywhere, and the Lord is working with them. All that I can say is – the mercy of the Lord endureth forever. He had abundantly met us in every way, filling us with joy and peace.[18]

More Voices from Taylor Women Abroad

Coalescing into an appropriate mix of the quality and amount of social and spiritual dynamics to sufficiently inspire and move fully 10% of Taylor University young people to lives of radical service through the 1890s into the initial quarter of the 1900s, the following personal letters, many of which appeared in university publications, tell us of the real-life challenges faced by Taylor graduates who undertook arduous journeys to assume demanding positions on the mission fields of Africa, China, Burma, Philippines, and others.

Ethel L. Mabuce (1916) was a prolific writer of informative letters to the Taylor University community. She writes about her work in Burma, even including a clipping from the local *Burma Mission Herald*. She tells us what it is like to spend her first Christmas in a foreign country, and she enlightens us by sharing her response to the international report that World War I has been brought to a close in 1918. Still more of Ethel's experiences abroad are told in the book of her compiled letters by Lucille Griffith, *I Always Wore My Topi: The Burma Letters of Ethel Mabuce 1916-1921*.

❦   ❦   ❦

My! How good that the war is over. I have had one continual time of rejoicing since the news of the signing of the armistice came. I am beginning to get calmed down a bit now, but really I have been so glad and happy inside I haven't known hardly what to do with myself. I was in Rangoon when the news came and for more than a week after. We had all kinds of celebrating there. Flags are floating everywhere, Old Glory along with the rest. It looks good to see her! I am sure they are having great celebrations in America. Wish I could run over and join in for a day.

and:

…After a number of Christmas talks by missionaries and workers, the presents were given out. The cancelled post cards arranged together for wall decorations, and other similarly inexpensive gifts, that would find no place at all in America, were received with highest appreciation. We felt a strange reviving in our own hearts as we observed how simply they entered into the Christmas spirit and how grateful they were for what they had received.

We missionaries are like preachers at home, subject to change at Conference time, so we never feel that we are a permanent fixture at any one place. I was perfectly willing and should have been happy to go to any station in the Conference, but since I am in Pegu it seems that it is the best of all. It is a city of nearly twenty thousand people and there is a large district with many villages, which is a part of my assignment. Most of these have been practically untouched. Now during the dry season and the cool season all evangelistic missionaries turn their attention to the district work.

and:

When we are out in these villages the people gather about

us, often just for curiosity, but anyway they come, and we are glad. We always take a picture roll along, and as crowds collect we teach them some Bible lesson as best we can, using the pictures. I say "we" – the Bible women do the most of that yet. I often talk a bit too, but most of my talking is the conversational informal kind as yet. I am making it a point to talk some at every Thursday evening prayer meeting and at each of our Saturday woman's meetings, so I get some practice at "public speaking."

I do love to have the little tots gather around me and ask questions and talk in a general informal way. Most of them soon lose their fright of the "foreigner" and we become good friends.[19]

Ruth Copley (1917) tells us about her journeys to the Pangasinau Province of the Philippine Islands and describes her writing as a "sort of diary-letter." She minces no words in describing the seasickness and suffering she endured during her ocean voyage to her initial destination of Manila. She describes the problems with the ship and the forced layover in Tokyo. Regardless of the difficulties Ruth encountered, the reader is buoyed by the zest and joy that come through her words.

Perhaps you are wondering about my voyage and so I will tell you about that first. Well I have been very seasick and that is an indescribable experience. After days of suffering, it just seemed I could not bear it any longer, somehow the dear Lord helped me to realize I could leave it all in his hands and I slowly began to improve. I was so weak they carried me up on deck to see what the fresh air would do for me. I am able to get up by myself now, am gaining a little every day, and am very thankful the worst is over.

...I am anxious to arrive in Lingayen, my future home. Yes,

I feel that these islands are going to be that to me. I am going to love the people, and feel they are my people. I have so much joy just to be here and to realize I am in my corner of the Master's vineyard. I shall need your prayers that I may have strength for my task and I know I will have them.[20]

Alice McClellan (1915) describes her encounters with life and culture in Thandaung, Burma. A creative, compassionate, and "can do" spirit fairly vaults from her words. If one approach is unproductive, try another, her letter reveals. If there are needs, respond to them, as Alice says in her own words, "My doctoring is interesting indeed." And by all means, explore ways to help in one way that may also help in another, "It is wonderful how a few simple remedies will open the way for telling the Gospel story," Alice delights in telling us.

When I first came I thought that I was busy indeed with my language study and evangelistic work, but last November I opened a Kindergarten for Chinese children, and now I do have my hands full, with this youthful institution, as most infants require much time and attention. The children are darlings. I love them every one.

When I am out working among the women, time after time my heart is gladdened by the response which they give when the light begins to dawn upon their darkened spirits. At first they are likely to say when I ask them to come to church that they can't read, and what's the use. If one gives up then nothing is gained. It is often necessary to begin teaching them to read in their homes before you can succeed in getting them out to the services. How their faces do light up when they find that they can actually read. It is worth days of toil and weariness to see the joy and satisfaction of a smile like that.

My doctoring is interesting indeed. It is wonderful how a few simple remedies will open the way for telling the Gospel story. One old lady had a badly scalded foot. She had not the least idea what to do for it, so she pasted a piece of paper over it and sat down to growl and complain at her daughter-in-law and her grandchildren. One day I was calling there and looked at the foot. It had been sore for about a week and was in a bad condition. Every day for four weeks I visited her and kept the sore clean and at last it healed. The old lady is very willing to hear the Gospel and always, when I see her, she points to her foot and says, "I thank your God."[21]

Bertha Freeman (writing during 1922) takes us to Shanghai, China. Her letter describes the beggar-crowded streets, the hungry, and the homeless. Bertha also tells the story of the manner in which she was able to help a little Chinese boy she calls Billy to earn some badly needed money and to help others in the process.

It was just a few days before I left for China. I was sitting on the porch when a lady, leading a child by the hand, came and said, "I want to say good-bye, and please give the preacher this for preaching Billy's funeral."

"Well," I said, "I will take it to China. We will call it 'Billy's Five Gold Dollars,' and we will see how far we can make it go."

When I reached Peking, I began at once to look about, for the money was burning a hole in my pocket. Miss Gray could use it in her day schools. Then Miss Bess, in the kindergarten, was getting ready for Christmas. There never was enough money and those children were quite like Billy.

I walked through the ward with the beds full of suffering

children. "Ikey" was there, whose mother had slipped away and left him; the little mite with the tubercular spine, upon whom Dr. Manderson had performed such a marvelous grafting operation. They almost got Billy's money.

I went out into the streets, which were full of beggars. They were thin and old and cold and hungry and everybody was talking about the famine and how one preacher, coming in from the country, had passed twenty dead by the roadside. I was told that five dollars would save a life until the harvest time came. It was hard to keep that five dollars!

Then one day I talked to those splendid thirty-five medical girls and they had a plan that I thought Billy would like best of all. They had found some of the hungriest people among those wretched ones, who were to come to the hospital Christmas morning and one of the girls was to tell them the blessed story of the Christ child.

*I was told that five dollars would save
a life until the harvest time came.*

Exchange was away up and Billy's five dollars were transformed into $9.21 Mexican. It bought 161 packages and was given to 161 starving people to go into 161 different homes. The girls talked to the people and sang for them and I think some angel must have taken Billy by the hand and told him how his little life was going on and on even though he had slipped away.[22]

Jessie Edwards (writing during 1923) elevates with her ebullience. She writes of her new residence in Fobchow, China, a place of crushing need, and yet through it all, Jessie exclaims, "I am so happy." As well as later in her letter when she says, "It just seems that our hearts can grow and grow and joy never breaks them."

...I have been praising God because He has been answering prayers that I have been praying for a long while. I have wanted to see real results and now I am. Praise His Holy Name – His mercy endureth forever! It is a wonder I don't shout out very loud, but I don't. Sometimes I feel like my heart would burst for joy, but it has not yet. It just seems that our hearts can grow and grow and grow and joy never breaks them. But we know Jesus died of a broken heart, at least His heart was broken because we know that blood and water came out when his side was pierced. I used to think a broken heart was a joke until I began to read the Bible and knew that He had a broken heart.[23]

More Voices of Compassion and Strength ...

The wonderfully personal voices speaking out from the previous pages now give way to the more formal voices of the oration, the address, lecture, even eulogy. The following are excerpts from those selections that communicate to the reader something of the breadth and intensity of the topics addressed by early Taylor women, as well as the skilled manner of thinking and expression demonstrated. The items are entered chronologically with the earliest being a First Place winning oration by **Annabelle (Belle) Guy**, which appeared in a **1915** edition of the Taylor *Echo*.

Two phenomena, among numerous campus opportunities, stand out in early Taylor life as providing fine forums for students to develop both intellectual prowess and leadership abilities. Based upon the original purpose for which Fort Wayne Female College was founded – that of providing full collegiate education to young women – this policy was reaffirmed following the change of name to Taylor University. Equal opportunity education was available to both genders. Both the debating clubs, initiated as early as 1903 – with the introduction of intercollegiate debating in 1922 – and the literary societies, offered students of both genders opportunities to hone their thinking and communication skills.

The orator, Annabelle (Belle) Guy, is distinguished as one of the few women students to be elected president of the Thalonians Literary Society, a position she held in 1913. She was both accomplished and entertaining. The November 2, 1914, issue

of the Taylor *Echo* says of Annabelle that she presented a reading that "held the audience practically spellbound from first to last."

Annabelle's winning oration is both historical in its scope and global in her consideration of the opportunities for the Christian to respond to the call to continue the work of her forebears in spreading the Gospel to all humanity.

The people of every age, from time immemorial, have been called to do a noble work, but in selfishness and sin many have turned aside from true service for God and have wilfully neglected His call. In the beginning of the world's history, God looked with favor upon the Israelites and desired to make them a kingdom of priests and a holy nation, if they would keep His covenant. But the nation would not. Seeking their own pleasures, and serving their own idols, the Israelites refused the divine guidance and blessings. We remember that there was one tribe, the sons of Levi, who were faithful and God covenanted with them to be a royal priesthood. Time passed by; and the Levites, too, failed Him. Then the family of Zadok was divinely set apart for this great commission. But they also failed the Great Covenanter.

God looked upon the world and beheld the nations, a hopeless and sin-cursed people. They could no longer hear God's voice, so He sent prophets to call them back to righteousness.

Day after day, year after year, and through the centuries rang the voice of the prophets, but the appeals of these holy men were ridiculed and set at naught.

The people rejected the message from God and stoned the prophets. In infinite and boundless mercy, God said, "My people have forgotten their covenant, neglected my call, and killed my prophets. I will send my Son to proclaim my love for them and they will reverence Him."

Soon a world listened to that song of the heavenly host, "Glory to God in the highest and on earth peace and good-will to men," heralding through the gloom and despair of earth the birth of the holy child, Jesus. Well we know the story of the Christ as He walked on earth; how He was rejected by the learned and the influential of that age; how He gathered about Him a few Galilean peasants who were willing to forsake all and obey God's voice; how the Jews hated Him and cried out, "Crucify Him." They, the once chosen, committed the blackest crime in the history of the world. "They nailed the Son of God to the accursed tree." His blood flowed from Calvary, proclaiming the love of God unto a lost world. But Christ not only died for all; conquering sin and death He arose from the grave that all might know His resurrecting power.

Nineteen hundred years have passed since then; yet one billion of the sons of men have never even heard the message of salvation. We have neglected to tell them of our wonderful Savior. Did not Christ command us to proclaim His love? Behold that small band of disciples as with bowed heads they hear the risen Savior's last command, "Go ye into all the world and preach the gospel to every creature," and then with upturned faces they reverently behold Him as He is taken from their midst, and as He vanishes from their view into the celestial heights they come face to face with the stern reality of the vast and solemn mission placed in their hands. Were they faithful unto the trust assigned them? Yes! Ah yes! from the depths of their suffering and from their crosses of martyrdom the answer comes, "Yea, they were faithful even unto death." By this weak yet mighty

band were disseminated to different parts of the world the most
vital and precious truths known to the human heart.

Since then ages have rolled by and we may ask again, "Has
each succeeding generation obeyed God's call?" And from the
multitudes suffering untold agony in heathen darkness, from the
millions who are dying daily without knowing the name of Jesus,
from these comes the wail, No! No! and with this wail there
comes the piteous appeal, send the Light that we too may know
Him....[24]

Professor **Bertha Munro** gives the **1919** *"Senior Day Address,"* and offers a timeless challenge to graduating students.
She inspires to the pure ideal of learning and encourages her
listeners to reflect on the spirit of Socrates, Plato, and others of
the Greek Academy. She offers an historical overview of the history of education. Professor Munro's message both educates and
elevates the consciousness of the listener.

...Yours is a consecration, first to knowledge. The academic
spirit stands for a definite attitude to knowledge, an attitude that
is reverent, simple, genuine, pure. Our oldest American college
bears on its seal the single word, "Veritas," Truth.

"First pure." The object of study is not facts in and for
themselves, but facts as fragments of the great scheme of things
– the scattered, shattered limbs of the lovely form of the Virgin
Truth (you know the legend), which scholars are forever seeking
throughout the world; that truth we shall begin to comprehend
when we "know as we are known." Pure science – chemistry,
not merely because it will help you to become a physician or a
food specialist, but because it opens a new avenue to vast fields
of truth. Pure study of the classics even – not because you can
prove they are practical, but because there you find a whole

realm of the truth of beauty, the matchless beauty of symmetry and prose.

...I have purposely spoken of the academic spirit and not of the Christian, though I believe neither can reach full perfection without the other. We are cowardly Christians if we make our religion in any sense an excuse for superficiality of work, for smallness of soul, for meagerness of outlook. All this should we be, and all the more that the constraining, transfiguring love of Christ makes possible.

This is what we pray and earnestly desire for each of you who shall this year go out from Taylor. May you today have been consecrated to lives of unceasing, clear-visioned labor for great Christian ends. And so may the months which remain be precious indeed in helping you to realize the dignity of your last half-year in college.[25]

In her own words, **A. Amy Spaulding (Spalding) (1916)** talks to us about what she calls "Americanization work" – the term for assisting immigrants in their adjustment to American culture. The structure of her presentation, together with the information and opinions advanced, demonstrates Amy's well-developed abilities in highly effective communication.

Editor's Note: Owing to the disastrous fire that destroyed the Taylor University Administration Building in 1960, valuable historical information was lost. For this reason, some names appear with alternative spellings such as the above Spaulding or Spalding found in institutional publications. Effort has been made to retain completeness and accuracy where possible.

Among the questions, concerning my work, which come to me most frequently are: "What is Americanization?" "Why are you doing that work?" and "Won't you tell us about your work?"

The first I will answer last. To the second, I would say, "God has called—"

"Where the fog is thick,
And clouds are veiling the sun.

And souls are sick,
And souls in the dark are undone."

And to the request that I tell you about my work, I would answer: No question is so important in national and public polity as Americanization, and yet so little understood.

Charles Brooks says, "Americanization is the achievement of national unity for world-service." At this time, after all America has been united to win the war, one hesitates to turn a page so shameful in American history and to show that America is still continuing in the former indifference which she has taken toward the immigrant for so many years, and her practices of discrimination, ridicule, humiliation, exploitation and industrial degradation.

But it is time for us to face the inevitable truth. Americanization is not welfare work nor philanthropy; neither is it naturalization nor language qualifications. The man who comes here expecting opportunity, fair remuneration for his day's work, fair working conditions, friendly personal relations, and the opportunity to be at his best, cannot be met with discriminations and limitations and still be Americanized. He comes to escape the brutality of government and religion systems and he finds the brutality of the industrial system, ruthless in its destruction of life and property and morality.

…Some one asked me a little while ago if I had lost my vision because I had taken up Americanization work instead of going to the Foreign Field. I ask you. Is not the most efficient way to do Americanization work to train the foreigners who have come here, that they may return to their own countries, and carry the gospel message with them.

We need not be alarmed about the kind or number of immigrants who are coming to America. All that is easily regulated and needs no discussion here. But we do need to be alarmed about what reception and contact the immigrant receives when he comes here because that is the thing which determines his understanding of America and his reaction towards it. That is our own responsibility. The immigrant looks to us to exemplify our Constitution and Christian ideals and respects us the less for not doing so.

…Americanization for you and me means the fulfillment of the second greatest commandment; for our neighborhood it means mutual cooperation for the highest good; and for our nation, "national unity for world service."[26]

Following her graduation from Taylor University, **Olive Mae Draper (1913)** continued her service to the university with a 41-year career teaching in the Department of Chemistry and Mathematics. She passed away in 1982 at the age of 94. Miss Draper is still warmly remembered by faculty and university alums alike. From a 1918 Taylor *Echo*, we are fortunate to have Miss Draper's actual words as she explains the manner by which she sought to reconcile science and religion. The following is an excerpt from her presentation.

From the time of the earliest scientists, who were persecuted as heretics by the ecclesiastics of their day, up to the present, when the follower of Darwin unites with the rationalistic higher critics in the attempt to rob us of our Bible and of our faith in God, the battle between science and religion has raged continuously. The result is that in some sections today the term scientist is synonymous with skeptic. Much of this conflict has arisen from two sources. The first is the failure to distinguish between fact and theory, both scientists and religionists in many cases arguing the same authority for the theories of men as for the indisputable facts. There are some men who will allow the opinion of a few men to blind them to the importance and weight of many facts. The second is the failure on the part of many Christian people to claim for the facts of Christianity the same consideration in their realm as is accorded the facts of science in nature. The application of some of the rules of scientific research to the study of spiritual laws would prove helpful to many people.

…Christianity operates primarily in the realm of the spiritual, and works in the physical only in so far as this reacts upon 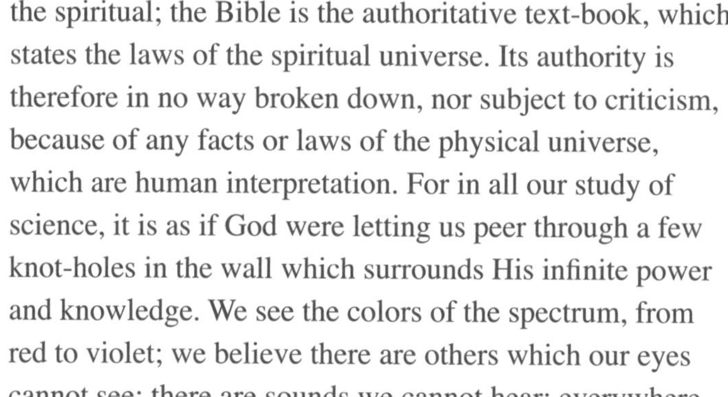 the spiritual; the Bible is the authoritative text-book, which states the laws of the spiritual universe. Its authority is therefore in no way broken down, nor subject to criticism, because of any facts or laws of the physical universe, which are human interpretation. For in all our study of science, it is as if God were letting us peer through a few knot-holes in the wall which surrounds His infinite power and knowledge. We see the colors of the spectrum, from red to violet; we believe there are others which our eyes cannot see; there are sounds we cannot hear; everywhere there are things we cannot understand nor explain. So many times the student asks Why? or, What is the cause of this phenomenon? to which the scientist can only reply, We do not know. We are often reminded of the words of the great apostle "Now we see through a glass darkly; but then face to face."

How foolish to cast away our hope of heaven and our faith in Him who may be our Saviour, Friend, Keeper and Guide, for such imperfect knowledge of the material world. Let us therefore hold fast our confidence in Christ and our faith in the Bible as the Word of God, knowing that such an attitude is an evidence of the highest intelligence, and is, in the nature of the case, a strictly scientific and rational one.[27]

Susan Ruby Breland Lamb (1928) is recognized for developing a comprehensive history of the women's missionary

organizations of the United Methodist Women, a study about
which Dr. Lamb speaks personally in the following excerpt
taken from her introductory remarks. A copy of this document is
housed in the Taylor University archives.

For a long time we have felt that there should be a History
of the missionary zeal of Methodist women in the Memphis Conference, but not until the fall of 1980 did we begin work on this
volume. As we have done research in pursuit of information our
appreciation has grown for the many heroic women who labored
so sacrificially, especially in the early days of this movement.
Many of them were pioneers in the missionary faith and led succeeding generations into fields of service.

Perhaps it is significant that this story is being written and
published near the time of our Centennial, (the first Woman's
Missionary Society was organized in 1878 and the Memphis
Conference Woman's Missionary Society in 1879). We have
divided the history into periods, such as the first twenty-five
years (Silver Jubilee 1903), the second twenty-five years (Golden
Anniversary, 1928), and afterwards into decades for our chapter
divisions....

Most of the early records were not preserved and even with
intense research the information is often very incomplete and
not available. As you read this History please keep in mind that
there are gaps and omissions over which we had no control. The
Records which we do have in the Archives at Lambuth College
consist mostly of the ANNUAL REPORTS, 1937-1980, and they
in turn record the events of the Conference as they were reported
at the Annual Meetings. Hence this has determined the style and
format of this History. The style is that of a factual account according to the records available....

The research and writing consumed more than a year and
a half. It has been a labor of love, worth all the effort if it is of

service to you.

We hope that you will read this History not only for personal information and inspiration, but that you will treasure it for future reference and use it in program planning....[28]

═══════════════ ❦ ❦ ❦ ═══════════════

Iva Durham Vennard is recognized in the Taylor *Echo*, 10-17-**1923**, by the unanimous recommendation of both the Taylor University Faculty and Board of Trustees to receive the first-ever Doctor of Divinity conferred upon a woman. In his eloquent introduction of Mrs. Vennard, the then President of Taylor University, John Paul, states boldly that in addition to her many accomplishments she also "has a model family of children," regardless of those who might question "whether or not a woman can rear a family and at the same time have a career." President Paul's support of well educated, creative, women professionals is noteworthy for his time and place in history. As of this printing, Mrs. Vennard's acceptance speech remains to be located.[29]

❦ ❦ ❦

Nominated for State Senator and longtime Indiana State President of the Women's Christian Temperance Union (WCTU), **Culla Johnson Vayhinger**, was the wife of Taylor University President Monroe Vayhinger, who served from 1908 to 1921. The "most dynamic member of the Vayhinger family was not the president but rather his wife."[30]

From a speech delivered at the Indiana State Temperance Convention held in Indianapolis, December, 1911, **Culla Johnson Vayhinger** said:

We are told the hand that rocks the cradle is the hand that rules the world, and that woman accomplishes more by indirect influence than she could possibly accomplish with the ballot. Let any man who will exchange places with me and try to get what he wants by indirect influence instead of the ballot, stand to his feet. Not a single man arises. So for the sake of truth never make an assertion of that kind again.[31]

From the 1913 Taylor *Echo*, "We hear it frequently stated that of all the lady speakers people have ever heard, Mrs. Culla J. Vayhinger, State President of the WCTU, beats them all. Well may we be proud of her as the wife of our College President."[32]

VENERABLE VOICES/MODERN MESSAGES

INTRODUCTION

[1]Miller, Sadie Louise (1910) *"The Uncommon Common," Dreams of a Decade,* Copyright: Sadie Louise Miller, 1940, Upland, Indiana: Printed by S. D. Freese & Son, (no publisher name), p. 27.

[2]Olson, Grace (1925) *"A Prayer,"* Taylor *Echo*, 3-30-25.

[3]Winquist, Dr. Jessica Rousselow and Dr. Alan H. Winquist. *God's Ordinary People: No Ordinary Heritage,* Upland, Indiana: Taylor University Press, 1996. (See Chapters 1,3,5).

A DISTANT, SOLITARY VOICE: 1848

[4]Smith, Susan Davis Marsters (1848) Personal letters written by Susan to her husband, Hezekiah Smith, between 1848-1849. Transcriptions, together with introductory comments, are reprinted by courtesy of the Lilly Library, Indiana University, Bloomington, Indiana, and by the generosity of Taylor University Professor, Dr. Robert Lay.

VOICES OF HUMOR AND WHIMSY

[5]Miller, Sadie Louise (1910) *"It Can Be Did," Dreams of a Decade,* Copyright: Sadie Louise Miller, 1940, Upland, Indiana: Printed by S.D. Freese & Son, (no publisher name), p. 43.

[6]Lohnge, Jessica L. *"Slang,"* Taylor *Echo*, 5-1-1916. (Jessica L. Lohnge is referred to in both the Taylor *Gem*, 1917, and the Taylor *Bulletin* and Taylor *Catalog*, 1917, but no graduation date is located).

[7]Goyings, Fernmae (1916) *"The Test,"* Taylor *Echo*, 5-15-1914.

[8]Miles, Inez (1921) *"Inspiration or Work"* Taylor *Gem*, 1921, p. 78.

[9]Freese, Dorothy (1928) *"The Most Embarrassing Moment in My Life,"* Taylor *Echo*, 11-16-1927, p. 4.

And then, THE UBIQUITOUS GENDER ISSUES …

[10]R.M. *"Our Aim,"* Taylor *Echo*, 1918.

[11]Miller, Sadie Louise (1910) *"In the Rough,"* *Poems*, approximate date 1925, p. 22.

[12]Author Unknown. *"My Ideal Husband,"* Taylor *Echo*, 3-1-1916, p. 9.

[13]Corson, Juliette *"To Cook a Husband,"* Taylor *Echo*, 2-14-1922, pp. 5-6.

[14]Wray, Mary G. (Taylor University Professor of History, 1909-1915) *"Marriage as a Career,"* Taylor *Echo*, 12-21-1920, p. 6.

VOICES FROM TAYLOR WOMEN ABROAD

[15]McAllister, Agnes A., *A Lone Woman in Africa: Six Years on the Kroo Coast*. New York: Eaton & Mains, 1898. (This book was acquired in 2004 by Taylor University and is housed in the university archives.)

[16]Wengatz, Susan Talbott Moberly (1910) Taylor *Echo*, 4-11-1918, p. 9.

[17]Miller, Sadie Louise (1910) *In Jesus' Name* by John C. Wengatz, compiled by Sadie Louise Miller, with a personal entry by Cecilia L. Cross in which Ms. Cross describes the remarkable courage demonstrated by Susan following an attack by a rabid dog while engaged in mission work in Angola, West Africa. Copyright: J.C. Wengatz, 1932, Upland, Indiana: Taylor University Press, pp. 69-74.

[18]Roseberry, Edith (mother of Taylor University graduate, Ruth Roseberry Herber 1942) *"Kansas Prairies to African Forests,"* (no publisher), 1956, pp. 41-47.

MORE VOICES FROM TAYLOR WOMEN ABROAD

[19]Mabuce, Ethel L. (1916) Letter: *First Christmas in Burma,* Taylor *Echo*, 10-12-1918, p. 7. Letter: *Ethel L. Mabuce Writes from Burma,* Taylor *Echo*, 11-12-1918, p. 9.

[20]Copley, Ruth (1917) *Letter from Ruth Copley to Mrs. McIntosh,* from Lingayen, Philippine Islands, Taylor *Echo*, 11-23-1918, p. 8.

[21]McClellan, Alice (1915) Letter: *A Message from Distant Burma: From San Francisco to Rangoon, Burma,* Excerpt from Taylor *Echo*, 3-1-1916, pp.1-2.

[22]Freeman, Bertha. Letter from Shanghai, China: *Billy's Five Gold Dollars,* Taylor *Echo*, 2-28-1922, p. 7.

[23]Edwards, Jessie (1921) Letter from Fobchow, China: *Miss Edwards Writes of Work in China* (dated 9-18-1923), Taylor *Echo*, 11-28-1923.

MORE VOICES OF COMPASSION AND STRENGTH ...

[24]Guy, Annabelle (Belle) (1915) Oration: *The Neglected Call,* Taylor *Echo*, 11-1-915, pp. 3-4.

[25]Munro, Bertha (Taylor University Professor of English, 1916-) "Senior Day Address," Taylor *Echo*, 1919.

[26]Spaulding (Spalding) A. Amy (1916) "The Work of Americanization" Taylor *Echo*, 6-7-1921, p. 11.

[27]Draper, Olive May (1913) "Science and Faith," Taylor *Echo*, 5-9-1918, p. 4.

[28]Lamb, Susan Ruby Breland (1928) *The Spreading Flame: History of Methodist Missionary Women,* Short bio- of Susan Lamb provided by Mrs. Robert E. Carson, Historian for United Methodist Women, followed by the book Introduction by Dr. Lamb.

[29]Vennard, Iva Durham: First woman to receive D.D. from Taylor U. Taylor *Echo*, 10-17-1923, p. 3.

[30]Ringenberg, William C., *Taylor University: The First 150 Years*, Grand Rapids, Michigan, William B. Eerdmans Publishing Co., and Upland, Indiana, The Taylor University Press, 1996, p. 91.

[31]Winquist, Jessica L. Rousselow and Alan H. Winquist, Excerpt: Vayhinger, Culla Johnson, wife of Taylor University President Monroe Vayhinger. From a speech delivered at the Indiana State Temperance Convention, Indianapolis, December 1911. *God's Ordinary People: No Ordinary Heritage,* Upland Indiana, Taylor University Press, 1996, pp. 103-104.

[32]Vayhinger, Culla Johnson. Wife of President. Died – Letter in Memoriam, listing her achievements in life. Taylor *Echo*, 11-21-1924, p. 3.

WRITERS' BIOS

*The date following the writer's name indicates
the year of graduation from Taylor University
or last year attended.*

Anderson, Hazel Butz Carruth, Ph.D. 1938
Named the first Chairman of the Division of Language and Literature in 1956, Dr. Hazel was a 1938 graduate of Taylor University. She earned the Ph.D. from Indiana University in 1955, then returned to Taylor and taught until her retirement in 1978. Dr. Hazel received the Alumni Merit Award in 1958, was named Professor of the Year in 1969, and received honorary membership in Chi Alpha Omega. In 1987, the recital hall in the Smith Hermanson Music Building was named the Hazel Butz Carruth Recital Hall in her honor.

Bagshaw, Linda Carlson 1968
A graduate of Fort Wayne Bible College, Linda grew up in Indianapolis, Indiana. She and her husband lived in several states over the next 20 years. They now reside in Sioux City, Iowa, where she enjoys writing poetry, teaching Sunday school, reading, and working outside.

Bergwall, Jean Francis 1981 (Honorary Alumna)
The First Lady of Taylor University, Jean was the wife of Dr. Evan H. Bergwall '39, President of Taylor University from 1951 to 1959. In addition to earning a preacher's license, Jean was instrumental in developing a faculty-wives prayer group that continues to the present. Jean engages in volunteer ministries at her local church and is actively involved with Alzheimer visitation in her community. At this printing, Jean is pleased to say she continues to lead a full life and has now reached the age of 88.

Berst, Janet R. 1959
A Taylor University Distinguished Alumna for Personal Achievement in 1998, Janet has distinguished herself in the field of systems analysis and videography. In addition to receiving four

EVVY awards for television programming, she authored *Christianity and the Real World.*

Blume, Kathy Lauber 1960
Kathy shares her powerful story of God's faithfulness by speaking at colleges, churches, and retreat centers across the country. She delights in living her life for the Lord, and she inspires others to seek the joy in life's mourning moments through the healing power of God's mercy. Kathy and her husband share a blended family, including five sons, five daughters-in-law, and eight grandchildren.

Boado, Valerie Wilson 1987
Valerie Wilson graduated from Taylor University in 1987 with a degree in elementary education and a minor in early childhood education. Valerie lives on the southern island of Mindanao in Tagum City, Philippines. She and her husband, Mike, run the NEOS Fellowship Center, where young people and families can go to feel the love of Jesus through the many opportunities available there. Since 1991 Valerie has written most of the children's curriculum for the children's ministries at NEOS and is in the process of preparing this material for publication. Besides her roles as wife, mother, and teacher, Valerie is also a Traditional Birth Attendant – lay midwife – and a volunteer with the local community health centers.

Boren, LaRita Gibbs 1994 (Honorary Alumna)
The Vice President of Avis Industrial Corporation, LaRita resides in Upland, Indiana. She has served on the Taylor University Board of Trustees since 1977, and continues to serve on the WBCL Board, Heartland Film Festival Board, as well as the Lyford Cay Foundation. She and her husband, Leland '75, have three children and five grandchildren.

Boxell, Dana Tucker 1977
Dana received her bachelor of science degree in education followed by a master of science degree in education from Indiana University in 1981. She taught elementary school fulltime, and

later, held substitute teaching positions after she began her family. Dana and her husband are the parents of three children.

Brightly, Beverly Jacobus, J.D. 1964
Beverly has amassed an impressive vitae of both academic and professional accomplishments. Following her B.A., Beverly earned the M.A. in 1968, and the doctorate in Educational Administration and Supervision in 1984. In addition, she completed the Juris Doctor degree in 2003. Beverly has utilized her training in influential positions such as in developing the Jacobus Foundation for Children, a consultation and training facility, and is currently with the Office of Special Education and Rehabilitative Services: U.S. Department of Education, Washington, D.C. Beverly has had extensive professional positions in the areas of Exceptional Children, Bureau of the Handicapped, Pupil Personnel Services, and has held university professorships. Beverly has been a member of the Taylor University Board of Trustees from 1992 to the present, holds commendations from Concerned Women of America, the Susan B. Anthony Society, the Council for Exceptional Children, and has received Government Performance Recognition and Awards for Internal Exchange and World Congress on Allied Health.

Britton, Joan Haaland 1960
A native of Brooklyn, New York, Joan graduated from Taylor University with a degree in Bible and Missions. She also received a Master's degree in mass communications from Columbia University in New York City prior to her position with Trans World Radio, a missionary radio organization. She and her husband, Skip, officially retired from 39 years of missionary work in December, 2002.

Brown, Marion E., Ph.D. 1946
Marion graduated from Taylor University in 1946 with a B.A. degree. She received the Chamber of Achievement Award from Taylor in 1971. She also received an M.R.E. degree from Asbury Seminary in 1951 and a Ph.D. from Ohio State University in 1971. Marion was a Diaconal Minister in 1985, and a Seminary

Professor from 1967-1987. She was a Retired Professor Emerita in 1987 and now resides in Largo, Florida.

Brummeler, Alicia Helyer 1992

Alicia graduated from Taylor University with a bachelor of science degree in English Education. She taught language arts to Junior High students for two years while husband Brad '90 served as a Youth Pastor in Van Wert, Ohio. Alicia has spoken to MOPS (Mothers of Pre-Schoolers) groups and written for *Momsense,* a division of MOPS International, and loves being mother to Jacob and Anna. Now living in Vancouver, British Columbia, while Brad attends graduate school, Alicia home schools, enjoys reading, drinking coffee, and Regent College community life.

Chaddock, Robin Chernenko, D.Min. 1981

Through her ministry, Wisdom Tree Resources, Inc., Dr. Robin is a conference and retreat motivational speaker. She is the author of three books designed to assist and encourage today's Christian woman. She is educated in psychology and theology, holds a doctorate in organizational development, and resides in Indianapolis with her husband and two children.

Chapman, Mildred Stratton, Ph.D.

Recipient of the 1991 Professor of the Year award at Taylor University, and the 1997 Asbury College Alumni Award, Mildred was professor of English at Taylor University for 22 years. Having completed her doctoral degree in 1962 from the University of Kentucky, Mildred also taught at Asbury College, Marion College, and Indiana Wesleyan University.

Chechowich, Faye E., Ph.D. 1974

Named *Professor of the Year: 2000*, Faye has held a faculty position in Christian Education at Taylor University for 14 years, is the Associate Dean of the Division of Letters, and before that she worked for 13 years with Youth for Christ. Faye's current and on-going research interest is in the area of spiritual development in older adults.

Chupp, Heidi Halterman 1986

Heidi grew up as a missionary kid in Peru, Bolivia and Guatemala – living in the Amazon basin, the foothills of the Andes, and along the Central American volcanic range. Heidi and her family have served with Gospel for Asia, helping to plant churches. She is managing editor of *Send!* magazine and has developed an in-house writing course. Heidi currently lives with her husband Dave '85, and two children in Texas.

Coburn, Jewell Reinhart, Ph.D. 1955

President Emerita of the University of Santa Barbara, Dr. Julie is the author of an award-winning series of books designed to foster cross-cultural understanding for which she has traveled widely into remote cultures of the world. *Authentic Voices: Women of Insight Talk about Real-Life Challenges* is assembled and edited by Dr. Julie, with Joyce Smith Helyer, and contains personal vignettes by women affiliate with Taylor over the years. A poignant inclusion are the voices of Taylor women past, those who left writings valuable to us today. *The Power of Knowing Who I Am In Christ*, one of the nineteen books authored by Dr. Julie, is designed to foster spiritual and emotional health, the result of her work with deeply hurting Christians. The recipient of honorary doctorates of Laws and Humane Letters, Dr. Julie and her husband, William, M.D. '55, together with their four children, worked in medical missions, including Tanzania, East Africa.

Cunningham, Paige Comstock, J.D. 1977

A Taylor Board member, Paige Comstock Cunningham is a Senior Fellow at the Center for Bioethics and Human Dignity, a Fellow at the Wilberforce Forum's Council for Biotechnology Policy, a Fellow at the Institute for Biotechnology and the Human Future, an adjunct professor of law at Trinity Law School and an adjunct instructor at Wheaton College. Cunningham, Esq., lectures and has published numerous articles, editorials and book chapters in the area of law and bioethics, has testified before congressional committees at the state and national level, and has appeared frequently on radio and television. She is a 1977 graduate of Taylor, and is married to Jay Cunningham '77. They have three children (including a current Taylor student), and live in Mt. Zion, Illinois.

Davenport, Barbara E. 1988

Barb began her academic career at UCLA and completed her degree in History at Taylor University in 1988. She earned the M.A. in Student Personnel Administration in Higher Education from Ball State University in 1989. Barb has been employed in the Registrar's Office of Anderson University, and was the Registrar at Taylor University from 1993 to 1998 and Director of Learning Services and Student/Athlete Academic Support from 1998 to 2003. Barb has biked across the U.S. and throughout various countries worldwide. She has guided students on short-term mission trips in six countries. Barb is the mother of four adult children, has 14 grandchildren and one great granddaughter.

Dechert, Wendy Loney 1996

With a major in Communication Arts and English Education, plus seven years as an English and drama teacher, Wendy completed her Masters in Education in 2004. She is the mother of a twenty-month old daughter and is currently a stay-at-home mom, having recently relocated from Georgia to Indiana. Wendy enjoys acting, singing, and travel.

Duke, Serena Thrush 2004

A 2004 appointee as Editor of the *Taylor Magazine*, Serena is a graduate in Communication Studies. Serena brings to her new position experience working in the department of University Advancement. She enjoys fitness exercise, scrapbooking, and spending time in nature.

Dusckas, Nancy E. 1975

The second recipient of the Taylor University G. Roselyn Kerlin Women in Leadership Award in 2001, Nancy is recognized by many awards for her professional expertise and community contributions. In addition, she received a certificate from the

Pittsburgh Institute of Mortuary Science before taking over her father's funeral business in 1981.

Earhart, Stephanie Golden, M.D. 1991
Stephanie received the 1991 Taylor University Citizenship Award. She graduated from Pennsylvania State College of Medicine in 1995 and served as an army doctor from 1995 to 2002. During that time Stephanie completed her Family Practice Residency and served in Germany. Stephanie was granted the 1995 Roche Award for Excellency in Psychiatric Research and is Board Certified in Family Practice. She left the military with the rank of major and currently lives in Pennsylvania where her husband serves as an Associate Pastor and she works part time in a local private practice. She and her husband have two daughters.

Ford, Lisa Curless 1992
Upon graduate from Taylor University, where she majored in English, Lisa taught at the American School of Kuwait, and later at Damascus Community School in Syria. In the United States, Lisa experienced a diverse teaching career over ten years, having taught 6-12 graders English, drama, speech, writing, history, and physical education. She now enjoys full-time motherhood. Lisa lives in Indiana with her husband and son.

Germain, Tamara Hittle 1990
Tamara is employed part time in Christian radio and serves as editor of Blackhawk Ministries women's newsletter, *Tapestry*. She lives with her husband and three children in Indiana and enjoys reading and keeping in contact with her friends via email.

Godfrey, Carole Hoel 1981
Carol lives in Edmonton, Alberta, Canada, is the recipient of many professional an community recognitions for her generous service, and lives with her husband and their two children. Both Carol and her husband are practicing attorneys.

Gormanous, Sherry Perkins 1959
Sherry was instrumental in starting a three-year olds class in her

church and has taught there for 23 years. She is the president of
the Interfaith Council in her area. Having received her Master
Gardener Certificate in 1999, she serves on the Advisory Board
of the Chicago Botanic Garden and also volunteers there. Sherry
served on the Taylor University National Alumni Council for two
terms and has been the Class Agent for 1999 and 2004. Sherry
is now a widow, has two grown children and two grandchildren,
and lives in Illinois.

Grimstead, Caryn P. 1996

Caryn is a full-time graduate student pursuing a Ph.D. in leadership in higher education from Indiana State University. After
graduating from Taylor University in 1996 with a BA in psychology, she received an M.A. in counseling psychology from Trinity
International University and then returned to Taylor to serve as
the Gerig Residence Hall Director for five years. She currently
resides in Maryland where she works part-time in student services at the College of Southern Maryland while completing her
doctoral studies.

Gudeman, Mary Ellen (Fort Wayne Bible College) 1964

As a missionary with the Evangelical Alliance Mission, Mary
Ellen served in Japan for 26 years. She is the author of *Survival
of the Unfit: Learning through Weakness, Failure, and Rejection*,
which describes her experiences, first, as a girl born on a farm in
Wolcott, Indiana, and later as a missionary. Mary Ellen attended
Indiana Business College and worked as a secretary at Purdue
University, and other local business firms before graduating from
Fort Wayne Bible College. Mary Ellen continues to work with
international students and volunteers in local refugee outreach.

Haak, Rebecca Kerlin, M.D. 1978

Rebecca graduated from Indiana University School of Medicine in 1982 with a specialty in Obstetrics and Gynecology. She
began her medical practice in Indiana and the group has now
grown to a four-physician OB/GYN practice. Rebecca developed a Women's Unit in her regional hospital. She lives with her
husband, also a physician and professor at Indiana University
School of Medicine, and seven children.

Hall, Sara Oyer 1996
Working in College Residence Life as Houghton College Residence Hall Director, teaching at the Junior High level, as assistant to the Dean of the Chapel, employed in church ministry support, and having completed graduate studies in 1999, Sara is recently married and is planning the next phase of her life.

Heavilin, Marilyn Willett 1959
Marilyn is the author of five books, an international speaker, a wife of 46 years, the mother of five and the grandmother of four. She is best known for her book, *Roses in December,* which tells her life story including the deaths of three of her sons. Marilyn and her husband live full time in a motor home and enjoy traveling throughout the country. Says Marilyn, "Home is where we park it."

Helyer, Joyce Smith
Joyce is the Associate Vice President for University Advancement, Taylor University. She has a B.A. in Speech from Biola University, a Certificate in Middle Eastern Studies from Jerusalem University College and her M.A. from Ball State University. Joyce has served at Taylor University for almost 20 years with primary responsibilities as Assistant Director of Admissions, and for the last 12 years in University Advancement. Joyce served as the Council for Christian Colleges and Universities Steering Committee Chair for Women in Advancement. In 1997, Joyce was instrumental in launching the annual Taylor University *Women's Forum* that brings to campus Taylor alumnae and special guest speakers.   Joyce and her husband, Biblical Studies professor, Dr. Larry Helyer, have two adult children and two grandchildren.

Jaeger, Paige Sheard 1978
After graduating from Taylor University, Paige worked four years in business prior to staying home to raise her children. She went on to earn a MLS, and she is now a librarian. She has been published in *Today's Christian Woman, Marriage Partnership, Sunday Digest,* and the *New York Times*, among other local magazines and newspapers.

Kehr, Heather Gladhill 1995

Heather Anne graduated from Taylor University with a bachelor of arts in psychology. Upon graduation, she worked as Executive Director for Tender Care Pregnancy Centers in Gettysburg, Pennsylvania, for over four years. Heather Anne lives with her husband Ken and their two children on their dairy farm. She is currently involved in her church nursery, missions committee, and young family Sunday school class.

Keller, Judie Assad x1972

Judith attended Taylor University for two years prior to graduating from Kent State University in 1972. She taught elementary school for 19 years before home schooling her children. She currently teaches art part-time at a local Christian school. She and her husband have two daughters.

Kerlin, G. Roselyn Baugh 1955

Elected the first woman Chair of the Board of Trustees of Taylor University from 1996-1999, Rosie has been honored by the Board with an award to be offered in perpetuity to women of achievement, the Roselyn G. Kerlin *Women in Leadership*. She began her career with a major in Elementary Education. Following her initial teaching position in Indiana, she worked at the Gila River Indian Reservation while her husband, Joe '56, took a medical residency there in Public Health. Rosie has been active on her local public school Board of Education, was Board President and Chief Negotiator in Board-Teacher Negotiations, and is current Board Chair of Kingdom Building Ministries. Rosie and her husband live in Indiana and are the parents of four daughters, all young professionals.

Key, Eleanor Radtke 1958

Listed in Who's Who in American Education 1991-1993, Eleanor was recognized as Outstanding Graduate Student in Education, 1983. Eleanor was awarded the Am-South Bank Grant for Multicultural Children's Books and holds a degree from Taylor University, and the M.A. and Ed.S. from the University of Alabama in Birmingham. In 1962, she was commissioned by the

Salvation Army School for Officers' Training, Chicago. A retired teacher of 18 years, she is mother of 5 children, and grandmother of 4.

Kittleman, Heather Myers 1997

Coordinating services in the Taylor University archives, Heather graduated with a major in Environmental Biology. When Heather is not contributing her organizing skills to the historical holdings of the university, she enjoys activities of, as she describes them, an "artsy-crafty" nature. She enjoys the outdoors, feeding stray cats, and learning the scientific names of flowers she grows in her garden. Heather and her husband live in Indiana.

Knight, Angela Lyons 1994

Angie graduated from Taylor University with a bachelor's degree in elementary education. Married in July 1994 to T.R. Knight, Angie returned to Upland in 1997 with her husband. Apparently not challenged enough by teaching middle school, Angie gave birth to twins in 1999 and finished a Master's degree in 2001. She is currently spending her time being a wife, a mother, and an adjunct professor in the Taylor Department of Education while she learns how to balance multiple sclerosis with life's varied roles.

Macomber, Angia, Ph.D.

Since 1999 the Education Department at Taylor University has been enriched by Angia's teaching. She holds several degrees from various institutions with the most recent being her Ph.D. from Michigan State University in 2003. Angia and husband, Phil, are both employed at Taylor University and recently adopted two-year-old Charlie from Haiti.

Manor, Billie Dusing

Billie graduated from Ball State University in 1972 with a BA in Home Economics and Library Science. She also earned her master's degree in Reading Education from Ball State. She has been employed at Taylor University for 32 years where she has served as the Director of the Academic Enrichment Center for 29

years. Billie has authored the <u>Advanced Study Skills Manual</u> in
1987. Billie married, has two daughters and one granddaughter.

Manor, Rochelle, Ph.D. 1987
Having completed her Ph.D. in Counseling and Neuropsychol-
ogy at Ball State in 1994, Rochelle has been in practice in
Michigan for the past 10 years. Currently, she is with the Hope
Network Rehabilitation Center specializing in traumatic brain
injury rehab. Rochelle spends the remainder of her time nurturing the creativity and spirit of her young daughter.

McKuhen, Lois S. Haycock (Fort Wayne Bible College) 1968
Lois graduated from Fort Wayne Bible College in 1968 with a
BRE. For the past 20 years she has been Executive Assistant to
the CEO of Wood-Mizer Products, Inc. in Indianapolis, Indiana.
She has been married for 32 years and has two sons and three
grandchildren.

McLaughlin, Beth Waldrop 1978
Beth holds a Master in Ministries and is currently working
on her doctorate in Communication Studies. She has a broad
background in advertising, public relations, local not-for-profits,
account executive and copywriter. Beth has been a partner in
a local advertising agency for five years. She teaches writing,
speech and public relations in the Bethel College Writing Center.
Beth is married to Donald '75, has two teenage daughters, and
lives in Indiana.

Medhurst, Pauline Getz 1952
Since graduating from Taylor University in 1952, Pauline has
served as an elementary teacher in the public schools, a college
professor at Bethel College and two years in teacher training in
Uganda, East Africa. In 1981 Pauline received a Specialist in
Reading degree. For the past 18 years she and her husband have
hosted many guests at the Queen Anne Inn Bed and Breakfast
in Indiana. Her pastimes include singing in the church choir,
ringing hand bells, serving as a Stephen Minister, doing counted
cross stitch and cooking.

Miller, Dorothy Hislop 1942

Dorothy is actively involved with Telephone Pioneers, serving as a Member at Large on the local board. She has also served as president of the local chapter, president of the Camelia Club (retired group), and Member at Large on the John I. Sabin Chapter Area Board. Dorothy is married to her 1943 Taylor classmate, Gavin.

Miller, Janice Spaulding 1972

Janice, a former teacher and librarian, is currently Site Coordinator for the Adult Studies program for Indiana Wesleyan University. She enjoys reading, writing, editing, and visiting with family and friends. Janice lives in Indiana with her husband of more than 30 years.

Miller, Lisa Moritz 1990

After graduating from Taylor University with a degree in English education, Lisa taught junior high and high school language arts for six years, then worked at her church as communications director for two years. Since then she has been a full-time homemaker and enjoys sharing her life and home with Joe '89, her husband of nearly 14 years. They have two daughters, Grace and Sophie, and live in Carmel, Indiana.

Morehouse, Dawn Deak 1994

Dawn received a bachelor of arts in Christian education. She and her husband, Ryan, live in Mishawaka, Indiana, where Dawn is a stay-at-home mom to their two children.

Nader, Sara Sigworth (Mother of Taylor alumna, Cindy Nader Moore 1972)

Sara has never known life outside of full-time ministry. As a child, she traveled with her father and sister leading worship in evangelistic meetings. She graduated from Bible College in Binghamton, New York, before studying at Moody Bible Institute. It was there she met and fell in love with her husband, Fred. Together, they served congregations in Illinois, Pennsylvania, New York, Michigan, and North Carolina. Sara now resides in Upland, Indiana.

Nieveen-Phegley, Trishena (Missy) 1991
Missy plans to complete her doctorate in Rhetoric and Composition within the year from Southern Illinois University. She serves as Assistant to the Director of Undergraduate Studies and is the author of an enviable list of scholarly papers and publications. Missy is a member of the National Council of Teachers of English, College Composition and Communication, and Missouri State Teachers Association. Missy lives with her husband and two young children.

Novak, Barbara Rioux 1952
Named Outstanding District Administrator in Gifted Education in 1979, and the author of *Dare To Be Different*, used by the Wisconsin Council for the Gifted, Barb has taught over the years most grade levels from first grade through college workshops. She continues membership in Phi Delta Kappa, Delta Kappa Gamma, Presque Isle Heritage Society, Wisconsin Historical Society, and the National Society of the Daughters of the American Revolution. Barb continues her active life maintaining her home on an island in northern Wisconsin. She has been widowed since 1995.

Prillwitz, Kristen 2003
Kristen is currently teaching literature at Henan College of Education in the People's Republic of China and working toward her M.A. through Azusa Pacific University. She likes spending time with her Chinese students, is partial to Chinese food, and enjoys fly fishing with her Dad whenever she is back home in Wisconsin.

Reusser, Kayleen Brewer x1982
Kayleen is a freelance writer with over 400 published articles, including essays, devotions, travel, business, celebrity, and testimonies. Since 2001, she has been the writer/editor of the Allen County Jail Chaplaincy News newsletter. She is married and is the mother of three young people.

Richmond, Rosalyn Coburn 1956

A 30-year leader of a neighborhood Bible Study representing
four denominations, Rosalyn also taught nearly eight years at
the Junior High School level. Having grown up on a large Iowa
farm, Rosalyn subsequently traveled widely throughout the
world. She lives with her husband near Minneapolis and has
three children and one grandchild.

Ringenberg, Frances Valberg 1978

Frances is a 1978 graduate of Taylor University with a Bachelor
of Science in Health, Physical Education and Recreation. She
received an M.A. degree in Biblical and Theological Studies
from Wheaton College, Wheaton, Illinois in 2001. For the past
five years she has served as Lay Minister of Worship at Lombard
Mennonite Church, Lombard, Illinois. She was also president of
the Taylor University Alumni Council from 1993-1994.

Ringenberg, Rebecca Lehman

A 1957 graduate of Bob Jones University with an academic
major and minor in Speech Education and English, Rebecca
holds the Distinguished Achievement American Legion College
Award and is listed with Who's Who in American Colleges and
Universities. With a rich experience in theater, opera, film, radio,
and television, Rebecca taught in the public schools for 32 years.
With her husband, Dr. William Ringenberg, Chair of the Taylor
University Department of History, they have a large family of
active young people.

Roggenbaum, Jayanne Housholder 1987

The past president of the Taylor University National Alumni
Council, Jayanne and her husband, Doug, graduated from Taylor
University in 1987. Residents of Michigan, they have one daughter. Jayanne is a psychologist in Birmingham Public Schools.
Currently, she serves as the Chief Elected Officer for the Michigan Association of School Psychologists and is a columnist for
several Detroit metropolitan area newspapers.

Rothrock, Mary Ellen Bidwell
Mary Ellen holds degrees in English Literature from Carnegie-
Mellon University (B.A.) and UW-Madison (M.A.). She is an
award-winning writer, sharing life-lessons from her experiences.
Her humorous and inspirational articles have appeared in *Moody,*
Christian Reader, Guideposts, War Cry and other Christian
periodicals. Mary Ellen and her husband, Paul, came to Indiana
in 1981 when Paul joined the Taylor University faculty in biology. City-bred Mary Ellen found living in a rural setting a major
adjustment, but now she values the peaceful surroundings as well
as the many friendships she has formed.

Rousselow-Winquist, Jessica, Ph.D.
Jessica grew up on what she describes as a subsistence farm in
northwest Wisconsin, and was the first person in her family to
obtain a college degree. After earning an M.A. at the University
of Minnesota, Jessica embarked on a career in higher education
– first at a small college in Minneapolis and one in Nebraska before coming to Taylor University where she has been on the faculty since 1967. Jessica earned the Ph.D. in 1980, co-authored,
God's Ordinary People: No Ordinary Heritage and *Coach Odle's*
Full Court Press, and in 2001, she married her best friend, university colleague, and co-author, Dr. Alan Winquist.

Sheard, Shirley Holmgren 1949
Shirley says of her life that she was born, reared, and careered
in New York City. She holds an M.A. in Library Science from
Queens College, NYC, has taught Special Education on Long
Island, and was an Aviation Librarian at JFK Airport. Shirley
is a chaplain of her county Gideon Auxiliary and is currently
engaged in jail ministry. She is married, has four adult children,
fourteen grandchildren, and is retired, living in the beautiful
Adirondack Mountains.

Smith, Carole Ann Shoup 1958
Author of *From Hopelessness to Hallelujahs*, Carole Ann reveals
a 17-month, day-by-day account of her life-changing cancer
diagnosis, through her transition from conventional medical

treatment, to a life-style change that she attributes to her current restored good health. Carole Ann is a frequent speaker in the Southwest. She and her husband are retired and reside in Texas.

St. Clair, Jessica 2006

Jessica was born and raised in South Bend, Indiana. She will be graduating with the class of 2006 at Taylor University with a degree in English Education and dreams of teaching young adolescents in an inner city. She enjoys writing as a means of expression and is gaining more appreciation for the value of sharing her work. Currently she is fostering a love for biography, reading each book from cover to cover before returning to school for her next academic year.

Stuart, Mary Ella Rose x1930

Married to the Rev. Bishop Marvin Stuart, who graduated in the class of 1931, Mary Ella and Marvin lived much of their adult lives serving the Methodist church. Mary Ella chronicled her debilitating, long-time struggle with clinical depression in her book, *To Bend Without Breaking*, with its fifth printing by Abingdon Press appearing in 1986. In 1994, Mary Ella updated her book with current medical and psychological information. Mary Ella died before *Authentic Voices* was published, and deepest gratitude is extended to her family for their permission to reprint her highly informative *Addendum* of 1994.

Tipple, Lori McGuffin 1989

Following completion of her undergraduate studies, Lori received a Master's degree in Community Counseling and a diploma in Christian Counseling. She married Kelly Tipple, who graduated from Taylor University in 1992, and they live in Tennessee where she has been employed as a professor of Psychology at Cleveland State Community College. Lori and her husband currently reside in Georgia where she reports that she is engaged in her life's greatest work to date, that of full-time, stay-at-home, home schooling Mom to their two young daughters.

Toney, Lisa Huber 1997

Lisa was born and raised in Michigan before moving to Indiana to attend Taylor University. After graduating with a communication studies degree, she worked for the Office of Admissions at Taylor University. In 2001, she graduated with her master of divinity degree from Fuller Theological Seminary and became an ordained pastor in the American Baptist Denomination. She now lives with her husband in California and serves as part of the pastoral staff at their church.

Truman, Ruth Dixon, Ph.D. 1952

Only two days after graduating from Taylor University with a degree in education, Ruth married her husband, Lee '52. She later received a master's degree in counseling from CSULA and a doctorate in higher education from UCLA. She is currently retired from California State University, Fullerton, where she served as acting associate vice president for research and external programs. She enjoys spending time with her family, writing, sewing, and interior decorating.

Wade, Linda R. (Taylor University Fort Wayne)

Linda is a retired elementary school librarian after serving 23 years in the same school. She has had a total of 36 books published since 1989, earning her the "Writer of the Year" award by the American Christian Writers Association in 2000. In addition to writing, she enjoys spending time with her husband, five children, five stepchildren, 22 grandchildren, and three great-grandchildren. Linda participated in two writing classes taught by Dennis Hensley at Taylor University Fort Wayne.

SUBJECT and NAME INDEX

---

*Subjects followed by an asterisk may be found in most vignettes in ways unique to the individual writer and her real-life experience.